An Environmental History of Northeast Florida

The Ripley P. Bullen Series
Florida Museum of Natural History

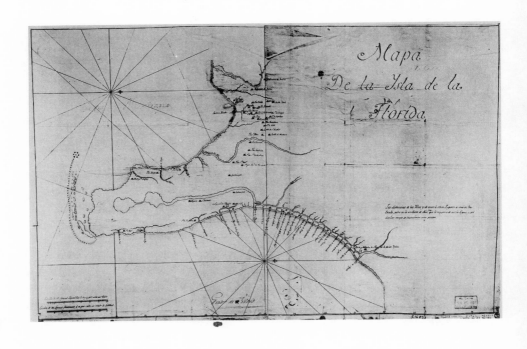

An Environmental History
of Northeast Florida

James J. Miller

University Press of Florida
Gainesville Tallahassee Tampa Boca Raton
Pensacola Orlando Miami Jacksonville

03   02   01   00   99   98   6   5   4   3   2   1

Library of Congress Cataloging-in-Publication Data
Miller, James J., 1948–
An environmental history of northeast Florida / James J. Miller.
p. cm.—(The Ripley P. Bullen series)
Includes bibliographical references and index.
ISBN 0-8130-1600-2 (alk. paper)
1. Human ecology—Florida—History. 2. Landscape changes—
Florida—History. 3. Nature—Effect of human beings on—Flor-
ida. 4. Florida—Environmental conditions. I. Title. II. Series.
GF504.F6M55   1998   97-43564
304.2'09759—dc21

The University Press of Florida is the scholarly publishing agency
for the State University System of Florida, comprising Florida
A & M University, Florida Atlantic University, Florida International University, Florida State University, University of Central
Florida, University of Florida, University of North Florida, University of South Florida, and University of West Florida.

University Press of Florida
15 Northwest 15th Street
Gainesville, FL 32611
http://nersp.nerdc.ufl.edu/~upf

For Cindy and Joey

Contents

Tables

Maps

Figures

Foreword

Stand by the railing of Jacksonville Landing on the St. Johns River, close your eyes, and try to envision what the landscape around you looked like 100 years ago. Now try 500. How about 15,000?

Difficult at best, isn't it? If you took a canoe and paddled up a quiet, isolated stream flowing into the St. Johns River in a less-developed locale you might enjoy more success, but even then you would be hindered by the present appearance of the land. In most areas in northeast Florida, what we see today—the trees, shrubs, and animals—is a far cry from what was there even 150 years ago.

In this skillfully researched and well-illustrated volume James J. Miller describes the changing landscape of northeast Florida over the past 18,000 years. He documents the reasons for the transformation that took place and the interaction between the succession of human cultures and the dynamic environments in which they lived.

Can visualizing and understanding the past help us today and in the future? As Miller points out, it can indeed. Knowledge about the changes that occurred in the past, their causes, and their effects on human populations is a powerful tool, one that can help us plan for future use of the environment and our place in it.

I take great delight in the publication of this volume by the Florida Museum of Natural History and the University Press of Florida. Not only are books on archaeology and natural history near and dear to my heart, but in addition Jim Miller is someone I admire and for whom I have great professional and personal respect.

For 15 years as chief of the Bureau of Archaeological Research, an office of the Florida Division of Historical Resources, Jim has guided the informed management of the state's archaeological resources. He has worked tirelessly and successfully to investigate and preserve sites, provide aid in the passage of appropriate regulations and legislation, and promote archaeology. As a result the state of Florida has one of the most successful and effective state archaeological offices in the nation; the informed management of Florida's archaeological resources is a reality.

Jim Miller can envision the past; more important, he has used that vision to chart the future of archaeology. In *An Environmental History of Northeast Florida*, the past, present, and future come together, providing a unique view of Florida.

Jerald T. Milanich,
series editor

Preface

This work is, in part, an attempt to reconcile the past and the future, to examine whether an understanding of what happened to people and environments in history can be of value in making decisions about people and environments in the future. Dissatisfied with the limited relevance of archaeology for finding solutions to modern problems, I have tried to understand the content and the practice of two very different professions: archaeology and regional planning. This look into the past and the future could not have occurred without the understanding and assistance of people in both fields, as well as the help of many others along the way. I sincerely hope that they will have found worthwhile the investment of their time and effort in what must have sometimes seemed an odd combination of specialties.

My interest in planning and the recognition of its power to influence the future of people and land I owe to John Ormsbee Simonds and Jack Scholl of the Environmental Planning and Design Partnership of Pittsburgh. The opportunity they and the ITT Community Development Corporation provided to develop many of the data and ideas in this work was instrumental in my later decision to study planning. Ian McHarg, then chairman of the Department of Landscape Architecture and Regional Planning, University of Pennsylvania, graciously encouraged my application for doctoral study in a field for which I had little preparation, and arranged financial and other support that made my residence in Philadelphia possible. Dan Rose, of the same department, introduced me to the application of anthropology to planning and served as a trusted adviser in matters academic and otherwise. Dan's friendship is exceeded only by his patience, and I am grateful for both. Seymour Mandelbaum of the Department of City and Regional Planning has been a steady supporter, providing solid advice, especially in times of doubt. The present work is based on a dissertation guided by that committee.

In the field of archaeology I am indebted to many colleagues and friends. For the past 15 years I have been employed in the Florida Division of Historical Resources as State Archaeologist. My supervisors and staff have been not only understanding in accommodating my outside obligations over the years, but many have also been valuable and enjoyable sources of intellectual stimulation over the years. I would particularly mention L. Ross Morrell, Randall Kelley, George Percy, John Girvin, Mable Revell, Henry Baker, the late Calvin Jones, James Dunbar, and Drs. John Hann, Gary Shapiro, Bonnie McEwan, Roger Smith, Brent Weisman, Marion Smith, and David Dickle.

Finally, many archaeologists and historians in Florida and elsewhere have influenced my thinking in a variety of ways over the years, particularly Drs. Jerald Milanich, Kathleen Deagan, Bennie Keel, Eugene Lyon, Patricia Griffin and Michael Gannon. My greatest debt, which I am most pleased to acknowledge, is to the late Dr. John W. Griffin, whose archaeological and historical knowledge of northeast Florida was unmatched. John was a colleague, partner, adviser, and friend for 15 years. Not enough scholars are also gentlemen; in both accomplishments John set a high standard.

I thank Charles Poe for inking and lettering the maps. Dr. Jerome Stern kindly reviewed an unfinished draft and offered encouragement as well as advice on style. Many others have been helpful along the way; I apologize for omitting acknowledgement and offer my sincere thanks.

Chapter 1

People and Land

[We] enterd and veued the cuntry therabowte, which is the fairest, frute-
fullest and plesantest of all the worlde, habonding in honney, veneson,
wildfoule, forrestes, woodes of all sortes, palme trees, cipers, ceders,
bayes, the hiest, greatest and fairest vynes in all the wourld with grapes
accordingly, which naturally and withowt mans helpe and tryming
growe to the top of okes and other trees that be of a wonderfull greatnes
and height. And the sight of the faire medowes is a pleasure not able to
be expressed with tonge, . . . and to be shorte it is a thing inspeakable, the
comodities that be sene there and shalbe founde more and more in this
incomperable lande, never as yet broken with plowe irons, bringing
fourthe all thinges according to his first nature, whereof the eternall God
endued yt.

Ribaut 1927:72–73

So wrote Frenchman Jean Ribault of his first impressions of the new land of
Florida upon landing at the mouth of the St. Johns River in 1562. The
wonder of these first European settlers conveys a vivid impression of the
lushness of the northeast Florida landscape, particularly in comparison
with their European homeland, which had been under the plow for millennia. Yet this was not a pristine wilderness inhabited by an innocent and
simple people. The northeast Florida environment, like that of most of the
New World, had been inhabited for more than 10,000 years. Natural and
human factors had already caused profound environmental changes. This
continuing development gives the region its present appearance.

Purpose of the Study

In the last several decades modern society has begun to comprehend the
importance of the environment as the foundation for continued human
existence. We realize that people and nature are inextricably related, so

much so that now the concept of people without environment is impossible. It remains, however, for us to understand the proper place of humans in the environment. We know that people affect their surroundings, whether they intend to or not, and that the environment influences the lifeways of people, providing opportunities as well as limits. Even so, we are just beginning to realize the implications of this current interdependence.

For example, the pristine environment, unspoiled by humans and existing in some perfect "natural" state, is usually considered to represent the state of the land at the time of the European "discovery" of the American continent. It is believed that in the absence of human intervention such an environment would have continued to exist in equilibrium, changing in replacement of individuals but remaining essentially the same in its "natural form."

The question of ecological stability versus change, of an ideal or correct environment versus a continually evolving and perpetually different environment, is one that can be best answered by a study of environmental history. It is a question of more than academic interest. Public agencies at the federal, state, and local levels are now largely committed to environmental protection in some form or other. While regulatory and incentive programs strive to influence environments, this costly exercise often lacks a sound foundation for making decisions. Environmental decisions can reflect public opinion more than scientific understanding of cause and effect.

A more thorough understanding of how environments function should form the basis for concepts that help determine how environments are "managed" in the future, that is, how planning decisions are made. Managers of public land have most recently embraced the concept of ecosystem management, recognizing that local landscapes are part of regional ecosystems and can't be managed independently. Planning strategies based on the goal of achieving an ideal, equilibrious environment, one that exists in a pristine state and that changes little over time, may well be "unnatural." This goal may be impossible to achieve; if such an environment never existed, it cannot be re-created. It is worth exploring in detail the basis for making environmental decisions and testing some of the underlying concepts about ecological change.

My goal is to use the northeast Florida environment as a historical case study to show how and why environment and people have developed through time. This book will explore the concept of nature undisturbed by people, the ways in which we affect other aspects of the environment and it affects us, and finally the question of proper role for humans in the environment: How do we make correct environmental decisions (Botkin 1990)? The value of environmental history for formulating and implementing public policy is that it explains how local environments achieved their modern form, what environmental processes operate within the region, what the consequences of environmental change have been in the past, and what the possible effects of naturally occurring or human-induced environmental change might be in the future.

Like any other region, modern northeast Florida is the product of a long human and natural history. Its appearance is due to a complex interaction of physical, biological, and cultural factors operating over millennia. What makes northeast Florida of special interest is the comprehensive documentary record of human settlement and landscape modification beginning at such an early date. Northeast Florida may be considered a historical environmental laboratory in which a number of unwitting environmental experiments have been conducted. Each successive pattern of settlement and adaptation in the region, beginning more than 10,000 years ago, may be seen as a manifestation of the complex interactions of people and environment, of culture and nature.

Were this a perfect laboratory, all variables would be held constant save one under investigation; in the real world, the problem is not so straightforward. Most relevant environmental factors are dynamic; on analogy, the laboratory itself changes, both as a result of large-scale and long-term changes in environment, and as a result of previous experiments. To some extent, it is possible to control many of these variables: for example, by comparing Spanish and English adaptations in the same place and close together in time while environmental factors remain relatively constant. In certain cases it will also be possible to observe how persistent and stable cultural patterns are influenced by environmental change. For instance, prehistoric Indians of northeast Florida adapted successfully to new hydrologic conditions associated with rising sea level about 5,000 years ago.

Environmental history has been of interest to geographers, biologists, ecologists, anthropologists, archaeologists, human ecologists, and landscape specialists, all of whom have contributed to a full and diverse literature over the last several decades. Historians, who should have been active participants in this dialogue, have only recently recognized the importance of environment in understanding history.

There is a pressing need to understand local environments in sufficient detail to anticipate the consequences of our decisions and actions. The historical record can be of use in showing the impact on the environment that past activities have had recently and over the long term. The historical perspective demonstrates that environments are dynamic and provides information not otherwise available on how human ecosystems have reacted to major modification. Such activities as burning, clear-cutting, plowing, farming, dredging, filling, ditching, and draining are all evident in the historical record, and in many cases it is possible to locate and examine areas identified in historical sources to observe their present condition and determine the long-term effects of earlier actions. By this method a fairly complete environmental history can be constructed, but more important, an inventory of local environmental processes and their effects becomes available.

Anthropologists were the first to pay attention to how people fit in the environment; they did so around the beginning of the twentieth century, when some of the last surviving non-Western societies in North America were still available to be studied. Indeed, for the great ethnographers such as Franz Boas and Clark Wissler, one function of anthropology was to record the last surviving elements of aboriginal cultures before they were lost to acculturation. Another function, of course, was to explain by some means how such cultures operated, how non-Western people lived. Anthropological theory has been built on examples of contemporary and antiquarian cultures much more intimately related to their environments than our own culture.

American anthropologists have had the advantage of observing the vast range and great complexity of Native American culture over two continents. The "history" of Indian people was largely ahistorical; because there were no written records for the millennia before European contact, anthropologists could not base a historical or social analysis on significant individuals or events. The most obvious explanation for diversity in institutions and technology was environment.

In the 1950s, Julian Steward laid the ecological foundation for analyzing and explaining human behavior. A cultural evolutionist in the Marxist tradition, like Leslie White (1959), Steward recognized the primacy of the means of production. While it was generally recognized that most cultural elements were related somehow to environment, Steward saw that the elements of subsistence and economic activity—what he called the culture core—were fundamentally related to environment and should form the first level of analysis. Understanding the technology and behavior of people in relation to producing food and otherwise gaining a living reveals the most fundamental relationships between nature and culture. In addition, Steward argued, the factors of environment, to which technology is adapted, largely influence the organization of social institutions. Size and complexity of social groups, the seasonal patterns of movement and settlement, and the intensity of political organization and control can all be seen to be influenced by environmental factors. Finally, in Steward's method, it is possible to ask how the most abstract cultural elements—ideological elements such as religion, ritual, and philosophy—fit into the ecological cultural pattern. Steward's cultural ecology is recognized as a fundamental contribution to anthropological theory and provides a powerful basis for explaining human behavior.

Because anthropologists did not study Euro-American culture until recently, and because historians did not concern themselves with the nature of American Indian culture except as it affected the expansion of the frontier, the possibility that environment played a fundamental role in the history of the Americas since the time of European contact occurred to only a few historians, among whom the best known are Frederick Jackson Turner and William Prescott Webb.

The first historian to recognize the power of the theory developed by Steward and applied by other anthropologists was William Cronon. His *Changes in the Land, Indians, Colonists, and the Ecology of New England,* published in 1983, must be recognized as the first successful ecological history. Spanning two centuries, generally between 1600 and 1800, and restricted to New England, his study was firmly grounded in the fields of history, ecology, ecological and economic anthropology, and ethnography. By contrasting Native American and colonial environmental relations, Cronon explores the ecological dialectic: "Environment may initially shape the range of choices available to a people at a given moment, but then culture reshapes environment in responding to those choices. The reshaped environment presents a new set of possibilities for cultural reproduction, thus setting up a new cycle of mutual determination. Changes in the way people create and re-create their livelihood must be analyzed in terms of changes not only in their social relations but in their ecological ones as well" (1983:13).

Cronon's thesis is that all human groups consciously change their environments to some extent; the dynamic and changing relationship between environment and culture is as apt to produce stability as not. A historical account of environmental change is sufficient to demonstrate the fundamental weakness of the functionalist explanation of culture, which says that cultural traits exist for the purpose of maintaining a stable system of adaptation. In the sense that there is little stability to the environment to which a culture is adapted, such notions as self-regulating systems, homeostasis, and equilibrium can have meaning only when the analysis is ahistorical. As Cronon demonstrates, seventeenth- and eighteenth-century environmental change in New England was so profound that the Indians' way of life simply became impossible. As we will see in northeast Florida, major environmental change, even prior to the coming of the Europeans, was a common phenomenon; the success of a culture may well be measured not so much in terms of its stability but rather in its ability to adapt to instability.

By now, environmental historians have defined their subject as the dialectic between culture and nature: how environment affects people and how people affect environment. Certain approaches like narrative accounts of past environments (Stilgoe 1982), history of the conservation of environmental movements (Petulla 1977), and local ecological analysis without reference to larger economic relationship (Cronon 1991) have been explored. But environmental historians have largely adopted the cultural materialist theory of anthropologists, with common reference to Steward, and have rejected the ahistorical idealist theory of the functionalists. And finally, environmental historians have even begun to suspect that their work might be relevant to policy makers.

Environmental history is an uneasy combination of natural and social science; scientists and historians come to the same domain with quite different methods and theories about how the world works. Environmental history is more than interdisciplinary; it crosses the fundamental boundary between humanities and science, and hopes to inform not only scientists and historians but also those who make decisions about the contemporary environment (Liebhardt 1988:23–24). One means of advancing this possibility is by using methods of analysis that are compatible with historical as well as scientific study; that such methods would prove useful in making planning decisions would be an added benefit.

A recent consideration of the fundamental question of the relation between people and environment is Daniel Botkin's *Discordant Harmonies* (1990). Botkin is more concerned with how people have thought about environment than how they have specifically changed it. Despite dramatic improvements in scientific measurement and interpretation of environmental processes within this century, Botkin argues that we make public and scientific decisions about the environment on the basis of prescientific myths based mostly on a mechanistic understanding of the universe. Such concepts as "balance of nature" and "environmental equilibrium" have little basis in reality, yet they continue to underlie our modern thinking about how the biosphere operates and how it could be managed.

This study of northeast Florida relies on the ecological planning methods of Ian McHarg (1969), comprising analysis of a region by a series of consistently scaled maps, each depicting a different natural or cultural factor. By this means, the interrelated aspects of people and environment that comprise a complex system can be disassembled, understood in a simple way, and reassembled in a variety of complex ways. The extra dimension of historical time provides some additional complications, as the distribution and character of some factors change over time, but it is also the key to constructing a meaningful environmental history. Ecological planning by this overlay method allows rational planning decisions to be made about the future on the basis of relevant environmental factors that provide opportunities and constraints. It is a predictive exercise, based on the assumption that future impacts of a particular action can be understood in advance rather thoroughly and somewhat accurately. To apply the same method backward in time is an explanatory exercise. The relationships between land and people are still assumed to be primary, but the purpose of the analysis is to understand which environmental factors provided opportunities and constraints for which activities at different historical periods and to arrive at reasonable explanations for certain behaviors and events.

The scope of the study is northeast Florida from before the time of the first inhabitants to the formation of contemporary landscapes in the 1930s or so. It is a basic assumption of the study that changes in the environment were caused partly by people and that people changed because of the dynamic factors of environment, among other reasons. In addition, an environmental historical analysis should not only explicate but also explain, tell not only what happened but also why. And finally, if we can understand how people and environment affected each other in the past and do so in the present, we should be able to project those important relationships into the future and improve our ability to make planning decisions.

The Region

The selection of any region for study is a decision about inclusion and exclusion. Regions are, in a sense, arbitrary boundaries imposed upon continuously variable landscapes at some convenient scale. Northeast Florida, as it is defined here, includes primarily the basin of the northward-flowing St. Johns River from Lake George to the mouth, as well as the adjacent Atlantic Coast and the intervening coastal plain (map 1.1). This area, measuring roughly 120 miles north-south and between 25 and 60 miles east-west, about 5,000 square miles (roughly the size of Connecticut), takes in

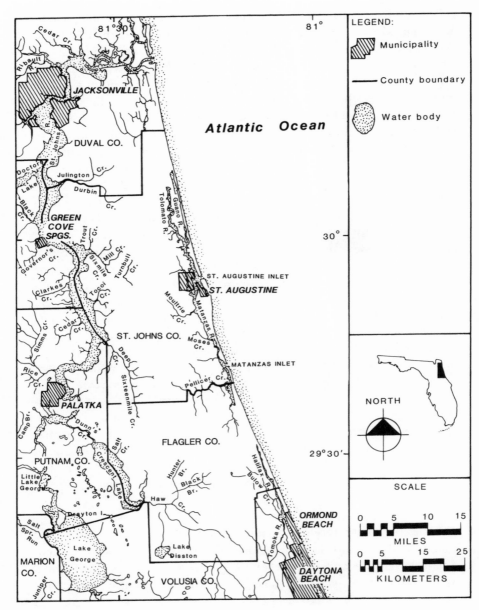

Map 1.1. The region. After U.S. Geological Survey 1:250,000 Jacksonville (1966), and Daytona Beach (1972) Topographic Sheets

Fig. 1.1. View of the St. Johns River at Fort Caroline. Florida Photographic Archives.

most of the significant historical developments in Florida of the sixteenth, seventeenth, and eighteenth centuries. Before European contact, it was also a cohesive culture area characterized by a range of riverine and coastal adaptive strategies practiced by Archaic, Woodland, and Mississippian period aboriginal groups, lasting some 10,000 years.

For convenience of mapping, the boundaries have been chosen as 29 degrees latitude on the south, 30 degrees 30 minutes latitude on the north, 81 degrees 45 minutes longitude on the west, and the Atlantic Ocean on the east. This area includes all of the floodplain and most of the drainage basin of the lower (northern) St. Johns River (fig. 1.1) as far upstream as the southern edge of Lake George, the sandy, relict Pleistocene terraces of the coastal plain east of the St. Johns River, the intermittent series of coastal lagoons, and the Atlantic coastline. The mainland part of northeast Florida consists of a broad peninsula bounded on the west by the St. Johns River Basin and on the east by the Atlantic Ocean. For the longest part of human occupation in the area, these bodies of water were the primary focus of settlement, transportation and resources. As it remains to some extent today, the intervening sandy mainland was sparsely occupied.

This northern portion of the St. Johns differs from its more southern course in being quite broad, navigable, and bordered by rich soils on adjacent uplands. As long ago as 5,000 years, aboriginal cultural patterns reflecting distinctive modes of subsistence, settlement choice, and technology could be recognized in northeast Florida. The region corresponds well with the territory of the Eastern Timucua Indians, as recorded in the middle of the sixteenth century. Throughout the First Spanish Period, between 1565 and 1763, effective European control of the entire Florida peninsula rarely extended beyond the boundaries of the study area. The British, upon acquiring Florida from the Spanish in 1763, fixed the Indian boundary north of Lake George, and although this line was not permanent, with the exception of the ill-fated New Smyrna colony on the coast, little British settlement in East Florida occurred south of Lake George. Between 1783 and 1821, when the Spanish again controlled Florida, patterns of settlement characteristic of northeast Florida extended farther south along the river and the coastal lagoons. It was not until the beginning of the twentieth century, however, that significant settlement was undertaken in the central and southern parts of the state. By this time northeast Florida no longer contained the majority of population in Florida, but it remained a recognizable culture area.

The Geology

Northeast Florida lies entirely within the Coastal Plain physiographic province of North America. Although basement rocks of pre-Cenozoic age are present at great depth, surface and bedrock features are restricted to Tertiary and Quaternary expressions. Surface landscape features of northeast Florida are mainly determined by geological processes of marine terrace development that occurred perhaps as early as Miocene times but definitely during the Pleistocene Epoch. In general, the region exhibits a series of flat, sandy plains of differing elevations, believed to have been formed by distinct episodes of advance and retreat of the seas. As the climate cooled over geologic time, glaciers locked up increasing amounts of seawater, and sea level became relatively lower with respect to the land surface. As the cli-

Table 1.1. Pleistocene marine terraces in northeast Florida

Terrace name	Approximate altitude of shoreline (feet)	Tentative age
Coharie	215	Yarmouth
Sunderland	170	
Wicomico	100	Sangamon
Penholoway	70	
Talbot	42	
Pamlico	25	Interglacial recession in Wisconsin glacial
Silver Bluff	5–10	Interglacial recession in Wisconsin glacial or Recent

Source: After Bermes, Leve, and Tarver (1963:38).

mate warmed, glaciers melted, sea level rose (often far above its present elevation), and coastal processes resulted in the formation of coast-parallel terraces.

The mechanics of terrace formation are presently being reinterpreted. The classic explanation by Cooke (1939, 1945) is that still stands of sea at certain levels were accompanied by wave and current action that formed a gently sloping or flat plain offshore, marked at the shoreline by a wave-cut bluff or low scarp. Coastal barrier islands could be associated with such abandoned shorelines and would provide some minor local relief. Cooke recognized seven, possibly eight, marine terraces in Florida; seven of these are present in northeast Florida (table 1.1). Distribution of the terraces designated by Cooke, as mapped by later authors (Bermes, Leve, and Tarver 1963), is shown in map 1.2.

In general, the pattern these form is like two broad series of steps, one rising from the Atlantic Coast and descending to the basin of the St. Johns River, the other ascending to a somewhat higher level on the western side of the river toward the middle of the Florida peninsula. Age of the terraces increases with elevation, so that near the Atlantic Coast and along the St. Johns River landforms and soils are relatively young. On the ridge between the river and the ocean and west of the St. Johns, soils have had somewhat more time to develop. Nonetheless, all of the region's soils are sandy, not unlike modern beach sand, and have little capacity to hold nutrients. The character of these sediments and their general distribution is shown in map 1.3, which illustrates the coast-parallel orientation of bands of different

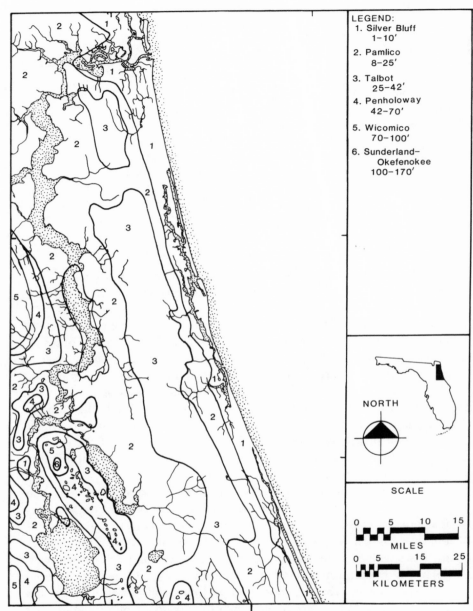

LEGEND:
1. Silver Bluff
   1–10'
2. Pamlico
   8–25'
3. Talbot
   25–42'
4. Penholoway
   42–70'
5. Wicomico
   70–100'
6. Sunderland–
   Okefenokee
   100–170'

NORTH

SCALE

0   5   10   15
MILES

0   5   15   25
KILOMETERS

Map 1.2. Marine terraces. After Bermes, Leve and Tarver (1963: fig. 3) and Healy (1975)

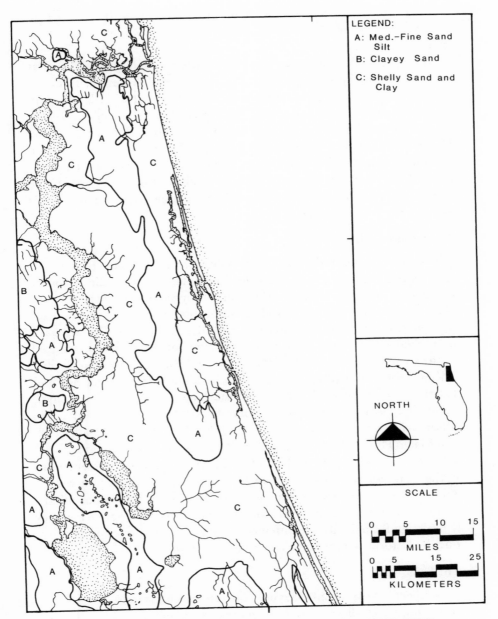

Map 1.3. Subsurface sediments. After Florida Bureau of Geology (1978, 1979)

types of subsurface sediments, as well as by the fact that the more recent coastal deposits contain a higher proportion of shells that have not yet decomposed.

The more modern interpretation of the formation of marine terraces has been developed by geologists in Georgia, where the same features are present but contemporary coastal processes associated with the development of beach, barrier island, and lagoon complexes are more evident. According to the model developed by Hoyt and others (Hoyt, Henry, and Howard 1966; Hoyt 1967; Hoyt and Hails 1974), the Pleistocene coastal deposits accumulated in barrier island environments, and the "terraces" are really former salt marsh lagoons. Regardless of the model of terrace formation that is followed, there is no doubt that the regional landscape is geologically young and coastal in origin.

The Physiography

The basic character of the regional physiography is illustrated in map 1.4, representing the later effects of erosion and redeposition on the originally continuous and level terraces. This map of physiographic divisions provides a convenient but broad-scale identification of surface features. Certain portions of the ridge associated with the Penholoway Terrace have been removed by stream erosion, and the remnant elevations are assigned to the Center Park Ridge, the Atlantic Coastal Ridge, and Espanola Hill. The St. Johns River Basin is contained within the Eastern Valley north of Palatka; south of this point the river is much narrower, following a physiographic division known as the St. Johns Offset. East and just north of the offset is an area of high elevation containing Teasdale Hill, Palatka Hill, San Mateo Hill, and the Crescent City Ridge, within which an area above 100 feet in elevation is termed Welaka Hill. More accurate representations of these divisions are visible in map 1.5, a topographic map of the region. While these physiographic divisions may appear subtle compared with the more dramatic surface expressions common in areas with more relief, they exhibit significant landscape differences and were clearly recognized as distinct by historic and prehistoric populations of northeast Florida.

The Soils

Soils reflect in great detail the types of landscape characteristics that influence land use in all periods. Some means of summarizing the important characteristics of soils is necessary, because at the level of soils series or type there is simply too much information available for a region of 5,000 square miles. Modern soil classification is hierarchical; its smallest unit is the

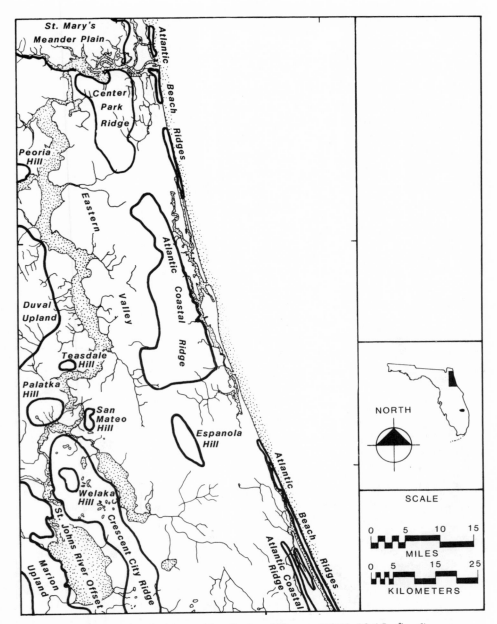

Map 1.4. Physiographic divisions. After Puri and Vernon (1964: 13.15, fig. 6)

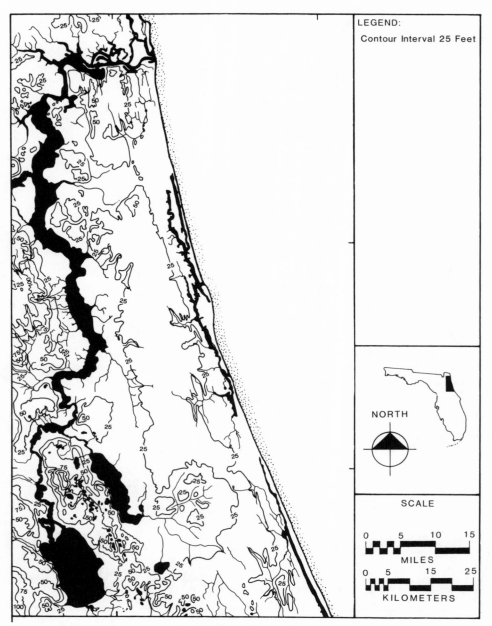

NORTH

SCALE

| 0 | 5 | 10 | 15 |

MILES

| 0 | 5 | 15 | 25 |

KILOMETERS

Map 1.5. Topography. After U.S. Geological Survey (1966, 1972)

pedon, defined as any mappable exposure of soil. Areas of identical soil characteristics comprise a soil type, which is usually defined at the county level, although adjacent counties may share soil types or series of types. The next largest classification is the *association,* a commonly occurring group of types that exhibit patterned landscape variation. Even this level of information may prove too detailed for a region the size of northeast Florida.

For purposes of mapping and analysis soil associations have been further grouped into three broad types. Map 1.6 shows these broad categories in northeast Florida, combinations of soil associations based on drainage characteristics for the eight counties within the region as classified in the Florida General Soils Atlas (Florida Division of State Planning 1975). Table 1.2 presents the individual soil associations for each county in each mapping category. Analyzing this information from the Florida Division of State Planning reveals more detail than has been revealed by any other mapping category yet presented.

Map 1.6 shows in black the areas of permanently flowing or standing water, rivers, lakes, and lagoons. The vertical lines represent areas dominated by poorly and very poorly drained soils subject to flooding—freshwater swamps, floodplains, and coastal marshes—and are closely associated with permanent bodies of water. The horizontal lines represent the opposite extreme of drainage, areas dominated by sandy, droughty soils not subject to flooding. Such soils are generally distributed along the coast, where they represent geologically young sediments with poorly developed soil profiles, and also occur adjacent to the St. Johns River, especially on the higher terraces. Finally, unshaded portions of the map show areas dominated by moderately well to poorly drained soils not subject to flooding. These areas comprise most of the interior portion of the region and are interrupted by the other two drainage types in regular patterns.

It is useful to note not only the specific occurrence of a particular drainage type but also the relationship between drainage types. For example, bodies of water have been attractive for settlement throughout prehistoric and historic times, yet wherever they are bounded by poorly and very poorly drained soils subject to flooding, certain land uses are unlikely to have occurred. Alternatively, the combination of water bodies and sandy, droughty soils indicates a higher settlement potential for some periods, but agricultural activities on such land would probably be unsuccessful. Finally, those parts of the St. Johns River and the coastal lagoons that are bordered by moderately well to poorly drained soils not subject to flooding provide the most attractive combination of landscape features for settlement and many types of land use for a wide range of technologies.

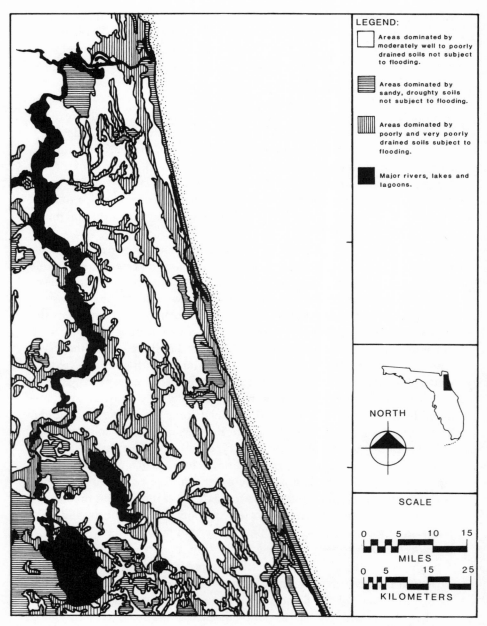

LEGEND:

Areas dominated by moderately well to poorly drained soils not subject to flooding.

Areas dominated by sandy, droughty soils not subject to flooding.

Areas dominated by poorly and very poorly drained soils subject to flooding.

Major rivers, lakes and lagoons.

NORTH

SCALE

| 0 | 5 | 10 | 15 |
MILES

| 0 | 5 | 15 | 25 |
KILOMETERS

Map 1.6. Soils by drainage type. After Florida Division of State Planning (1975)

Table 1.2. Soil associations comprising drainage categories

Areas dominated by sandy, droughty soils not subject to flooding

Fripp-Aquic Quartzipsamment association (Duval, St. Johns Cos.)
Lakeland-Tavares, variant association (Duval Co.)
Paola-Pomello association (St. Johns, Flagler, Volusia Cos.)
Palm Beach-Canaveral association (St. Johns, Flagler, Volusia Cos.)
Candler-Tavares association (St. Johns, Flagler Cos.)
Alpin-Blanton association (Clay, Putnam Cos.)
Astatula association (Putnam, Marion, Lake Cos.)
Candler-Apopka association (Putnam, Marion Cos.)
Astatula-Tavares association (Volusia Co.)
Astatula-Apopka association (Lake Co.)

*Areas dominated by moderately well to poorly drained soils
not subject to flooding*

Tavares, variant-Leon association (Duval, St. Johns, Clay Cos.)
Mascotte-Leon-Surrency association (Duval, St. Johns, Clay, Putnam Cos.)
Leon-Pomello, variant-Rutlege association (Duval, St. Johns Cos.)
Scranton, variant-Leon-Rutlege association (Duval Co.)
Wabasso, Thermic variant-Leon association (Duval, St. Johns Cos.)
Stilson-Pelham-Mascotte association (St. Johns, Clay, Putnam Cos.)
Adamsville-Immokalee-Pompano association (St. Johns Co.)
Myakka-Wauchula-Placid association (St. Johns, Flagler, Putnam, Volusia Cos.)
Olustee variant-Placid-Myakka association (St. Johns, Flagler, Putnam Cos.)
Meggett variant-Wauchula-Chobee association (St. Johns, Putnam Cos.)
Chipley-Leon-Osier association (Clay, Putnam Cos.)
Tavares-Myakka-Basinger association (Clay, Putnam, Volusia Cos.)
Olustee-Rutlege-Leon association (Clay, Putnam Cos.)
Myakka-Pomello-Basinger association (Flagler, Volusia Cos.)
Wabasso-Myakka-Felda association (Flagler, Putnam Cos.)
Meggett-Felda association (Flagler Co.)
Bladen, variant-Wauchula-Chobee association (Flagler Co.)
Pomello-Satellite-Immokalee association (Putnam, Volusia Cos.)
Pomello-Myakka association (Putnam Co.)
Myakka-Sellers association (Putnam, Marion Cos.)
Copeland-Wabasso association (Volusia Co.)
Pomello-Paola association (Lake Co.)
Myakka-Placid-Swamp association (Lake Co.)

(continued)

Table 1.2—*Continued*

Areas dominated by poorly and very poorly drained soils subject to flooding

---

Chobee, Thermic variant association (Duval Co.)
Freshwater swamp association (Duval, St. Johns, Clay, Flagler, Putnam, Volusia Cos.)
Saltwater marsh association (Duval, St. Johns, Flagler, Volusia Cos.)
Pompano-Anclote association (St. Johns, Flagler Cos.)
Dredge spoil (St. Johns Co.)
Brighton association (Clay, Flagler, Putnam, Volusia Cos.)
Iberia, variant-Manatee-Felda association (Flagler Co.)
Placid-Myakka association (Volusia Co.)
Iberia, variant-Manatee-Felda association (Volusia Co.)
Basinger-Myakka association (Marion Co.)
Sellers-Pamlico association (Marion, Lake Cos.)
Montverde-Ocoee-Brighton association (Lake Co.)

Source: After Florida Division of State Planning (1975).

The Climate

The climate of northeast Florida is classified as humid subtropical and is characteristic of the Gulf and Atlantic coastal plain of the southeastern United States. Rainfall averages about 52 inches per year, decreasing slightly toward the north at Jacksonville to around 50 inches per year. Within the region rainfall is slightly heavier along the immediate coast. The majority of precipitation falls in the summer, from June through September, when showers and thunderstorms are common, and it averages between six and eight inches per month. In the winter, rainfall is more moderate; two to four inches per month is normal.

The monthly extremes follow the same annual pattern; maximum recorded rainfall per month ranges from 5.3 inches in December (1941) to 15.67 inches in July (1960). All months other than June through September have experienced minimum precipitation of less than one inch. The minimum recorded for the summer rainy months is less than four inches (Bradley 1972:16). Precipitation in the form of snow and ice is negligible. Traces were reported at Jacksonville in 1955, 1961, and 1962, and measurable amounts, less than two inches, were recorded in February 1899 and 1958. Snow produced a white Christmas in 1989, when more than three inches fell in some parts of Jacksonville (Henry, Portier, and Coyne 1994: 135).

Throughout Florida, warm-season rainfall is at its maximum near the coast, where surface heating and sea breezes interact. The typical summer rainfall pattern includes frequent afternoon thunderstorms and occasional hurricanes or tropical storms. The proportion of annual rainfall attributable to thunderstorms is difficult to evaluate, but such storms occur approximately 70 days per year, and about 70 percent of this total occurs during the summer months; summer thunderstorms may drop two to three inches of rain in a few hours. As much as 30 percent of the total annual rainfall can be expected from hurricanes and tropical storms. Over the period 1891–1980, for the entire state of Florida 10.7 hurricanes and 10.6 tropical storms were reported per decade, an average of about one per year for each type. Major storms of this type are not as common in northeast Florida as in south Florida.

Seasonal variation in temperature follows that of rainfall. A summer period of high temperatures occurs between June and September, and a cooler period extends from December through March; these are separated by more moderate transitional seasons. The annual mean temperature for Jacksonville is just above 68 degrees Fahrenheit. Average daily summer temperatures are between 70 and 90 degrees; highest temperatures are reached in early afternoon but are frequently reduced by afternoon thunderstorms. In winter, average daily temperatures range from 45 to just below 70 degrees.

Extremes of temperature on an annual basis are consistent with this pattern. Between 1940 and 1970, five months experienced maximum extreme temperatures above 100 degrees, May through September. Temperatures below freezing were experienced in four months, November through February. The lowest of these was 12 degrees, recorded in December 1962 (Bradley 1972:16).

Freezing temperatures may be expected about 12 times per year, but in most such cases the temperature will rise above 32 degrees sometime during the day. Only on five days during the period of record (since 1851) has the temperature remained below freezing for an entire 24-hour period. Several of these occasions mark memorable and agriculturally damaging freezes, like those of 1835 and 1899. The earliest recorded date of freeze is November 3 (1954) and the latest recorded date of freeze is March 31 (1964) (National Oceanic and Atmospheric Administration 1978).

Of all the continental states, Florida is most exposed to the risk of severe tropical storms. Bounded on the west by the Gulf of Mexico and on the east by the Atlantic Ocean, the peninsula is directly in the path of many storms of tropical origin. Between 1886 and 1992, 85 hurricanes struck Florida

(Henry, Portier, and Coyne 1994:207). Hurricanes are most frequent in the southern part of the state, but no part is immune from their damage. Several means are used to predict the probable point on the coastline where a hurricane may strike land.

The coast of the United States from Texas to Maine has been divided into equal segments 50 nautical miles in length for purposes of assessing storm probability and season. In northeast Florida (Sector 33) there is a 5 percent probability that a tropical storm will occur and a 2 percent chance a hurricane will occur in any one year. A tropical storm or cyclone has wind speeds between 39 and 73 miles per hour, a hurricane between 74 and 124 miles per hour. Great hurricanes, storms with winds in excess of 125 miles per hour, have almost no probability of occurring in northeast Florida. Of all of Florida, the northeast part of the state has the lowest hurricane risk. In fact, between St. Augustine and Jacksonville no hurricane was noted in official records until September 1964; however, hurricanes are suggested by historical records in 1565 (Henry, Portier, and Coyne 1994); 1765 (De Brahm 1773:39); 1837, 1848 (Ludlum 1963:26); and 1894 (Graham 1983:204). The hurricane of 1565 played a crucial role in Spain's successful defeat of a French force near St. Augustine (Ludlum 1963:8). Tracks of five hurricanes passed through the region in the twentieth century, but none caused great damage (Doehring, Duedall, and Williams 1994:99–108). Before 1964, Jacksonville was the only large city on the Atlantic Coast south of Boston that had never experienced an officially recognized storm of hurricane intensity (Bradley 1972:4).

The earliest and latest dates of tropical storm or hurricane occurrences between 1886 and 1970 in northeast Florida are June 6 and October 17. These dates are not inconsistent with other parts of the Florida coast and generally reflect the hurricane season.

Although the probability of a hurricane or tropical storm affecting northeast Florida in any year is quite low, these storms are among the most forceful and potentially damaging natural phenomena in the area. The massive energy of hurricanes is primarily felt in winds that may often exceed 100 miles per hour and that are believed for certain storms to have reached more than 200 miles per hour. Such winds will often break off trees high above ground level and cause considerable damage to buildings and other structures. Rainfall during a hurricane is heavy but might not exceed that likely to be dropped during a typical thunderstorm. Some hurricanes are accompanied by very little rain. By far the most potentially damaging characteristic of severe tropical storms is storm surge of seawater along the coast. Depending on the time of the hurricane within the daily and annual tidal cycles, as well as the speed of the wind, storm surge can be very high, sometimes above 10 feet. In such an instance, the coastal region to an elevation of 10 feet above mean sea level can be inundated, and the damage to natural and cultural features near the shore can be extensive.

The Hydrology

Pleistocene and Recent sediments of Quaternary age account for the upper 50 feet or so of surface sediments. They follow to some degree the slight contours of the underlying limestone but generally mask any structural characteristics with a relatively level, homogeneous deposit. The surface expression is the result of Pleistocene erosion, deposition, and reworking of sediments rather than any processes occurring in earlier geologic periods. The geologic map of the region is shown in map 1.7.

While the region is relatively flat, the landscape is quite varied, owing mainly to the importance of surface water. Relief is not pronounced, ranging from sea level to less than 150 feet, yet a few feet in elevation at a locale can mean the difference between dry, habitable, cultivable land and freshwater swamp or coastal marsh. The slope of the St. Johns River from Lake George to the Atlantic Ocean is only about five feet in 100 miles, but at certain locations the banks of this slow and large body of water provide rich soils and high, dry, commanding elevations. In the interior, between the river and the ocean, drainage courses are usually poorly defined and bordered by extensive freshwater swamps. In addition, the presence of impermeable clays below the surface results in areas of poor drainage that remain wet for at least part of each year.

Although the region is entirely covered by a mantle of Pleistocene and Recent sediments, the nature of which is distinctly determined by their marine origin, certain aspects of the subsurface geology have influenced patterns of human settlement and resource extraction. Bedrock formations consist mainly of limestones of Tertiary age forming relatively undeformed beds of horizontal sediments. From oldest to youngest a typical section exhibits the Lake City and Avon Park limestones of the lower Eocene, penetrated usually in wells only over 200 feet deep. The next three limestone beds, the Inglis, Williston, and Crystal River Formations, have been designated the Ocala group, and are upper Miocene in age. These have no surface expression in northeast Florida but comprise the uppermost and most productive beds of the Floridan Aquifer, the main supply of nonsurface water for the region. Overlying the Ocala Group is the Hawthorn Formation of Miocene age, which is sandier than the purer limestones below and contains sufficient clay to act as an aquiclude (a confining impermeable

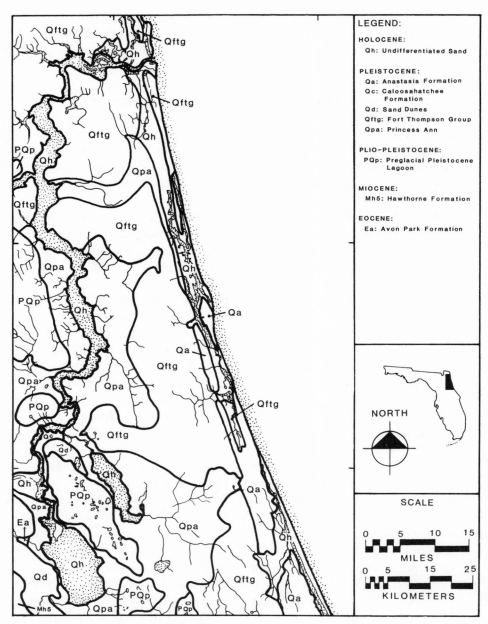

Map 1.7. Surficial geology. After Brooks (1981)

layer) for the Floridan Aquifer. The next youngest sediments are of sand, shell, and silty clay. They are generally undifferentiated and are usually grouped together as upper Miocene and/or Pliocene deposits. They may yield small quantities of water but have low permeability. There are two major subsurface bodies of water that participate in the regional hydrology, the deep artesian reservoir and the shallow nonartesian reservoir, which includes the groundwater table. As illustrated in the generalized diagram of hydrologic conditions (fig. 1.2), the artesian aquifer is several hundred feet below the land surface. This aquifer consists of the important Floridan Aquifer, which is made up of the Eocene-age Ocala Group of limestone formations as well as the overlying Miocene or Pliocene beds of marl, clay, and dolomite of the Hawthorn Formation that comprise an aquiclude of very low permeability. Wherever the land elevation is below the piezometric surface (that elevation to which water will rise in a tightly capped well), water will flow freely from any open well or sinkhole that penetrates the Floridan Aquifer.

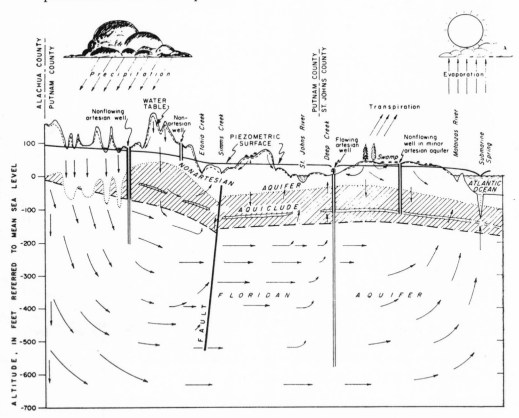

Fig. 1.2. Generalized hydrologic conditions. From Bermes, Leve and Tarver (1963: fig. 10)

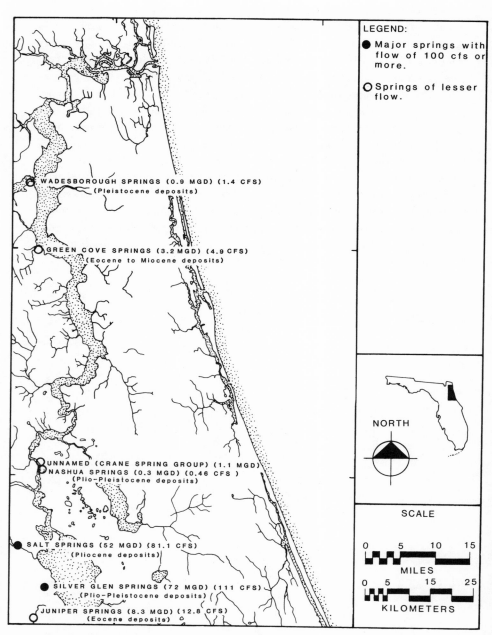

WADESBOROUGH SPRINGS (0.9 MGD) (1.4 CFS)
(Pleistocene deposits)

GREEN COVE SPRINGS (3.2 MGD) (4.9 CFS)
(Eocene to Miocene deposits)

UNNAMED (CRANE SPRING GROUP) (1.1 MGD)
NASHUA SPRINGS (0.3 MGD) (0.46 CFS)
(Plio-Pleistocene deposits)

SALT SPRINGS (52 MGD) (81.1 CFS)
(Pliocene deposits)

SILVER GLEN SPRINGS (72 MGD) (111 CFS)
(Plio-Pleistocene deposits)

JUNIPER SPRINGS (8.3 MGD) (12.8 CFS)
(Eocene deposits)

NORTH

SCALE

0   5   10   15
MILES

0   5   15   25
KILOMETERS

Map 1.8. Springs. After Ferguson and others (1947)

Above the aquiclude is a reservoir of groundwater known as the non-artesian aquifer, which does not have sufficient hydrostatic potential or head to cause artesian flow but will have surface expression, depending upon the relative elevations of the land surface and the water table. Wherever the elevation of the water table is above the surface of the land, water will stand in ponds or swamps, or flow in streams. Height of the water table is locally variable and depends upon the supply and demand experienced by the nonartesian aquifer. Both the deep and shallow aquifers exchange water by slow seepage through the intervening aquiclude, and both are replenished by recharge in their respective areas of high hydrostatic potential. The aquifers may be more directly connected to the surface by sinkhole springs, which depending upon local conditions, may provide great volumes of water for surface flow or may serve to recharge the aquifer with surface water. There are seven permanently flowing springs in northeast Florida, all situated near the St. Johns River (map 1.8). They range in size from Silver Glen Springs, west of Lake George, which has an average flow of 72 million gallons per day (111 cubic feet per second), to Nashua Springs near Satsuma, with an average flow of 0.3 million gallons per day (0.46 cubic feet per second) (Ferguson et al. 1947).

The deep artesian reservoir, consisting of the Floridan Aquifer and overlying aquiclude, underlies all of Florida and the south part of Georgia. Its importance to modern settlement cannot be overemphasized, as it supplies the public, agricultural, and irrigation water supply of the region. Despite the huge quantity of water represented by the Floridan Aquifer, its maintenance in certain areas, particularly around Jacksonville and Palatka, is in question. Whenever local demand by pumping exceeds replenishment from the recharge areas, the level of the aquifer declines, particularly at the location of deep wells, where cones of depression are formed. Since the Floridan Aquifer is underlain by permeable beds containing water of high chloride content, freshwater is replaced by saltwater. Coastal areas are especially prone to such saltwater intrusion, which, although easily caused, is not so readily corrected.

The Drainage

The dominant factor in the northeast Florida landscape is water, both as it occurs in the defined drainages of the St. Johns River, the coastal lagoons, and various streams and at or below the ground surface in intervening areas.

Drainage refers to that part of the hydrologic cycle involving water on the surface. The pattern and quantity of drainage depends not only on topography and rainfall, as is true in any area, but also on the characteristics of the groundwater table. Within northeast Florida, water is present on the surface, in the shallow aquifer, and in the deep Floridan Aquifer. There are areas of recharge for the shallow and deep aquifers, as well as areas where water escapes the Floridan aquifer by artesian flow. At the beginning of the twentieth century, nearly all of northeast Florida was subject to artesian flow, occasionally through sinkhole springs and more commonly through uncapped, free-flowing wells; more recently, water pumping has reduced the elevation of the piezometric surface, and less of the region is now subject to artesian flow.

Hydrologic units or drainage basins of northeast Florida are shown on map 1.9. At the northern extreme of the region is the Nassau River Basin, an area of tidal marsh and low elevation drained by the Nassau River, which empties into the Atlantic at the north end of Duval County. Along the Atlantic Coast is the Upper Coastal Basin, a narrow strip drained by small streams that empty into a series of lagoons: Guano River and Tolomato River north of St. Augustine, Matanzas River south of St. Augustine, and the Halifax River north of Daytona Beach. These lagoons contrast with dendritic interior drainages in being wide, coast parallel, and entirely tidal. They have been formed as a series of bays behind barrier islands that front the Atlantic. There is a very small portion of the Oklawaha River Basin in the region at its confluence with the St. Johns River north of Lake George, and this marks the boundary between the Lower St. Johns River Basin, already mentioned, and the Middle St. Johns River Basin to the south, which includes Lake George. The distribution of surface drainage is presented in map 1.10, which includes names of the major rivers, streams, and coastal lagoons.

The St. Johns River is Florida's largest river and one of the few large rivers in the United States that flows northward. Within the region it averages one mile in breadth and is tidally influenced for its 120-mile length. Because of this tidal influence, water may flow upstream (south) during periods of high wind and high tide, and the volume of such flow is considerable. Although the average discharge at the mouth of the St. Johns in Jacksonville averages 8,300 cubic feet per second, the total upstream and downstream flow at the same station can reach 130,000 cubic feet per second (Snell and Anderson 1970). This significant movement of water is characterized more by volume owing to the river's width than by velocity, as the river appears at all times to be only slowly moving. Nonetheless, it stores a great volume of surface water in its low flood plain, which may reach 10 miles in width. The very shallow gradient, around 0.05 feet per

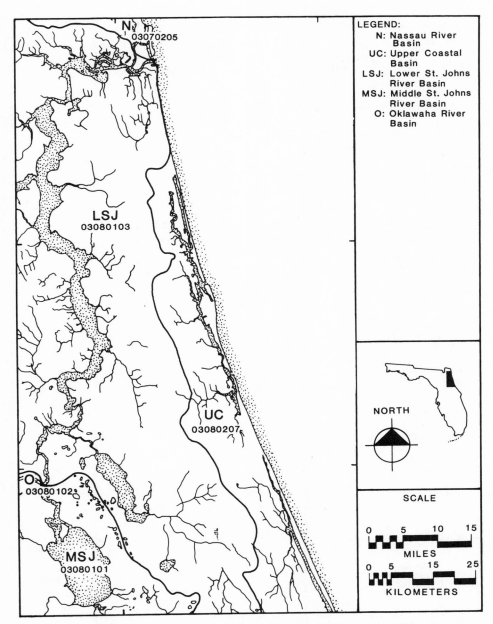

Map 1.9. Hydrologic units. After U.S. Geological Survey (1975) and U.S. Water Resources Council (1970)

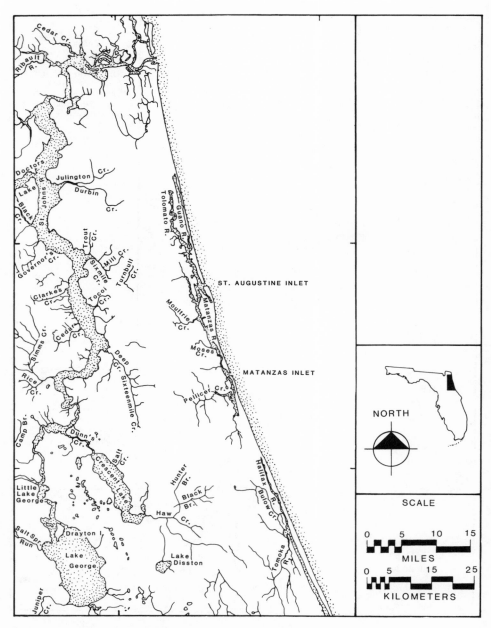

Map 1.10. Surface drainage. After U.S. Geological Survey (1976)

Fig. 1.3. The St. Johns River Offset. View of the St. Johns River south of Lake George in the late 1940s. Florida Photographic Archives.

mile, combined with tidal influence allows water to remain in the basin for a long period of time.

Geologically, the St. Johns River within northeast Florida may be divided into two parts, a very broad northern course following the Eastern Valley physiographic division and, south of Palatka, a considerably narrower section following the St. Johns River Offset physiographic division. The northern part of the river represents an estuary or coastal lagoon formed by the Pamlico Sea during Pleistocene times that was subsequently isolated by development of seaward marine terraces. South of Palatka (fig. 1.3), the river is offset west of the Eastern Valley and separated from it by an older Plio-Pleistocene terrace ridge exhibiting remnants of the Talbot, Penholoway, and Wicomico terraces. In fact, the broad character of the Lower (northern) St. Johns channel is reflected in the orientation and shape of Crescent Lake within the Eastern Valley, from which the flow of the St. Johns was likely captured during the Pleistocene Epoch (White 1970). The intervening terrace ridge, which comprises the Crescent City Ridge and some associated hills, is the only part of northeast Florida characterized by solution sinkholes and lakes.

The Upper Coastal Basin (map 1.9), extending in a band about 10 miles wide inland from the Atlantic Coast, was formed by the same geologic processes as the St. Johns River Basin, but in geologically more recent times. It consists of a linear series of coast-parallel estuaries or lagoons entirely within the limits of the Silver Bluff terrace. These coastal features may be in some cases no more than 5,000 years old, having been formed in association with coastal barrier islands at a time of rising or stable sea levels during the current glacial recession.

A few freshwater dendritic streams, including Moultrie, Pellicer, and Bulow Creeks along with the Tomoka River, drain the inland flatwoods eastward to the coastal lagoons, but the predominant character of drainage along the coast is coast-parallel, brackish lagoon bordered by salt marsh. An important effect of the coastal barrier islands is to shield the mainland from the high energy of the coast and to provide stable areas along the lagoons. These sheltered areas have been important for settlement, transportation, and food throughout prehistoric and historic times.

The Vegetation

Like soils, the natural vegetation of northeast Florida can be mapped and studied at different levels of detail. A classification is required that can be mapped accurately at the scale selected for this study and has a sufficient number of categories to distinguish broad regional patterns of vegetation. Map 1.11 presents natural vegetation (vegetation that would be expected without severe human intervention), which is divided into eight categories. Following the patterns already recognized in physiography and soils, the region is seen to comprise a coastal strip characterized mainly by coastal strand, coastal marshes, and small areas of cabbage palm hammock and sand pine. The broad interior between the coast and the St. Johns River is characterized simply as an expanse of pine flatwoods interior interrupted by hardwood swamp forests and cypress swamps. Along the St. Johns River, which interrupts the pine flatwoods continuing to the west, are large areas of longleaf pine forest; these occur on the high terraces east of Lake George as well as near the mouth of the river. West of Lake George, on the sandy soils of Ocala National Forest, is a sand pine forest formed on well-drained relict dunes. Table 1.3 presents Davis's (1967) vegetation descriptions as depicted in map 1.11. Because the original soil mapping was completed at small scale, finer detail of drainage patterns is available from the soils map (1.6).

Modern vegetation in northeast Florida is a reflection of many centuries of land use as well as the introduction of a broad variety of exotic species.

Table 1.3. Classification of natural vegetation

1. Coastal Strand. A zoned vegetation on sand dunes and rock, composed of pioneer herbs and shrubs near the shore with scrub and forest zone more near the interior.

2. Pine Flatwoods. Open woodlands of one to three species of pine: longleaf, slash, and pond pines. Many herbs, saw palmetto, shrubs and small trees form an understory. Included in general flatwoods areas are small hardwood forests, many kinds of cypress swamps, prairies, marshes, and bay tree swamps.

3. Sand Pine, *Pinus clausa*, Scrub Forests. These occur mostly on excessively drained deep sandy soils, especially on old dunes of the coastal strand and old dunes or dry sands in the interior.

4. Forests of Longleaf Pine, *Pinus palustris*, and Xerophytic (dry site) Oaks. Mostly on well-drained uplands. The turkey oak, *Quercus laevis*, and wiregrass, *Aristida stricta*, are common.

5. Cypress Swamp Forests. These are found mostly in depressions and bordering rivers and lakes. Forests of many shapes, as round domes and long strands. Some have hardwood species associated.

6. Swamp Forests. Comprised mostly of several kinds of hardwoods bordering most rivers and growing in basins. Some Bay Tree, Gum, Nyssa, Titi, and cypress zones occur in many of these hardwood swamps.

7. Mangrove Swamp Forests and Coastal Marshes. Usually there are tidal conditions which vary from saline to brackish. Grass, sedge, and rush marshes along more temperate coasts.

8. Forests of Abundant Cabbage Palms, *Sabal palmetto*. Vary from scattered palms to groves of palms and oaks in hammocks.

Source: After Davis (1967); number refers to map symbol.

Virtually all virgin forest in the region has been cut; in fact most timberlands have been cut over several times. According to surveys conducted between 1908 and 1910 by Roland M. Harper approximately 95 percent of the pine flatwoods in the region remained uncultivated at the beginning of the century, and 99 percent of the coastal strand retained its natural vegetation (Harper 1914:395). Since that time, considerably more land has been cleared of vegetation for agricultural use, and, as agricultural land requirements change, many previously cleared areas have reverted to forest. The greatest change in vegetation, however, is that associated with residential and commercial development. With few exceptions, the result of

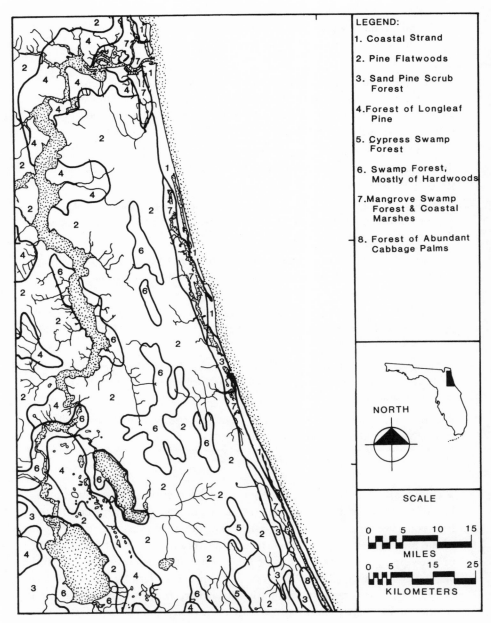

LEGEND:

1. Coastal Strand

2. Pine Flatwoods

3. Sand Pine Scrub Forest

4. Forest of Longleaf Pine

5. Cypress Swamp Forest

6. Swamp Forest, Mostly of Hardwoods

7. Mangrove Swamp Forest & Coastal Marshes

8. Forest of Abundant Cabbage Palms

NORTH

SCALE

0   5   10   15
MILES

0   5   15   25
KILOMETERS

Map 1.11. Natural vegetation. After Davis (1967)

residential development is to replace a naturally occurring landscape with an intensively managed one composed primarily of exotic species and impermeable surfaces.

The Fauna

Many animal species have been important to people in northeast Florida. The principal land animals historically used for food have been white-tailed deer, black bears, gray and fox squirrels, raccoons, opossum, marsh and cottontail rabbits, red and gray foxes, gopher tortoises, several kinds of snake, and perhaps cougars, bobcats, and weasels. Of aquatic and marine animals, the most important have been fish and shellfish, but otters, porpoises, manatees, several types of freshwater turtles, alligators, sea turtles, and bullfrogs also provided sources of meat (fig. 1.4). The principal shellfish have been oysters, quahogs, and donax along the coast, and apple snails and *Viviparus,* a gastropod, along the St. Johns River. Subsistence, sport, and commercial fishing have had long histories on the St. Johns, in the coastal bays and estuaries, and offshore. Shrimping has been the most important regional fishery on a commercial scale.

Fig. 1.4. *Killing Alligators*, de Bry engraving, 26 years after the painting by LeMoyne; published in 1591. Florida Photographic Archives.

Modern Land Use

Modern land use based on 1973 United States Geological Survey satellite data is shown in map 1.12. Forest lands account for slightly more than 60 percent of the total acreage and are almost all in private ownership, as there are no national or state forests in the region shown. Most forest land, when suitable, is managed by large paper companies for pulpwood production. Nearly 14 percent of the region is mapped as wetlands, which include both freshwater and saltwater wetlands. They occur directly along the coast and the St. Johns River, as well as scattered throughout the intervening pine flatwoods of the terraces in a pattern generally parallel with the coast. Ten percent of the region is mapped as water: coastal estuaries, the St. Johns River, and associated large lakes. Urban and built-up land comprises 8.3 percent of the total and includes Jacksonville and its suburbs, and Green Cove Springs and Palatka along the St. Johns River, as well as Jacksonville Beach, St. Augustine, Ormond Beach, and Daytona Beach along the coast. Not represented in the 1973 imagery on which the analysis is based is the planned community of Palm Coast in Flagler County, now one of the fastest growing counties, in terms of population increase, in the United States. Some 100 square miles will be under development over the next several decades, and this particular land-use conversion would account for approximately 2 percent of the region being removed from forest land use and added to urban or built-up use.

The Regional History

The development of the northeast Florida environment will be traced within this context of natural and cultural factors. The study will begin with a discussion of environment as it can be reconstructed before the arrival of people, which occurred sometime around 12,000 years ago. Prehistoric Indian occupations of northeast Florida will be summarized with reference to their particular modes of adaptation to local environments and the resulting settlement patterns during several periods of very different environmental conditions (table 1.4). The arrival of Europeans in the early sixteenth century begins the longest documented written history in the United States (table 1.5).

The starting point for understanding environmental dynamics is before human occupation—not in search of pristine nonhuman environments against which later environments might be compared but rather because the relationship between people and environment is continuous. The study begins with a reconstruction of conditions during the Late Pleistocene some 18,000 years ago when climate was cooler, sea level was much lower,

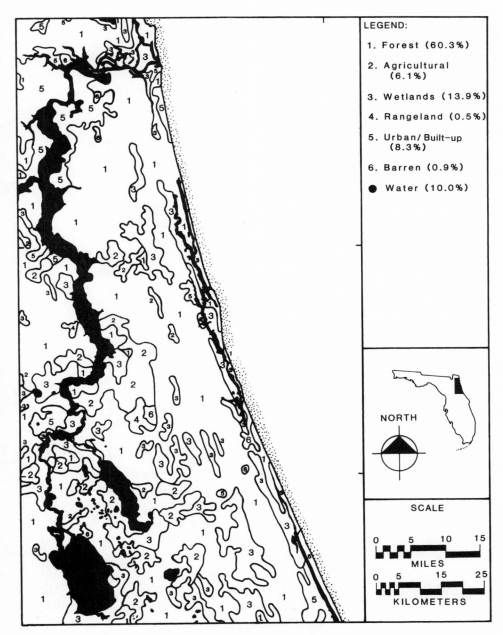

Map 1.12. Modern land use. Based on 1973 data after Fernald and Patton (1984: 163)

Table 1.4. Archaeological chronology

Years ago	Archaeological period	Geological epoch	Glacial stage
0	Historic		
1000	St. Johns II		
2000	I		
3000	Late Transitional		
4000	Archaic Orange	Holocene or	Postglacial
5000	Mt. Taylor	Recent	
6000	Middle Archaic		
7000			
8000	Early Archaic		
9000			
10,000			
11,000			
12,000			
13,000	Paleo Indian	Late Pleistocene	Late glacial transition
14,000	???		
15,000			
16,000	Prehuman environments		Full glacial
17,000			
18,000			

and the last Wisconsin glaciation was at its maximum. As global climate warmed and environments responded accordingly, terrain, drainage, fauna, and flora were all different from the present. The first inhabitants of northeast Florida adapted to Late Glacial conditions with a technology and settlement pattern suited to the hunting of scarce and large animals in a dry environment. Even at quite low population densities the environmental influence of these Paleo Indians may have included hunting to extinction a number of vertebrate species.

The most fundamental environmental changes between 10,000 and 5,000 years ago, however, were natural in origin and of such magnitude as to require different patterns of settlement, subsistence, and technology. As sea level rose to its present position, water sources, small game, and plant resources became more accessible with increased sedentism as the result.

Table 1.5. Historical chronology

Date A.D.	Historic period	Historic event
1975		
1950	Twentieth century	World War II
1925	World War I	
1900		
1875	Civil War and Reconstr.	Civil War
1850	Early statehood	Statehood, 1845
1825	Territorial period	Adams-Onis Treaty, 1821
1800	Second Spanish period	Treaty of Paris, 1783
1775	British period	American Revolution
1750		Treaty of Paris, 1763
1725		
1700	First Spanish period	
1675		
1650		
1625		
1600		
1575		St. Augustine founded, 1565
1550	Exploration and discovery	Ft. Caroline, 1562
1525	Protohistoric	
1500	Precontact	Ponce de León landing, 1513

Social organization likely increased in complexity as groups became larger, and new tool technologies were developed.

By about 5,000 years ago the environment of Florida and much of the southeast United States had become essentially like that of today. The sea had reached more or less its present level, barrier islands had formed on the coasts, stream gradients had become reduced and stabilized, vegetative complexes and their associated fauna were essentially modern, and the climate and landscape were much wetter than before. Indians living on the coast and along the St. Johns River were able to take advantage of stable and abundant fish and shellfish, an important source of protein, and as populations became more sedentary in response to more stable conditions, opportunities for specialized collection and domestication of plants increased.

With the introduction of agriculture about 3,000 years ago, environmental effects increased in some areas, particularly respecting vegetative cover and the use of fire for clearing (Larson 1980, Pyne 1982). Freshwater and estuarine locales continued to be favored for settlement; however, inland regions with fertile soils were also utilized and modified. By the time of first European contact, complex social and political organizations had developed based on a broad variety of wild foods as well as some crops (Deagan 1978).

The first permanent colony in North America, Fort Caroline at the mouth of the St. Johns River, was established by the French in 1564 and occupied by them until 1565. The French accounts provide the first detailed historical descriptions of the rich environment of northeast Florida and its native populations. Subsequent Spanish settlement at St. Augustine beginning in 1565, along with the destruction of the French force, began two centuries of Indian-European relations dominated by the Spanish and resulting in the eventual decimation of nearly all Indians in northeast Florida. During the First Spanish Period (1513–1763) the Florida settlement, primarily military and missionary, remained centered around St. Augustine and was dependent upon outside support from Spain and other New Spain settlements.

English occupation of Florida for the next 20 years was more productive and intensive. The accounts of De Brahm (1773), Romans (1775), and the Bartrams (J. Bartram 1769, W. Bartram 1791) provide a detailed environmental and social picture of northeast Florida around the time of the American Revolution. In contrast to their Spanish predecessors, British officials supported the development rather than the mere survival of the Florida colony. Large tracts of land were granted for the establishment of plantations devoted to export agriculture, new crops were introduced and marketed, and during this period timber was exported for the first time. When Spain reacquired control of Florida in 1783 under terms of the Second Treaty of Paris, many agricultural settlements were abandoned by the British, and much of the previously cleared and cultivated land reverted to secondary growth; Spanish attempts to turn East Florida into a self-sufficient and prosperous enterprise were not entirely successful, although a number of plantations were established, often continuing at the locations of the earlier British settlements.

The historical environmental record of the region was enriched considerably in the 1820s as the U.S. government attempted to assess its new territory (Simmons 1822, Vignoles 1823). Federal survey of township and section lines resulted in a rich historical landscape record, and a number of travelers described the region over the next several decades (Proby 1974, Williams 1837b). The Seminole Indian Wars that followed led to white abandonment of the interior in the 1830s (Cohen 1836), and the region was only slowly resettled after the passage of the Armed Occupation Act in 1842. Following the Civil War, the United States again encouraged settlement by deeding "swamp and overflowed lands" to the state, which in turn distributed huge tracts to railroad and development companies at very low cost. The famous railroad development of Henry M. Flagler opened Florida's east coast during the late nineteenth and early twentieth centuries and swelled the population of St. Augustine for a short time, yet much of northeast Florida remained either rural or unsettled (Barbour 1882, Hawks 1887). Citrus, vegetable, and timber production dominated the region's rural economy throughout the early twentieth century (Hanna and Hanna 1950).

Following World War II and the development of an adequate regional highway system, the coast and interior were opened for settlement in Florida's second period of intense residential development. Although much of the region remains forested and agricultural, coastal development pressure is now intense. Contemporary technology and seemingly abundant energy have combined to overcome the once intimate relationship between humans and environment, allowing land-use decisions to be based primarily on economic rather than ecological factors. Whether this is a viable strategy over the long term, or whether future adaptations must rely more directly and more benignly on local natural systems, is a question that environmental history may help answer.

2

The Late Pleistocene: Environments and People of the Last Ice Age, 18,000–10,000 Years Ago

Prehuman Environments, 18,000–15,000 Years Ago

Our account of northeast Florida begins at the peak of the most recent glaciation of the Pleistocene Epoch, around 18,000 years ago. A series of climatic cycles during the previous million or so years of the Pleistocene had resulted in four major advances and retreats of the polar ice around the globe. As temperatures cooled, seawater became trapped in the ice sheets covering the polar and upper latitudes of the northern and southern hemispheres. At the present time, glaciers cover about 10 percent of the earth's surface; during one or another of the Pleistocene glaciations ice covered nearly 30 percent of the globe (Flint 1971:80). Ice sheets extended in North America nearly as far south as the 40th parallel below the Great Lakes, affecting local climate and vegetation well into the southeastern United States. With so much of the earth's constant quantity of water locked up in the ice sheets, sea level was much lower than at present and the continental land masses were correspondingly larger. Florida, for example, is estimated to have been about twice its present size during the Wisconsin maximum.

While air temperatures everywhere were lower than they are now, the amount of difference depended on several factors, including proximity to the ice sheet. In the Great Lakes and northeast regions of the United States near the margin of the Laurentide ice sheet, temperatures may have been as much as 20 to 27 degrees Fahrenheit colder than at present, with most of the change occurring in winter. In South Carolina, at 34 degrees latitude, summer average temperature is estimated to have been 13 degrees Fahrenheit lower, winter as much as 32 degrees lower. This latitude seems to have marked the maximum southern extent of the boreal forests associated with the margin of the ice sheet. South of this point previously existing deciduous forests remained (Barry 1983).

It is unlikely that the Florida peninsula experienced temperatures as low as those associated with the boreal forests, because it appears that the boreal-deciduous forest ecotone represented a sharp climatic gradient (Delcourt 1980 in Barry 1983). While Florida and the lower Southeast served as a climatic refuge for plant and animal species displaced by the ice sheet and its associated cold climate margins, the air was considerably drier than it is at present. Xeric (dry) forest conditions—noted in Alabama as well as Florida as late as 13,000 years ago, on the basis of pollen evidence—may have been partially a result of the relative scarcity of water on the land surface. As the water tables dropped along with the sea level, they essentially dewatered the peninsula (Barry 1983:401). This phenomenon had an important influence on human adaptations throughout the time of low sea level.

Before discussing the effects of glacial climate upon plants and animals, it is necessary to establish the shape and size of the region during the Late Pleistocene. The size of the landform exposed to air at a given level of the sea is a function of the topography of the continental shelf. The approximate location of old shorelines can be determined by following the depth contour corresponding to the level of the sea below its present shoreline. Determining the relative movement of the shoreline, however, is somewhat more complicated, as sea level does not rise at a constant rate, nor does the continental shelf exhibit a constant slope. Thus, relative change in shoreline position is a function of two complex curves.

Figure 2.1 shows the generalized bathymetry of the continental shelf off the shore of Florida. The slope of the shelf is quite gradual and constant to about 95 kilometers offshore. For this distance the rate of slope is roughly 1 meter of depth for every 20 kilometers of distance. At a depth of 50 meters or so, the slope steepens considerably, falling 100 meters at the edge of the continental shelf in about 5 kilometers, or, for comparison, 400 meters in 20 kilometers. Around 18,000 years ago, when sea level was at its lowest during the peak of the glaciation, it was estimated to be about 100 meters below the present level, and the shoreline was approximately 100 km seaward of its present location. Because the slope is so steep at this point, a rising sea is not accompanied by much landward movement or transgression of the shoreline; a rise of 50 meters in sea level is accompanied by a transgression of only 5 kilometers. While this may seem like a great distance, the movement occurred over some 8,000 years.

Once the shallow slope of the shelf is reached by the advancing shore, a

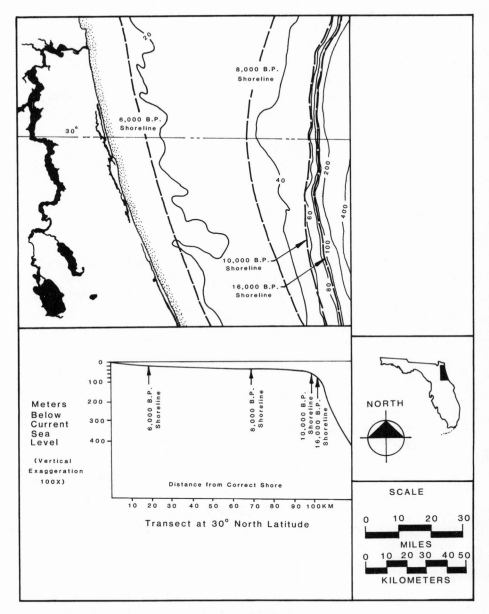

Fig. 2.1. Continental shelf bathymetry and Paleoshoreline location. Bathymetry from NOAA (1976); sea level stands from Bloom (1983b: 219).

comparable rise is accompanied by a much larger horizontal movement of the shoreline. Table 2.1 shows approximate relative levels of the sea and corresponding distance of the shoreline from its present position. For each 2,000-year period the rate of rise in centimeters per century and the rate of transgression in meters per year is given. The results show that the most dramatic environmental changes arising from the inundation of coastal areas did not begin to occur until about 12,000 years ago and were over about 5,000 years ago. During that period the sea rose about 1 meter per century, and the shoreline advanced over previously dry land as much as 15 meters in horizontal distance per year, or 1.5 kilometers per century. Approximate locations of the Paleoshoreline—at 6,000, 8,000, 10,000, and 16,000 years before the present—are indicated in figure 2.1.

The nature of the full glacial coastline is an expression of the geomorphology at the edge of the continental shelf. As shown by the bathymetric cross section at 30 degrees north latitude (fig. 2.1), the shelf edge begins at about 60 meters below current sea level and extends far deeper than the lowest level of the Late Pleistocene sea. Average slope at the shelf edge is about 1 in 50, or 2 percent, and the topography includes low ridges that have been interpreted as dunes associated with previous shorelines. Other processes could also account for the same features, however. In northeast Florida the shelf edge ridges have been lithified, a change that probably occurred after their submersion (Bloom 1983b:222). It is unlikely that the

Table 2.1. Sea level rise and shoreline transgression

Years before present	Sea level meters below present	Rate of rise cm/century each 2000 yr	Shoreline transgression distance km from present	Shoreline transgression meters/yr each 2000 years
2,000	0	20 cm/century	0.0	0.25 m
4,000	-4	70 cm/century	0.5 km	6.25 m
6,000	-18	100 cm/century	13.5 km	27.00 m
8,000	-38	100 cm/century	67.0 km	16.50 m
10,000	-60	110 cm/century	100.0 km	0.90 m
12,000	-82	110 cm/century	101.8 km	0.15 m
14,000	-88	30 cm/century	102.1 km	0.05 m
16,000	-90	10 cm/century	102.2 km	

Sources: Bathymetry after National Oceanic and Atmospheric Administration (1976); sea level stands after Bloom (1983b:219).

shoreline located at the shelf edge during the glacial maximum had a configuration like that of today.

The landscape of the glacial maximum was apparently a very dry one and is believed to be due to a combination of two factors: lowered water table and decreased precipitation. With the Atlantic shoreline some 100 kilometers away and the level of the sea some 100 meters lower, the hydrology of the peninsula would have been very different. It is unlikely that there was much standing water; pollen cores from Late Pleistocene ponds and bogs usually show a hiatus during the full glacial period indicating that they did not hold water. Stream base levels would have been lowered considerably and surface water may have found its way to the ocean by way of well-developed drainage systems with flows more rapid than today, given the greater drop in elevation to the sea. The surface water available on the Florida peninsula appears to have been restricted to those sinkholes and springs in the karst topography where the potentiometric surface of the groundwater aquifer was penetrated.

Little is known of the environmental communities that might have occupied the land mass that is now under the Atlantic Ocean. It seems reasonable to assume that, except for the dynamic region of advancing shoreline and the steep edge of the continental shelf, vegetation communities on the exposed shelf would have been similar to those on the part of the peninsula that remains above water today. Little information is available from the shelf itself. However, many mastodon and mammoth teeth have been recovered from fishing nets along the Atlantic shelf (Whitmore et al. 1967 in Bloom 1983b). The main body of evidence useful for inferring such vegetation communities is from identification of pollen preserved in bogs and lakes from which cores have been analyzed. No such work has been done in northeast Florida specifically, but several such cores have been analyzed from Georgia and other parts of Florida, and the results may be generalized for much of the lower southeast United States.

Three pollen sites in south Georgia and north Florida have been analyzed for Late Pleistocene flora. Mud Lake (Watts 1969) in north-central Florida and Lake Louise in southern Georgia (Watts 1971) provide good pollen information for the period before full glaciation as well as the later Holocene, but they are missing sediments from the full glacial period. This condition is not inconsistent with other cores throughout the Southeast (Watts 1983) and can be attributed to a climate and landscape so dry that bodies of surface water like lakes and ponds contained no water and provided no protection for pollen rain to be preserved. No information about full glacial vegetation was available from any southeast coastal plain pollen site until the analysis of a core from Sheelar Lake in north-central Florida (Watts and Stuiver 1980), where a pollen record between 24,000 and 18,500 years ago is present.

Spruce pollen is absent at Sheelar Lake, although it is recognized in full glacial vegetations from southern Georgia at the Pennington pollen site and appears to represent a boreal forest extending from this southern limit north to the edge of the ice around southern Pennsylvania, where a tundra is evident (Watts 1983). The pollen flora at Sheelar Lake is as high as 80 percent pine with significant amounts of oak and hickory. Mesic trees are represented, and herbs, especially species of prairies and sandhills, make up more than 10 percent of the pollen. On the basis of this evidence, William A. Watts interprets the full glacial vegetation in north-central Florida as "an environment dominated by *Pinus* forest and open herbaceous communities with small populations of broad-leaved trees, especially oak and hickory. The silty sediments and the presence of fossil sand dunes suggest that the Late Wisconsin may have had a very dry, windy climate with mobile dunes and deflation of silt" (Watts 1983:304).

The vertebrate fossil record for Florida is complicated in that it lacks the well-defined stratigraphic exposures of long duration that have provided the basis for firm chronologies in other parts of the country. Instead, many of Florida's fossils are from river bottoms, where bones may have accumulated from a number of different eroding bank deposits of different age, sinkholes that served as watering holes during drier climates, and such exposures as strip mines or canals, where exposure and stratification are often not clear or properly recorded (Webb 1974:9). Nonetheless, certain generalizations can be made and certain species established as residing in Florida during the full glacial period.

As mentioned, the climate was colder and drier. Previously existing pine and deciduous forests of the northern and middle latitudes of North America had been largely replaced by spruce boreal forest or tundra, and many of the animals dependent upon temperate climate and associated plant communities were displaced southward, especially into the Florida peninsula. Among the more distinctive animals of the Late Pleistocene of Florida were the large mammals that would later be associated with the earliest humans: mammoth (*Mammuthus jeffersoni*), mastodon (*Mammut americanum*), saber-toothed cat (*Smilodon* sp.), bison (*Bison antiquus*), horse (*Equus* sp.), ground sloth (*Megalonyx* sp.), giant beaver (*Castoroides ohioensis*) and giant armadillo (*Holmesina* sp.) (fig. 2.2). Two species of giant tortoise (*Geochelone* sp.) survived longer in Florida than anywhere else on the continent; the presence of these cold-blooded forms suggests an equable climate with little frost and periods of warm winter temperatures that allowed feeding. More moderate-sized mammals of this period would include the muskrat (*Ondatra zibethicus*), peccary (*Platygonus compressus*), dire wolf (*Canis dirus*), bear (*Tremarctos floridanus*), and jaguar (*Felis onca*) (Martin and Webb 1974, Lundelius et al. 1983).

Beginning 16,000 or 15,000 years ago, the full glacial conditions began to change. The climate started to become warmer and wetter; as glaciers melted, the glacial front retreated northward, water was released into the oceans, and sea level began to rise; coastal landscapes began to become inundated; plant and animal species died out or adapted to new conditions by extending or increasing their distribution ranges; and new complexes of species combined to form communities that had not previously existed. This period of deglaciation and rapid environmental change is known as the Late Glacial Transition and represents the interstadial period between the time of maximum glaciation, around 18,000 years ago, and the time of minimum glaciation, around 5,000 years ago. That part of the Late Glacial Transition before 10,000 B.P. is termed by geologists the Wisconsin Period of the Late Pleistocene Epoch. The onset of the Holocene or Recent Epoch is generally agreed to have occurred 10,000 years ago.

The full glacial environment described so far is without people. It is not possible to say with certainty that no people were present in the Florida peninsula 18,000 years ago. Indeed, the question of the first peopling of the New World is both complex and controversial. It may be simply characterized by two different positions: People using a recognizable tool tradition termed Clovis arrived in the Americas around 12,000 to 13,000 years ago, and people using a less distinctive pre-Clovis tool tradition arrived as early as 20,000 or 30,000 years ago (claims for even earlier dates have been made). A comprehensive review (West 1983) probably represents the majority opinion of archaeologists on this subject: Candidates for pre-Clovis sites are suspect for a variety of reasons, and the unequivocal evidence supports the first entrance of people into the Americas at about 13,000 to 12,000 years ago. A more recent summary of Paleo Indian colonization dates the first arrival of people between 12,000 and 11,500 years ago (Anderson and Sassaman 1996:49). In the absence of any definitive evidence for people in northeast Florida, or even the southeast United States, before 13,000 years ago, it seems most likely that the proper period for introducing humans into the reconstructed northeast Florida environment is during the Late Glacial Transition. This was a period of very rapid environmental change, made all the more interesting by the appearance of a new species with an ability to manipulate the environment on a scale never before experienced.

Fig. 2.2. Giant armadillo in a Late Pleistocene landscape. Florida Division of Historical Resources.

The Paleo Indians in the Late Glacial Landscape, 15,000–10,000 Years Ago

The Late Glacial Transition was a time of rapid and profound environmental change. Melting of the glacial ice and the corresponding rise in sea level
were rather slow at first, accounting for, in Florida, a change of only 10
meters or so in depth between 18,000 and 12,000 B.P. As the position of
the shoreline was at the steep shelf edge, the transgression of the shoreline
was also small, on the order of 5 to 10 kilometers, or around 1 meter per
year. The whole of the continental shelf plain was still exposed, although its
vegetation was changing quickly as a result of warming and increased precipitation.

A record of Late Glacial sedimentation in the Florida peninsula is preserved in the Sheelar Lake core beginning at 14,600 B.P. and shows a replacement of the previously existing pine forest by one of broad-leaved
trees and herbs. Unfortunately, the details of this transition are not preserved in any of the Florida pollen cores, because climate was so dry and
the water table so low that ponds were dry and sediments were deflated
rather than deposited. Between 14,600 and 14,000 years ago at Sheelar
Lake, the pollen record shows a predominance of oak (*Quercus*), hickory

(*Carya*), hackberry (*Celtis*), juniper (*Juniperus*), or white cedar (*Chamae-cyparis*), and herbs including ragweed (*Ambrosia*). This assemblage is interpreted by Watts (1983:305) to represent a drought-adapted forest or woodland with some prairie. Implications of this vegetation type are warmer climate, increased precipitation, and rise in water table. By 13,540 B.P. mesic trees increase at the expense of the prairies, and beech (*Fagus*) becomes evident. Climate is inferred as continuing to warm, although not to its present state, and precipitation continues to increase.

Between 13,500 and 11,200 years ago the mesic species decline in importance, being replaced by pine, oak, and herbs. An assemblage of this type is consistent with a climate like that of today. This association continues to the beginning of the Holocene at 10,000 B.P. Wide variation in pine pollen frequency in the core may result from periodic natural fires (Watts 1983:305).

Change in vegetation communities occurs as a result of each plant species responding independently to those climatic factors that determine its distribution. The specific associations are a reflection of the availability and adaptability of species, which respond at different rates of migration. Thus, associations are unstable, responding to frequent invasions or losses, and are not likely to have modern analogues.

The fossil record for animals does not provide the chronological control available for pollen cores, and it is not possible to establish the appearance and disappearance of fauna so precisely. It is reasonable to assume, however, that as vegetation communities responded to changes in temperature, precipitation, and water table depth, the animals were similarly changing their ranges. As habitats disappeared and competition relationships changed, many species that had adapted to cold, dry climates became extinct.

Sometime between 15,000 and 10,000 years ago the first people entered the Florida peninsula. No sites of the Paleo Indian culture have been found in northeast Florida, although a small number of Paleo Indian projectile points have been discovered. It is not known whether the lack of sites is due to the absence of people or because sites of this period are unavailable (buried or submerged) or unrecognizable (lacking the types of artifacts that would be either preserved or readily identified). Elsewhere in Florida there is abundant evidence for the presence of people more than 10,000 years ago.

Some idea of the range of Paleo Indians in Florida has been obtained by plotting the distribution of their artifacts. Of more than 1,200 artifacts known in 1983, some 400 representing 126 sites with good provenience information were plotted, revealing a distribution covering about one-third of the Florida peninsula and corresponding very closely to the karst topography of Florida's exposed Tertiary limestone beds. Within this region in the central Gulf part of the state, there is good access to the chert inclusions in limestone beds, which provided raw material for making stone tools. In addition, the karst topography is characterized by solution features, springs, and intermittent rivers that very likely comprised the few reliable sources of water during the Late Pleistocene (Dunbar and Waller 1983).

The plotted distribution done in 1983 shows only one Paleo Indian artifact from northeast Florida and a general absence or scarcity of such material from the Florida Panhandle, the east coast, and the southern third of the peninsula. Negative evidence of this sort does not necessarily mean that people were not present in these areas during Paleo Indian times, but it is possible that the landscape might not have been conducive to regular occupation. First, it will be useful to review what is known about the Paleo Indian way of life and the environmental relationships of this time.

Most artifacts that can be confidently assigned to the Paleo Indian Period have been found in spring fed rivers of the Tertiary karst region already described. In some cases, diagnostic Paleo Indian projectile points or tools are found in clear association with extinct animals, particularly large game species such as mammoth, mastodon, horse, and bison. Until recently, it was widely believed that underwater deposits of this type did not provide reliable evidence of association, as artifacts and bones were thought likely to be carried by water currents far from their original source of deposition and to be mixed with materials from other locations. The result would be a secondarily deposited site with material from many different times and many different sources, all in one place.

In fact, it is now apparent that bones and artifacts do not move appreciably in many cases, and several examples of articulated skeletons of extinct megafauna associated with artifacts have been reported (Hoffman 1983, Waller 1983) from karst rivers. Another significant Paleo Indian site from an underwater context is Little Salt Spring in Sarasota County on the southwest Florida Gulf Coast. This site has yielded the oldest radiocarbon date in the southeast United States for undisputed human occupation, 12,030 ± 200 years before the present. At a depth of 26 meters below the current water level, dry land deposits of Paleo Indian times yielded the remains of a giant tortoise (*Geochelone crassiscutata*) believed to have been killed by a wooden stake driven through its shell. Slightly shallower sediments yielded a wooden nonreturning boomerang and a mortar made from an oak log. Besides the giant tortoise, other now-extinct animals possibly eaten by people at Little Salt Spring include the giant sloth (*Megalonyx* sp.), an elephant (mammoth or mastodon), and an extinct bison (Clausen and others 1979).

In the region of Tampa Bay extensive excavations have been completed at the Harney Flats Paleo Indian site. This dry land site is deeply buried in acidic sandy soils where no remains other than stone are preserved. As at many land sites, the entire organic component of the archaeological record is absent, and interpretations of Paleo Indian lifeways are based on analysis of chert tools and waste from tool manufacture. Harney Flats is believed to have been a base camp, that is, a location occupied somewhat permanently and repeatedly over the years. In addition to base camps, sites of the Paleo Indian Period include: quarries, locations where raw stone material for tools was collected and partially worked; camps, which were occupied for short periods during the process of exploiting some nearby resource not available near the base camp; and kill sites, locations where game animals were hunted, killed, and sometimes partially butchered. Finally, there are isolated finds of projectile points of the Paleo Indian Period, but it is difficult to interpret their origin or meaning in the absence of other remains (Borremans 1989).

Harney Flats provided a comparatively large assemblage of stone tools and tool manufacture waste. Two separate categories of tools were believed to be represented: formal tools of recognizable types that required a fair amount of skill and effort to produce; and informal or expedient tools quickly made, used, and discarded. It is suspected that formal tools made up the permanent tool kit of the Paleo Indian. Given the need to travel frequently to exploit distant resources, the tool kit needed to be carried or new tools manufactured later. Tools that were used on a permanent basis have been interpreted as being general in function rather than specialized; that is, a few tools could be used for a wide variety of tasks (Daniel and Wisenbaker 1987). Despite the usefulness of the formal tool kit, however, it seems likely that Paleo Indians required a constant and reliable source of chert to make new tools, whether expedient or permanent.

The Paleo Indian way of life reconstructed on the basis of evidence from Florida and other parts of the eastern United States is one of nomadic or seminomadic hunters and gatherers in small extended family groups characterized by a band level of social organization. The nature of the archaeological evidence available has until recently emphasized the stone tool technology of these first people, as no organic components of the material culture were preserved, and has likely led to an overemphasis on their supposed reliance on the hunting of now-extinct big-game animals. It is reasonable to

assume that plants, small animals, and perhaps shellfish also played important roles in the diet.

Two environmental factors appear to have played a crucial role in Paleo
Indian settlement: the availability of reliable sources of fresh water in an
arid landscape and access to cryptocrystalline rock suitable for stone tool
manufacture; in Florida the only available material is chert or flint. Not
only was permanent fresh water necessary for people, but it also attracted
and concentrated game animals, which could be more easily killed at water
holes than in forests or prairies. With these requirements in mind, it is
possible to suggest several reasons that Paleo Indian remains are absent in
northeast Florida. First of all, as shown in figure 1.3, the lithified limestones that could contain chert inclusions are buried beneath tens of meters
of unconsolidated sandy sediments of the Pleistocene marine terraces. Depth
to this rock ranges on average from 10 meters at the southern boundary of
the region to over 100 meters in the northern part. Buried limestone that
might yield chert occurs, from north to south, in the Crystal River, Williston,
and Inglis formations, but geologic maps (maps 1.3 and 1.7) do not show
these limestone beds being penetrated and exposed by river channels or solution holes. Any stone, whether in the form of finished tools or prepared
preforms, that would be available to Paleo Indians in northeast Florida would
have to have been transported into the area.

The matter of fresh water availability is more complicated. Recall that
during the period from the glacial maximum to the beginning of the Holocene 10,000 years ago, sea levels were between 100 and 60 meters lower
than at present. There was a corresponding decline in the level of the local
water table, but it is not possible to relate the two levels directly. In northeast Florida there are two aquifers that could contribute to the exposure of
fresh surface water: the surficial or nonartesian aquifer, composed of un-
lithified sandy sediments underlain by relatively impermeable clay layers,
and the Floridan or principal aquifer, which may be artesian and is made up
of deeper limestone beds.

The nonartesian aquifer of surficial sandy sediments averages around 50
meters in depth and receives recharge from local rainfall. Local water tables
are seldom perched or held near the surface because the impermeable beds
of clay are at considerable depth. Rather, surface water readily penetrates
the permeable sandy sediments and has little surface expression. Setting
aside the possible contribution of the artesian aquifer to surface water for
the moment, water of the nonartesian aquifer will be exposed at the surface
only when the aquifer is saturated between the underlying impermeable
clay layers and the surface (Bermes, Leve, and Tarver 1963:43). Evidence

from pollen cores in lakes and bogs suggests that these factors did not occur at the time of lowest sea level (Watts 1983).

The deeper Floridan Aquifer is a massive body of subterranean water extending throughout most of the Florida peninsula as well as the southern part of Georgia. It resides within a single hydrologic unit composed of limestone beds of Eocene, Oligocene, and Miocene ages. The surface of these limestone beds lies as much as 100 meters below the present land surface and averages 30 meters or more in depth throughout the region. The Floridan Aquifer does not depend on local recharge for surface expression; rather, water will be exposed at the surface in springs and sinkholes wherever the piezometric surface is higher than the land surface. Exchange of water between the nonartesian and artesian aquifers will occur where the aquiclude formed by impermeable clay layers is penetrated by solution cavities like sinkholes or where such confining beds are absent.

There are only a few locations in northeast Florida where these conditions might exist. Map 1.8 shows the springs of northeast Florida along with an indication of their measured flows and which deposits supply their water. These data are summarized in table 2.2. The northern springs are all situated at the edge of the St. Johns River and have flows less than five cubic feet per second. Of these, Wadesborough Spring, Whitewater Springs, Satsuma Spring, Nashua Spring, Welaka Spring, Forest Spring, and Mud Spring are unlikely candidates as reliable sources of surface water during a period of low sea level and arid climate. They have low flows even today and appear to be fed by the nonartesian surficial aquifer. Green Cove Spring, however, has a moderate flow that seems to originate in the artesian Floridan Aquifer. Beecher Springs in Putnam County has a comparatively strong flow and might have a deep source. The four southern springs in northeast Florida are all situated some distance from the St. Johns River and have flows in excess of 10 cubic feet per second (Rosenau et al. 1977). Salt Springs, Silver Glen Springs, Juniper Springs and Fern Hammock Springs are all possible sources of water during the Late Pleistocene, given their independence of the St. Johns River surface water system, their large discharge, and, in the case of Juniper Springs, an apparent source in the Floridan Aquifer. Although no Paleo Indian remains have been reported at these locations, the probability of their being found either surrounding the springs or in the associated spring runs would seem to be higher than anywhere else in northeast Florida.

Another possibility for Paleo Indian settlement is within the physiographic zone known as the Crescent City Ridge, located between Crescent Lake and the St. Johns River (map 1.4). In this hilly upland area a number of sinkholes breach the aquiclude of the Floridan Aquifer and currently provide a means

Table 2.2. Springs of northeast Florida

Name	County	Flow in cfs	Depth in m
Wadesboro Spring	Clay	1.0	
Green Cove Spring	Clay	3.0	46 m
Whitewater Springs	Putnam	1.4	seep
Satsuma Spring	Putnam	1.8	
Nashua Spring	Putnam	0.5	
Welaka Spring	Putnam	tidal	
Beecher Springs	Putnam	10.7	
Forest Spring	Putnam	0.3	
Mud Spring	Putnam	2.3	
Salt Springs	Marion	83.2	
Silver Glen Springs	Marion	112.0	
Juniper Springs	Marion	12.8	
Fern Hammock Springs	Marion	15.8	

Source: After Rosenau and others (1977).

Note: cfs = cubic feet per second; 1 cfs = 0.64 mgd (million gallons per day)

of local recharge (Bermes, Leve, and Tarver 1963:62). They may have provided a reliable water source during the Late Pleistocene Epoch.

The preceding argument is based on the supposition that the St. Johns River has not always been a major flowing river, at least during times of very low sea level and arid climate. Geologically, the St. Johns valley is a feature of the sandy marine terraces. It has been entirely estuarine throughout its length during times of higher sea level, when the terraces were formed, and it has the appearance of having a broad channel consisting of shallow lakes extending from one valley edge to the other, separated by intervening stretches of narrow channel that have accumulated sediments by deposition or accumulation of vegetation (White 1970:108). It seems likely that the history of the St. Johns drainage has been complex, ranging from periods of little or no flow, to times when the Floridan Aquifer contributed substantially to its flow, to times when it was entirely estuarine.

Finally, there are other candidates for Paleo Indian remains on the continental shelf that remained largely exposed during the Late Pleistocene. Characteristics of its surface drainage and topography are unclear, but at least one submarine freshwater spring is known to exist about 4 kilometers east of Crescent Beach (Stringfield and Cooper 1951 in Bermes, Leve, and Tarver 1963). This spring is fed by the Floridan Aquifer, and is probably

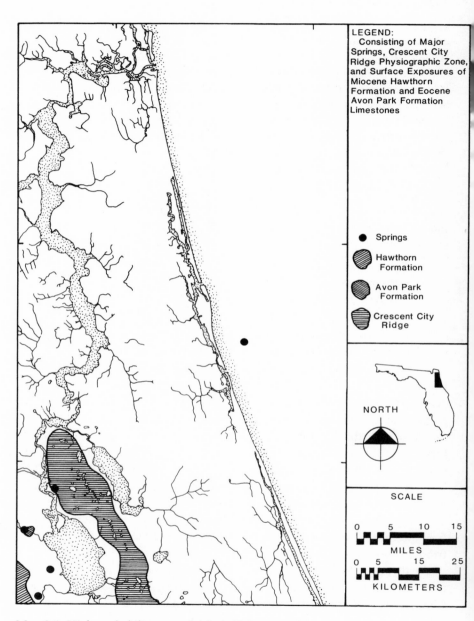

Map 2.1. High-probability areas for Late Pleistocene sites

not the only such feature on the shelf. Areas in northeast Florida having high probability for Paleo Indian archaeological remains are shown in map 2.1.

Geologists place the close of the Pleistocene Epoch at 10,000 years ago. While the effects of glaciation continued into the Holocene or Recent Period, the process of glaciation was at an end. Climate had become warmer and wetter, and the glaciers were beginning to contribute vast amounts of water to the world's oceans. Sea level was beginning to rise at a rapid rate and would continue to do so for around 4,000 or 5,000 years, until it reached its present level. For people adapted to the Late Pleistocene environment of Florida, the next 5,000 years would be a time of great environmental and cultural change.

3

From Postglacial to Essentially Modern Environments: Hunting and Gathering Adaptations, 10,000–2,500 Years Ago

The Early Archaic Period, 10,000–7,000 Years Ago

By the beginning of the Holocene Epoch 10,000 years ago the global extent of the ice sheets had decreased about 50 percent. The relative level of the sea was still low, variously estimated between −60 meters (Bloom 1983b:219) and −35 meters (Bloom 1983a:42). The shore was 70 to 100 kilometers east of its present position, and the climate approached modern conditions. According to the sea level curve for Florida (Bloom 1983b:219 after Clark 1981, fig. 1), the rapid rise between 12,000 and 6,000 years ago was well under way. As noted earlier (table 2.1, fig. 2.1), the shallow slope of the continental shelf had been reached by the rising sea and the shoreline of northeast Florida was transgressing at a rate of 15 to 30 meters per year.

The first 5,000 years of the Holocene were marked by a rate and degree of environmental change greater than that of the previous or following 5,000 years. From a cultural perspective, the importance of this change for Florida's aboriginal people may be considered as important as the introduction of agriculture or the coming of the Europeans. It would be difficult to imagine a better example of the close relationships among environment, technology, and social organization than that offered by the comparison of Paleo Indian to succeeding Archaic lifeways. Gradual but persistent environmental change leading to the extinction of Pleistocene animals as well as changes in composition and distribution of plant communities rendered Paleo Indian technology and exploitative strategies obsolete. As new means of adapting to new conditions were developed, human groups became more sedentary, and social organization increased in complexity.

Vegetation studies suggest that the climate was altered significantly at the beginning of the Holocene. On the southern Coastal Plain and in north Florida the late glacial, pre-Holocene vegetation was primarily mesophytic and included beech species. These forests were replaced by more xeric woodlands dominated by oak and pine. Davis (1983:176) interprets these changes in forest composition to suggest that the first millennium or so of the Holocene experienced a climate similar to essentially modern conditions. Around 9,000 years ago, it appears that the climate became somewhat warmer than it is today, at least through 5,000 years ago; these conditions continued, to a lesser extent, to the beginning of the Little Ice Age (A.D. 1450–1850). Based on analogous differences in the distribution of modern vegetation, Davis suggests that the early Holocene temperature was about two degrees centigrade higher than now and annual precipitation was about 125 millimeters lower; i.e., the climate was warmer and drier.

The implications for animal species at the onset of Holocene conditions were dramatic. In comparison to the range, diversity, and composition of Late Pleistocene fauna, the Holocene assemblage has been termed "depauperate" or "impoverished" (Martin 1967:110, Martin and Webb 1974 in Semken 1983:192). However, the cause of this change, which amounts essentially to the extinction of the major Pleistocene megafauna, is not clear. Two schools of thought exist: overkill and environmental change. Either species like mammoths, mastodon, caribou, musk-oxen, long-horned bison, horse, and saber-toothed cat were exterminated by Paleo Indian hunters, who represented a newly introduced and extremely effective predator in the Late Pleistocene environment, or the habitats of the megafauna were so modified that their niche was no longer available. The latter is most likely to have occurred at the base of the food chain, where the open prairies supporting grazing herbivores become more closed forests. Probably a complex combination of factors led to extinctions.

Whatever the reasons, the fact remains that for Early and Middle Archaic people in northeast Florida, potential animal resources for food, hides, and other products were substantially different than for Paleo Indians. Following the disappearance of the elephants, the largest common animal available in the Holocene environment was the white-tailed deer, which comprised the principal terrestrial source of meat (Stoltman and Baerreis 1983:254). Fish also assumed a greater importance. The disappearance of the herd animals living in open savannas and the dominance of smaller forest game that foraged in small groups or individually led to differences in hunting techniques, technology, and probably settlement patterns.

Throughout the peninsula of Florida and indeed the eastern United States, the Archaic was a time of growing population. The number of Archaic sites is greater than the number of Paleo Indian sites, and the Archaic sites are also larger. Archaeologists have divided the Archaic Period into early, middle, and late subdivisions. Roughly, the Early Archaic marks the end of the Paleo Indian way of life characterized by nomadic to semipermanent bands adapted to a relatively cold and dry Late Pleistocene environment.

Despite the comparative abundance of Archaic sites, the Early Archaic is a period about which we have only limited knowledge. The diagnostic tools or projectile point types of the period are widespread across the southeast United States and are readily recognizable, but our understanding of the period is limited by the fact that stone tools are often the only types of remains preserved in Early Archaic sites. Knowledge of Early Archaic people was greatly increased by the discovery and excavation of the Windover Pond site in east-central Florida. This peat-bog pond site had been used as a cemetery for about 1,000 years, beginning around 8,000 years ago. The saturated peats preserved the organic components of the burials, including soft tissue, woven textiles, bone tools, wooden objects, and plant and animal remains. The Windover excavations (Doran and Dickel 1988) provided important new information about well-developed technologies in textiles and wood that were never represented in typical Archaic sites with only stone artifacts. Interestingly, in the entire Windover burial assemblage, which included 168 individuals, there are only five stone tools, suggesting how incomplete and unrepresentative a picture of past life we create from lithic remains alone.

The life of Archaic people revealed at Windover appears to have been difficult. Human bones show many examples of injury and suggest poor health for some individuals, but it is also apparent that those needing help were well cared for. One child with spina bifida and osteomyelitis lived to the age of sixteen despite having lost a foot from infection (Milanich 1994:74).

It has been suggested that as the peninsula decreased in size because of rising sea levels and transgressing shorelines, and as the number of people increased, population pressure caused increased competition for food resources. Social changes may have occurred as a means of improving the exploitation of food, and settlement patterns may have changed to reflect the distribution and seasonality of important food resources (Milanich and Fairbanks 1980:50).

Within northeast Florida only one site (8SJ3134) is known from the Early Archaic Period, in contrast with no sites of the previous Paleo Indian Period (map 3.1). This, in itself, is insufficient evidence to support the notion of a population increase but may suggest that conditions for settlement were more attractive than they had been before 10,000 B.P. People had moved out of the restricted zone of the Tertiary karst landscapes, where chert resources, water, and probably big-game animals were available, and seem to have extended their occupation to almost all other upland environments. Site 8SJ3134 is assigned to the Early Archaic based on the discovery of a Bolen Beveled projectile point, and is situated on a high sand ridge adjacent to a swamp (Smith and Bond 1984). The site, 10 kilometers from the present coast in St. Johns County, is not associated with a coastal lagoon. Its inland, sandy marine terrace situation is similar to that of Middle Archaic sites and contrasts dramatically with sites of later ceramic periods.

It is difficult to judge the full range of either Archaic or Paleo Indian technologies, given the absence of preserved organic remains. We know almost nothing about tools of wood, about basketry and textiles, or about the uses of animal products like bone, skin, and antler in either period. However, we do have a large number of stone tools, both formal and informal, to compare, and it is clear that lithic technology declined in the Archaic Period, at least as far as this would be reflected in the quality of tools. Early Archaic stone tools are less well made than Paleo Indian tools, but there are many more functional varieties. In contrast to the small but highly efficient tool kit of the Paleo Indians, who would have had to transport all of their belongings frequently, the Early Archaic stone tool assemblage is much more varied, more expedient or less permanent, and composed of heavier tools, which would be difficult to transport. One implication of such tool forms is that the Early Archaic people of Florida were more sedentary, that is, that they lived at least part of the year in permanent villages. This inference would also be consistent with an environment typical of the Early Holocene, which would be composed of a variety of exploitable environments in which desirable resources like water, small game, and plant foods are more widely and evenly distributed.

The Middle Archaic Period, 7,000–5,000 Years Ago

The distinction between Early and Middle Archaic people is one that was originally defined on the basis of the appearance of ground stone tools in the archaeological record. It is a distinction that has greater validity elsewhere in the Southeast, where suitable metamorphic and igneous stone resources are common. In Florida, the Middle Archaic, lasting roughly from 7,000 to 5,000 years ago, is characterized by the presence of a particular type of stone projectile point, the Newnan point (Clausen, Brooks, and Wesolowsky 1975:28, Clausen et al. 1979:611, Jahn and Bullen 1978:22). Newnan points are more common in Florida than are any other type of

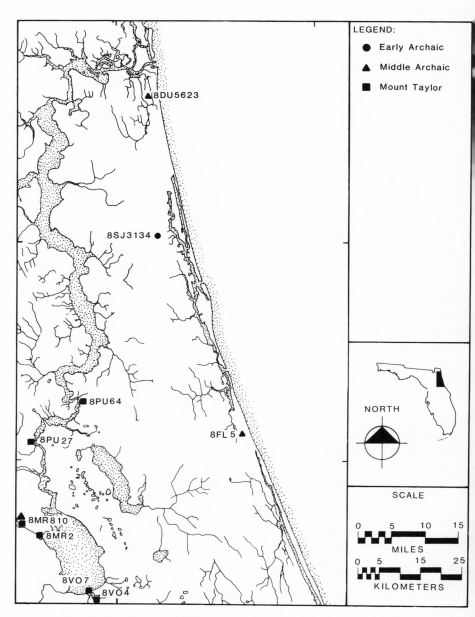

Map 3.1. Distribution of preceramic Archaic sites

projectile point, suggesting that the Middle Archaic Period was a time of increased population, continuing the trend noticed in the preceding Early Archaic (Milanich and Fairbanks 1980:57).

Within northeast Florida only three sites (8DU5623, 8FL5, 8MR10) are recorded as having material assigned to the Middle Archaic. Their distribution is shown in map 3.1. It should be noted that in many cases the sample of sites available for analysis in northeast Florida does not benefit from large-scale intensive archaeological survey. Rather, sites recorded outside of the few formal surveys are those that are prominent or readily identifiable. The use of these data for formal statistical analyses is unjustified, yet they are useful for making general comparisons of frequency and adequate for recognizing patterns of site location with respect to environmental features.

As in the Early Archaic, the locations of Middle Archaic sites are distinctive. Spencer's Midden (8DU5623) is nearly three kilometers from the present Atlantic coast and about one kilometer from the Pablo Creek estuarine marsh. Yet the site contains coquina and oyster shells, species of the beach and lagoon respectively. The association of the Middle Archaic projectile points (Newnan and Levy types) with the midden is unclear because they were found by local residents in a nearby ditch. Nonetheless, the midden itself yielded no pottery and must date to either the Middle Archaic or to the Mt. Taylor Period.

The second recorded Middle Archaic site (8FL5) is the Bon Terra Farm site, which was once believed to contain artifacts in association with extinct Pleistocene fauna (Connery 1932, Howard 1940). A more recent review of the evidence (Neill 1953) showed that the Pleistocene animals were unrelated to the Middle Archaic projectile point found there. Bon Terra Farm is nearly two kilometers from the Atlantic shore and twice as far from the nearest lagoon. Its location on the Atlantic Ridge corresponds not only with the other reported Early and Middle Archaic sites but also with the location of unconfirmed reports of arrowheads of unknown age discovered by local collectors. This site distribution pattern is, as yet, little understood and not readily explained. While it is clear that Early and Middle Archaic people of the Early Holocene did not locate their settlements on the lagoons, on what is now the coast, or the St. Johns River, it is not clear why these groups selected the Atlantic Ridge. It is possible that additional research will show a relationship between the relatively elevated locales where Early and Middle Archaic projectile points are found and the existence of a higher stand of sea level than at present (Fairbridge 1961, Stapor and Tanner

1977). This theory could explain site distribution during the period of the higher stand (probably not more than 1,000 years in duration) but would not account for the other 4,000 years of the Early Holocene, when sea levels were lower than at present. Perhaps the Ridge offered access to several nearby ecological zones.

Finally, a Middle Archaic Levy point is reported from 8MR810, Salt Springs. This second-magnitude spring is situated at the edge of a swamp forest bordering Salt Springs Run and Lake George in the St. Johns River Basin. No large midden accumulation is reported, but the site does yield artifacts from nearly every prehistoric period. It is possible, then, that Salt Springs has been a flowing source of fresh water, attractive to people as well as game animals since the Middle Archaic.

As discussed earlier, the complex relation between sea level and shoreline position during the Late Pleistocene and Early Holocene periods depends on two factors, slope of the continental shelf and depth of the water. Between 18,000 and 10,000 years ago sea level rose about 40 meters, from −100 to about −60 meters, corresponding to a shore transgression of only about three kilometers along the steep outer edge of the continental shelf. In contrast, during the Early and Middle Archaic, between 10,000 and 5,000 years ago, sea level rose about 50 meters, from −60 to about −10 meters, but the shoreline moved around 100 kilometers landward along the gradual slope of the shallow shelf itself (table 2.1, fig. 2.1). There are two important implications for Archaic Period people of northeast Florida: The interface between land and sea was an extremely dynamic environment, because shoreline position changed as much as 25 meters per year around 6000 B.P., and at some time during the Middle Archaic Period sea level rose sufficiently to affect the local water table dramatically.

There is essentially no evidence in the archaeological record that marine or estuarine resources played a role in Early or Middle Archaic adaptation. This pattern can be attributed to the fact that coastal sites are submerged, but it is more likely that the rapidly transgressing shoreline was too unstable to allow the development of exploitable populations of either shellfish or bony fishes at the coastline. Inland landscapes that previously had been characterized by quite well-drained soils became much wetter. This change seems to have had two major effects on the northeast Florida environment, providing new habitats for abundant freshwater and marine food resources. These dramatic changes in prehistoric ecology of the St. Johns River and the coastal lagoons set the stage for significant technological, social, and settlement changes in the Late Archaic Period.

The Late Archaic Period, 5,000–2,500 Years Ago

By about 5,000 years ago climatic and environmental factors were close to reaching their present, modern conditions. Depending on the model of sea level rise one follows, the level of the ocean was somewhere between three meters above and five meters below its current level. Climate had approached its modern configuration and vegetation associations present today essentially had been established. With respect to its major features, the environment of the Late Archaic people was like our own, or more accurately, like our own would be at a much reduced scale of human intervention. The major changes occurring around 5,000 years ago that form the basis for our discussion are the stabilization of sea level at roughly its present position on the coast and the corresponding rise of the water table in the interior part of the peninsula.

The level of the sea and the corresponding position of the shoreline are more difficult to characterize than they were for the Late Pleistocene and the Early Holocene periods. Most authorities agree that the rapid rise of sea level was finished around 5000 B.P., i.e., the rate of change decreased. What is not so clear is where the shore was at this time and whether the sea level rose above its present level or not. Much of the variation in proposed sea level curves can be attributed to the effect of regional conditions, and it is now widely accepted that because local position of the shoreline is not only a function of volume of water in the ocean but also isostatic adjustments of the land masses as they respond to removal of the glacial burden, different regions will have different sea level histories.

One of the more widely accepted models of sea level rise is that of Clark and Lingle (1979) who postulate separate curves for six global zones corresponding roughly to latitude. Their mathematical model takes into account glacial unloading and ocean floor loading by meltwater as well as the geoidal and gravitational responses of the crust (Bloom 1983a:43). Variation in sea level at 5,000 years ago outside the glaciated area is between –12 and +3 meters, with northeast Florida showing a position somewhere between –12 and –4 meters. These data are not as precise as one would hope, but they are adequate to support our argument regarding resource availability along the coast and in the interior rivers.

During Late Archaic times settlement is also concentrated along the St. Johns River. Shell middens of extreme size attest to the importance of freshwater snails for food and also to the comparatively high density of settlement after the end of the Early and Middle Archaic Periods. It is likely that this dramatic shift in location and size of population can be attributed primarily to environmental factors.

The presence of two aquifers within northeast Florida, the surficial aquifer and the deeper and larger Floridan Aquifer, has already been discussed. They differ in some important ways: The surface aquifer, also known as the water-table aquifer, generally has its surface a short distance below the land surface. The water in the water-table aquifer is not under pressure; it usually has a surface expression where the land dips sharply below the zone of saturation. The water-table surface is recharged through precipitation and discharges through seep springs or small streams. Usually the deep-water aquifer and the water-table aquifer are separated by impermeable beds of clay. Thus, the two systems do not readily exchange water.

The deep-water or Floridan Aquifer, in contrast, lying under the impermeable confining beds, is under pressure. It receives water in recharge areas (of which there are two in north and central Florida) where the aquifer is exposed at the surface or where it is overlain by porous and permeable material. It discharges water in areas of artesian flow where the potentiometric surface is above the land surface. In general, the entire St. Johns River Valley is an area of artesian flow (Rosenau et al. 1977:21), and the only part of northeast Florida where recharge occurs is on the higher sandy terraces between the St. Johns River and the Atlantic Ocean (Rosenau et al. 1977:fig. 7).

The character of the two aquifers is somewhat complementary; the water-table aquifer reflects the local hydrological budget and is sensitive to variation in rainfall and small differences in the elevation of land surface. The deep aquifer represents a comparatively massive body of water, one originally defined as the Principal Artesian Aquifer of the southeastern United States. It underlies all of Florida and extends beneath parts of Alabama, Georgia, and South Carolina (Rosenau et al. 1977:13). Its scale is much greater than that of the water-table aquifer, and the factors that influence its surface expression are different. The deep aquifer is not exposed at the surface as the water table would be in swamps or ponds; rather, its water appears at the surface only when there is a conduit between the deep confined beds where water exists under pressure and the surface where the elevation is lower than the piezometric surface. Conduits can be natural, as in the case of springs and sinkholes, or they can be artificial as in the case of wells.

A spring, then, represents a place where potentially large volumes of water from a virtually limitless source may be introduced into a local landscape. We have already reviewed the distribution of springs within northeast Florida in connection with potential settlement patterns of Paleo Indian Period people (map 2.1, table 2.2). It is necessary now to expand the geographic area to the larger St. Johns River Basin to account for water in the river system within northeast Florida that has a source outside the area under study.

Although there are some 54 freshwater springs within the St. Johns Hydrologic Subregion (Rosenau et al. 1977, fig. 12) only 16 of these are first or second magnitude, i.e., have average flows greater than 10 cubic feet per second; these 16 are listed in table 2.2. While it is difficult to be precise about the source of water in a spring, it is safe to say that all of the first-magnitude springs (flow greater than 100 cubic feet per second) have their source in the deep Floridan Aquifer, as do most of the second-magnitude springs (Rosenau et al. 1977:13). Combined, these 16 springs contribute on average approximately 1600 cubic feet per second or slightly more than one billion gallons per day to the St. Johns River System stream flow. The entire stream flow of the St. Johns River itself measured just south of Jacksonville averages 5,500 cubic feet per second. While it is not possible to reconstruct the entire water budget of the St. Johns River System, these figures suggest that spring flow from the Floridan Aquifer accounts for almost one-third of the water volume in the St. Johns River System. What would the region have been like without this contribution of "outside" water?

As we have seen, the St. Johns River is an extremely slow-moving, broad river system with an extremely shallow slope. As such, it is tidally influenced throughout its length. While the average stream flow is recorded at around 5,500 cubic feet per second, the maximum stream flow for the period 1971–74 was measured near Jacksonville at 64,000 cubic feet per second on June 20, 1972. During the same year in October a negative or reverse flow of 62,700 cubic feet per second was measured. This occurrence is not unusual; the frequency curves of negative and positive flows are, in fact, very similar (Fernald and Patton 1984:165). These authors point out that occasionally, during severe droughts, the combination of high tides and northeasterly winds may cause reverse flow as far south as Lake Monroe, 161 miles above the mouth.

In some respects, the modern St. Johns River is more like a lake than a river. Topographically it appears as a system of connected lakes within a broad channel and an even broader floodplain. Its slope is so shallow (less than 0.1 foot per mile) that the magnitude of flow in the channel is more a function of channel cross section than velocity. Finally, the river is tidally influenced throughout its length and will flow backward almost as rapidly as it flows in the normal direction. These are the conditions necessary to understand the settlement of the St. Johns River after the end of the Early Holocene.

The great majority of prominent archaeological sites on the St. Johns River and its tributaries are vast accumulations of snail shells, primarily of the species *Viviparus georgianus*. While more than 95 percent of the volume of such sites is made up of the shells of this species, the quantity and value of food represented by *Viviparus* is more moderate. Cumbaa (1977) has estimated that about 25 percent of the caloric intake of Late Archaic people at one representative shell midden on the St. Johns River was provided by these small snails. White-tailed deer provided another 25 percent, plant foods are estimated to have accounted for about 30 percent of the total calories, and the balance was made up by fish, small mammals, and birds.

It seems probable that the appearance of people on the St. Johns River in such great numbers around 5,000 years ago coincided with the appearance of habitats for the freshwater snails. According to Clench and Turner (1956:110) *Viviparus georgianus* is not generally found in larger rivers but rather in adjacent sloughs, creeks, lakes, ponds, and springs. The snails occur in colonies that usually exhibit uniform shell characteristics and are sometimes widely separated. They can exist where there is much soft mud or sand—but only in quiet water. These are the conditions that currently exist on the St. Johns, particularly in its upper, or southern, section, where springs and lake basins are common.

It has been suggested that the shift in settlement by Archaic populations from the highlands of north-central Florida to the St. Johns River was a result of climatic changes that affected the vegetation and water sources in the highlands (Milanich and Fairbanks 1980:146). Rather, it is more likely that the St. Johns River changed its character dramatically around this time, offering a new, rich environment for exploitation. Before sea level had reached its current position, the St. Johns would have behaved more like a river than an estuary or lake. Its mouth at the edge of the Atlantic would have been much farther below the elevation of its source and main body, stream flow more rapid, tidal influence diminished or absent, and the contribution of the Floridan Aquifer to the river system probably lower.

As sea level rose, and with it the piezometric surface, the aquifer became saturated, hydrostatic pressure increased below the confining beds, and springs began fairly suddenly to flow. In addition, as the level of the sea rose, the St. Johns Basin became essentially drowned. Its water surface level was very near sea level throughout its length. At Lake George, for example, at the southern edge of northeast Florida, average lake elevation above mean sea level was 1.26 feet between October 1982 and September 1983. The maximum elevation was 2.43 feet and the minimum elevation 0.29 feet. From this location to the mouth of the river is approximately 100 miles. At

Lake Monroe, another 60 miles south, the average lake level was 2.49 feet above mean sea level in 1983. During the period of record, 1920–1982, the maximum elevation was 8.23 feet and the minimum level, in April 1945, was 0.45 feet below mean sea level (United States Geological Survey 1984:214, 222).

Even a small decrease in the level of the sea would have a major effect on a river whose slope is so shallow. Throughout its geologic history the St. Johns River has been a product of sea level. Its broad floodplain channel is interpreted by White (1970:102–104) to be a former estuary, "a once continuous body of standing water," resulting from a higher stand of the sea. This must have been at least before the last Wisconsin glaciation and may correspond to the Silver Bluff or Pamlico Pleistocene terraces. During the maximum glaciation of the Wisconsin and through the period of rising sea level the St. Johns Basin would have been an unremarkable landscape, not unlike the adjacent sandy terraces, except where sinkholes or springs fed by the deep artesian aquifer provided a source of water for people and animals alike. It is difficult to determine from geological evidence exactly when the character of the St. Johns Basin changed so significantly, as the local sea level curve lacks precision and there is no way to determine the specific relationship between the level of the sea, the level of the piezometric surface, and the depth at which various springs penetrated the aquifer.

The Mt. Taylor Period, 5,000–4,000 Years Ago

From an archaeological point of view, it makes sense to correlate the sea level–induced flooding of the St. Johns Basin with the appearance in the archaeological record of the Mt. Taylor culture. Radiocarbon dates from the Tick Island site, located about 15 kilometers south of Lake George, show that between 6,000 and 4,000 years ago Archaic people began to occupy the St. Johns Basin on a regular basis, perhaps year round but certainly seasonally. In the opinion of Milanich and Fairbanks (1980:150), this transition "marks the time when this sporadic occupation became more sedentary and village life began." By definition, the Mt. Taylor Period is that portion of the Late Archaic Period before the introduction or invention of pottery. On the basis of artifacts, it would appear that Mt. Taylor people were little different than their Early and Middle Archaic predecessors. Based on settlement patterns and strategies of exploitation of the environment, however, the Mt. Taylor people differ in a major way. For the first time in northeast Florida an environment existed that was sufficiently productive in terms of food resources and sufficiently free from major change to support a permanently settled way of life. Whereas Paleo Indian as well as Early and Middle Archaic people were obliged to follow their food source, or at least to range widely during the course of the year, Late Archaic people occupying the St. Johns River Valley could spend at least part of every year in the same location, depending upon the rich aquatic environments of the newly watered valley for their subsistence and other needs.

The flooding of the St. Johns River Basin marks the beginning of a landscape that has maintained its basic character for 5,000 to 6,000 years. Beginning with the settlement of the Tick Island site on the St. Johns River about 15 kilometers south of Lake George, Late Archaic Mt. Taylor people were attracted to the newly available resources of the river valley. The stone tool technology of the Archaic has continued, and the common Newnan points of the Middle Archaic are still present. Banner stones of steatite and heavy, stemmed projectile points suggest the use of atlatls or spear throwers (Milanich and Fairbanks 1980:151). Bone points and other bone tools are found in Mt. Taylor shell middens, but in general the tool assemblage and the technology it represents are typical of the preceramic Late Archaic throughout the southeast United States.

The 10 sites in northeast Florida that have been assigned to the Mt. Taylor Period (map 3.1) are, without exception, situated on the St. Johns River or tributaries. Six are in the northern (lower) section between Palatka and Jacksonville that is characterized by a wide channel. Four are in the southern (upper) St. Johns Offset. The two segments differ in their geologic history and landscape features. The lower section has every appearance of being a drowned estuary. Its wide channel is clear of swamp and floating vegetation, its course is not braided, and its banks are well-defined upland margins. In a recent intensive archaeological survey of the Timucua Ecological and Historic Preserve in this section of the river, four Mt. Taylor shell middens were identified on the basis of radiocarbon dating. All were situated in marshlands and were partially submerged by a higher sea level. An additional 12 similar sites are thought to be Mt. Taylor in age, based on the absence of ceramics below layers containing Orange Series pottery (Russo 1993:8–9). South of Palatka in the offset section, the St. Johns has more the character of a series of shallow lakes connected by narrow, braided channels that wind through vast expanses of aquatic vegetation. No Mt. Taylor Period sites are known on the coast (Griffin and Miller 1978).

The Orange Period, 4,000–3,000 Years Ago

Pottery first appears in the archaeological record of northeast Florida around 4,000 years ago, and its presence is the distinguishing characteristic of the Orange Period, which lasted roughly 1,000 years. By this time, adaptation to the river environments must have been firmly established, and indeed, despite this new technological development, it is likely that the settled or semipermanent occupation of the Late Archaic hunters, gatherers, and shellfish collectors continued with little change until the introduction of domesticated plants. There is a dramatic increase in the number of sites recorded in northeast Florida throughout this period, attesting not only to the success of the adaptation but also to the relatively rapid growth of population. No sites of the Paleo Indian Period are present, and Early and Middle Archaic sites of the Early Holocene average only 0.075 per century. Late Archaic Mt. Taylor sites increase to 0.35 per century. During the Orange Period site count within northeast Florida jumps to 4.5 sites per century, increasing by more than a factor of 12 over the previous period.

These figures are useful in demonstrating trends in number and location of sites. They should not, however, be construed to represent actual numbers of sites or actual population levels, because many parts of northeast Florida have not been surveyed for archaeological remains, and many more sites have yet to be found. Moreover, the number of components does not take into account the size of the sites, a factor that would be necessary to construct any meaningful relationship between sites and population. Finally, not all periods are easily recognized at sites, especially in the absence of excavations; this difficulty may account for the apparent decline in number of components during the Transitional Period, which is defined on the basis of degree rather than the presence or absence of fiber tempering in pottery.

Along the coast, shell midden sites occur for the first time during the Orange Period (map 3.2). It would appear then that the formation of rich aquatic environments in the St. Johns Basin preceded the formation of comparable environments along the coast by at least 2,000 years. It is likely that this difference is due to a combination of factors. The drowning of the St. Johns Basin would have occurred when sea level rose sufficiently to raise the base level of the river above the bottom level of much of its channel. This stage probably occurred when sea level was five or so meters below the present level, based on the recorded channel depths today. The beginning of large-scale flow of the springs in the St. Johns Valley would have preceded the sea's reaching its present level because the piezometric surface is higher than the sea level; at present it is 5 to 20 meters higher in northeast Florida. Exactly when the major springs began to flow is not known, but they would have followed a step function in their behavior; either the piezometric surface was high enough and the flow was present, or it was below the elevation of the spring outlet and flow was absent. Finally, the coastal barrier system of beaches and lagoons may have been somewhat slow to develop a stable configuration that could reliably support exploitable populations of species like oysters that are sensitive to salinity.

The current configuration of the northeast Florida coastline can be generalized as a linear system consisting of a littoral zone, a beach and dune complex on a barrier island or barrier peninsula, a lagoon or estuary, and then a mainland landmass extending westward to the St. Johns River. In terms of landform development the key feature of this coastal landscape is the barrier island. The complex of seaward dune and landward lagoon is the dominant coastal pattern. Apparently absent during Early Holocene/ Early and Middle Archaic times, it forms a significant new exploitable environment that accounts for a dramatic increase in the number of sites and people living in northeast Florida.

The reason such sites do not appear earlier in the archaeological record is probably that the rich lagoon environments did not exist before sea level stopped its Early Holocene rapid rise. During its fastest period of rise, the sea was transgressing at a rate of more than 20 meters per year. Essentially no time existed for formation of coastal features; those incipient coastal features that did develop, such as storm- deposited dunes or small estuaries, were submerged within a year or two. Along such a rapidly eroding coast there was certainly insufficient stability for faunal and floral communities to become established and produce mature individuals suitable for food. More likely, for the 5,000 years or so of the Early Holocene the shore was a constantly eroding stretch of previously established upland vegetation whose origin and composition had little or no relation to the ocean or its edge. Some confirmation of this view is provided by study of barrier formation under laboratory conditions. Leontyev and Nikiforov (1965) found that submarine bars never break the surface when sea level is constant or rising, and no barrier beaches are formed under such conditions.

The Orange Period, with its distinctive pottery tempered with plant fibers, marks the first time in the archaeological record of Florida that regional cultural variations can be recognized. They appear as differences in ceramic designs and styles, but the degree to which they reflect more fundamental differences in ways of life is not clear. From the distribution of the different pottery series, termed Norwood on the Gulf Coast and Orange in northeast, central, and south Florida, it is apparent that distinct cultural groups are now more settled. Both Norwood and Orange people used resources obtained from outside their culture areas, but exploitation of particular local environments appears sufficiently well developed to alleviate the need for frequent movement from one region to another.

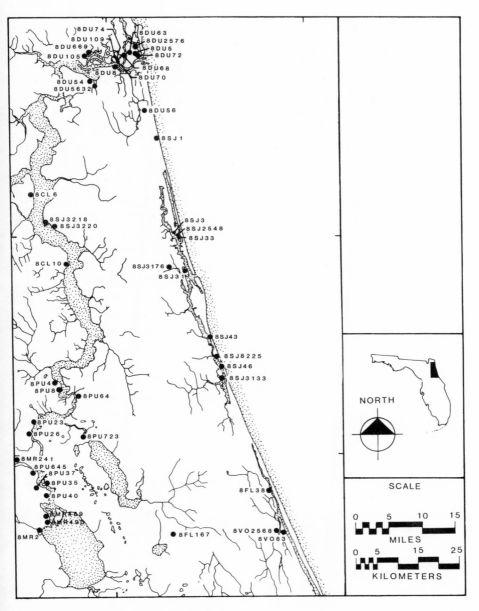

Map 3.2. Distribution of Orange Period sites

Bullen (1972) defines four subperiods of the Orange Period, based primarily on differences in ceramics. The occurrence of the marker pottery types for each subperiod shows that occupation during subperiods one and two is confined to the St. Johns River; the coast shows no fiber tempered Orange pottery until subperiod three, beginning around 3,300 years ago.

The earliest sites on the coast that have been excavated, Summer Haven Site (Bullen and Bullen 1961) and the Cotten Site (Griffin and Smith 1954), are largely composed of shells of coquina (*Donax variabilis*), a small species of surf-dwelling clam that is most abundant during fall and winter months (Miller 1980). Recent excavations at the Crescent Beach site (Bond 1992) also showed coquina layers of the Orange Period under oyster layers of the St. Johns periods. Coquina continued to be used during all subsequent prehistoric periods on the Atlantic Coast, but it would seem to be an inefficient source of meat in comparison to species like oyster and quahog. Perhaps it provided a necessary protein source when other shellfish were unavailable. Or perhaps it was so easy to collect comparatively large volumes of shells with a basket on the beach during times when large colonies were present that it was in essence a convenience food. Whatever the advantage of coquina in general, its comprising the predominant shellfish food at Orange Period sites is an indication that lagoon shellfish such as oyster, quahog, and moon snail were not available. At least one sea level curve (Fairbridge 1961) shows a high stand about three meters above that of the present, suggesting that the previously formed lagoons were inundated rather than protected.

Milanich and Fairbanks have reconstructed the basic life-style of the Orange Period as being similar in many respects to that of the Mt. Taylor Period: hunting, fishing, and gathering in the St. Johns River Valley, with occasional hunting trips into nearby hardwood forests (1980:154). In their view, the yearly round was split between the coast and the river, with winter collection of coquina, some clams and oysters, and fishing. Hunting of the standard Florida food animals—deer, bear, wildcats, and otters—along with collecting of the smaller species—opossums, rabbits, and turtles—would have occurred near the coast. Winter resident seabirds would also have provided some food. Winter camps are suggested to have been occupied by no more than 30 people, and camps were often moved as local resources were exhausted.

In the spring and summer, people would have moved across the sandy terraces of pine flatwoods to return to the St. Johns River. Here, villages would have developed alongside or near the river, especially at locations where the channel flowed adjacent to dry upland bluffs rather than meandering through swamps. Over the centuries of seasonal or permanent settle-

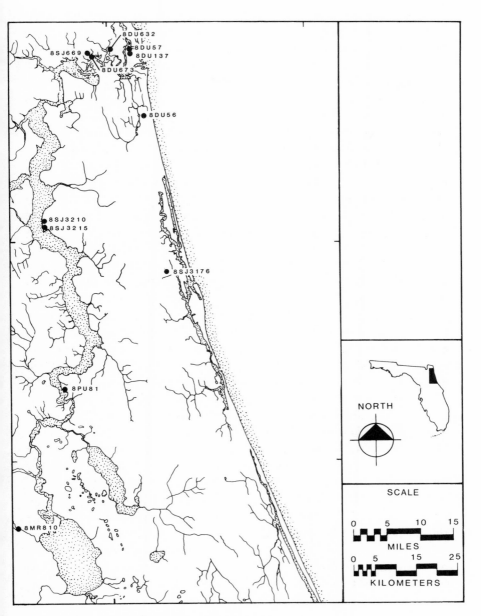

Map 3.3. Distribution of Transitional Period sites

ment the continuous deposition of shellfish remains and other refuse material formed large shell middens, themselves forming new high ground in the floodplain. The use of canoes, present in the archaeological record of the St. Johns as early as 5,000 years ago, would have opened up large bodies of water for exploitation, improved the efficiency of travel for people, and allowed the transport of comparatively large loads that previously could only have been carried on the backs of people. In this sense, the river is not only a new environment; it is, with the technology of the canoe, also a potentially larger environment. Until the introduction of the horse by the Europeans nearly 3,000 years later, travel and transportation of goods on land would be limited to the distance one could walk or run and the load one could carry. Not only did the rivers and lagoons provide new sources of food and raw material, they also facilitated communication and transportation, as they would continue to do even into the early twentieth century.

The Transitional Period, 3,000–2,500 Years Ago

The Transitional Period was defined by Bullen (1959) to cover a period of about five centuries immediately following the Orange Period and before the firm establishment of regional traditions that characterize the remainder of Florida prehistory. The distribution of Transitional Period sites is shown in map 3.3. Essentially, the pattern of settlement is identical to that of the preceding Orange Period, although only 3 of the 11 reported sites were occupied during both periods. St. Johns Incised pottery is the diagnostic characteristic of the period, and this pottery is rare, aside from controlled excavations. Thus, the relative number of Transitional Period sites per century is low. Before the Transitional Period, cultural traditions throughout the southeastern United States exhibited the same basic characteristics and shared many of the same recognizable artifact types. After the Transitional Period, aboriginal cultures throughout the region had established clearly recognizable identities, most of which are defined by archaeologists on the basis of styles and types of pottery. The major changes in post-Transitional cultures cannot be attributed to environmental changes but rather appear to be the result of social, political, religious, and technological innovations introduced from elsewhere in the eastern United States. While regional variations in culture are well established, in a broad sense many southeastern cultures are participating in a single complex of traits involving mound burial, social stratification, and status differentiation of goods, as well as shared symbolism, ceremonialism, and religious beliefs. At the core of this eastern U.S. complex is an initial reliance on domesticated plants for food. However, no evidence for horticulture is known from Florida during the Transitional Period (Russo 1992:114).

4

The Development of Indigenous Social Stratification, 2,500–500 Years Ago

The St. Johns Tradition

The remaining prehistoric and early historic aboriginal occupation of northeast Florida has been most thoroughly analyzed and summarized by Goggin (1952) who defined the St. Johns Tradition and recognized its divisions, both geographical and temporal. While the details of St. Johns chronology are less important than the broad outlines in understanding environmental relations of the St. Johns people, it is useful to review the basis for the different temporal divisions, keeping in mind that, as in many archaeological constructs, the differences are defined primarily on the basis of ceramic styles.

Within the 4,000 years of St. Johns Tradition occupation in northeast Florida, Goggin defined two major periods, St. Johns I and St. Johns II, separated at about A.D. 800 by the appearance of pottery decorated by a stamped pattern of checks. This diagnostic check stamped pottery is present in the later period and absent in the earlier period. On the basis of foreign ceramics from other parts of the southeast United States, the periods were subdivided into St. Johns Ia, early; St. Johns Ia, late; St. Johns Ib; St. Johns IIa; and St. Johns IIb (Milanich 1994:247). Assignment of sites to various subperiods depends upon rather specific distinctions based on the presence or absence of various pottery types, most of which are quite rare and unlikely to be adequately represented in small collections. Moreover, it is not clear that environmental conditions or adaptations differed significantly from one subperiod to the next, or at least not to a degree that can be reconstructed from the available information. For these reasons, we will focus on the settlement patterns and environmental relations of St. Johns I and St. Johns II, with additional reference to the subperiods where they are environmentally significant.

The St. Johns I Period, 2,500 B.P.–A.D. 800

The beginning of the St. Johns I Period is placed around 500 B.C., when the diagnostic St. Johns Incised pottery of the Transitional Period disappears. It ends around A.D. 800 with the appearance of St. Johns Check Stamped pottery. These major changes in pottery style do not appear to reflect important cultural changes; indeed, Goggin states, "St. Johns II carries on the tradition and is marked only by the introduction of check-stamped pottery. As before, temporal subdivisions have been made solely on the basis of foreign influences" (1952:70).

The St. Johns Tradition in northeast Florida reflects the broad patterns of cultural development evident throughout the eastern United States but is unusually conservative in maintaining its own distinctive characteristics in the local archaeological record. There is clear evidence of interaction with other traditions, especially along the Gulf Coast, represented by foreign ceramics and such status goods as platform smoking pipes, ground stone celts, copper masks, galena, and mica, as well as traits such as burial mounds and temple mounds. Nonetheless, the St. Johns Tradition has been persistent in its archaeological expressions of settlement patterns, technology, and artifact styles for 2,000 years and even continues the basic patterns established as early as the Orange Period.

St. Johns culture reflects the evolution of cultural patterns that have expression throughout the eastern United States and have their origin outside northeast Florida. The complex of characteristics, as expressed in most regions, has as its foundation the practice of horticulture or agriculture, and includes a range of technological, social, and ideological traits that would seem to support this distinctive means of adaptation. Although the divisions between the various periods and subperiods in the St. Johns Tradition are somewhat arbitrarily based on ceramic styles, there are clearly changes in cultural traits through time that correspond to different types of adaptation and different levels of cultural complexity. There is also considerable spatial variation in the St. Johns culture area in the importance of domestic plants. Among the Saltwater Timucua and the Western Timucuan groups, the St. Johns Tradition reflects an initial adoption and increasing reliance on the agricultural complex of maize, beans, and squash. At the same time, settlement patterns reflect increasing sedentism and increased population as evidenced by larger numbers of archaeological sites than in previous periods. Similarly, social organization becomes more complex, reflecting a change from the band organization of the previous hunter-gatherers to more stratified societies at the level of chiefdoms encountered by the first European explorers. As social complexity and status differentiation increased, so did the importance of religion. (Perhaps, as the cultural ecologists would argue, religion was a means of maintaining the controls necessary to organize production of crops on some scale.) In contrast, the Freshwater Timucua, especially the Mayaca, planted no crops, relying instead on hunting and gathering. In general, horticulture decreased in importance along the river and the coast, and was more important in the upland, central part of the peninsula (Hann 1996:94–95). Each of these developments has its characteristic signature in the archaeological record of the St. Johns region.

Throughout the St. Johns I and II Periods reliance on the river system for food resources remained paramount. People continued to occupy the same kinds of riverbank locations that had been attractive earlier, and the deposition of larger and more numerous shell midden sites attests to the continuing use of freshwater snails for food.

Although Timucuan subsistence is best characterized as sedentary horticulture, crops appeared to be important for some groups at the time of contact. Spanish and French documents of the mid-sixteenth century recount the reliance of Indians as well as Europeans on the annual corn crop (Sparke 1565:388, 392; Laudonnière 1586:62). Archaeology does not provide much direct evidence concerning the use of crops in northeast Florida during St. Johns I times. It is likely that cultivation of domestic plants was introduced at the beginning of the St. Johns I Period, along with a variety of cultural traits that constituted an associated complex of technology, social organization, and ideology evident throughout the Southeast (Milanich and Fairbanks 1980:159, 162; Milanich 1994:260–262). The adoption of this complex varied significantly throughout the St. Johns culture area, but in the St. Johns Valley itself wild foods continued to make up a significant part of the diet.

One way of examining the nature of increasing reliance on domestic plants is to compare settlement patterns of sites for different subperiods to see how they change over time. Two aspects of settlement pattern could be expected to depend upon degree of reliance upon cultivation. First, if it is correct that agriculture is a more successful adaptation than hunting and gathering, then greater populations should be supported, and sites occupied should increase in size or number or both through time. Second, site locations should change over time, indicating people's increasing preference for better agricultural soils. Maps 4.1, 4.2, 4.3, and 4.4 show relevant site locations. Although sites in each period must have been occupied during one or both of two subperiods, the ceramic markers that would allow this distinction to be specified are often not recorded. Thus, two levels of analysis are possible: All St. Johns I Period sites can be compared to all St. Johns II Period sites, and, where the necessary information is available, sites definitely assignable to various subperiods can also be compared. Site locations of the St. Johns I Period are shown in map 4.1. Locations of sites assignable to St. Johns Ia or Ib subperiods are shown in map 4.2. All site locations of the St. Johns II Period are shown in map 4.3, and locations of sites known to have been occupied during St. Johns IIa or IIb subperiods are shown in map 4.4. From table 4.1 it is apparent that the frequency of sites (number of sites per century) in the St. Johns II Period is more than twice as large as in the St. Johns I Period. This more general result, implying increasing population through time, is not replicated in the more specific case of comparing subperiods. Unfortunately, the numbers of sites that can confidently be assigned to the four defined subperiods are too small to present a statistically reliable sample.

The geographic distribution of sites assigned to St. Johns Ia and Ib subperiods (map 4.2) does not appear to reveal a change through time that might be related to increasing reliance on agriculture. Of 32 sites whose locations could be plotted all are closely associated with water; three are on or near the coastal lagoons, and the remainder are along the St. Johns River or its tributaries. Sites appear more common during the Ia subperiod within the coastal marsh systems at the mouth of the St. Johns River, while later sites of the Ib subperiod are distributed more regularly along the entire length of the river north of Lake George. For the St. Johns IIa and IIb subperiods (map 4.4), the picture is similar. Sites of both subperiods, of which only 14 have accurately recorded locations, are generally distributed along the St. Johns River system and along the Atlantic Coast.

Comparison of the site distribution patterns of the St. Johns I and II Periods taken as a whole is more instructive. Not only is the total number of sites greater in the later period, but the number of sites situated in inland environments away from rivers, streams, and lagoons is greater as well. In St. Johns I times, of 79 sites whose locations can be accurately plotted, five, or roughly 6 percent, are in environments that would suggest the importance of gardening or crop raising. In the St. Johns II Period, 10 percent of the 120 sites with known locations are in nonriverine and noncoastal locales. It would be misleading to assume that all such sites were situated to take advantage of soils suitable for crops; rather, the more conservative interpretation of this change in settlement pattern is that in St. Johns II

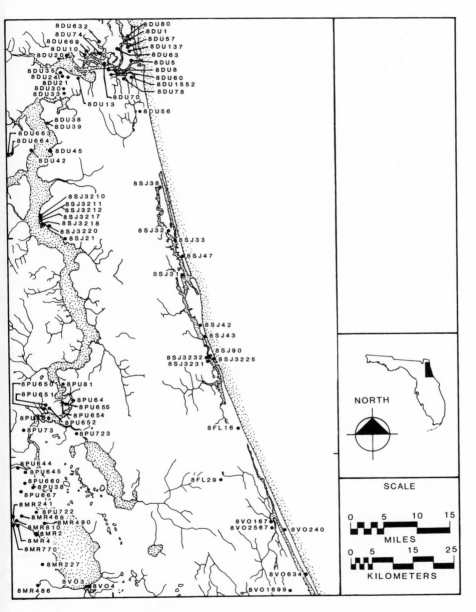

Map 4.1. Distribution of St. Johns I Period sites

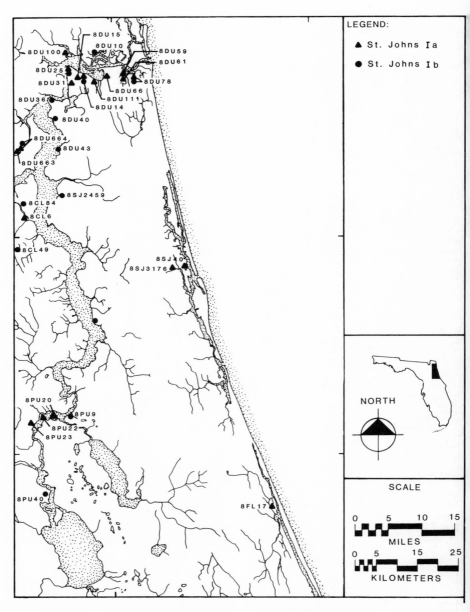

Map 4.2. Distribution of St. Johns Ia and St. Johns Ib Subperiod sites

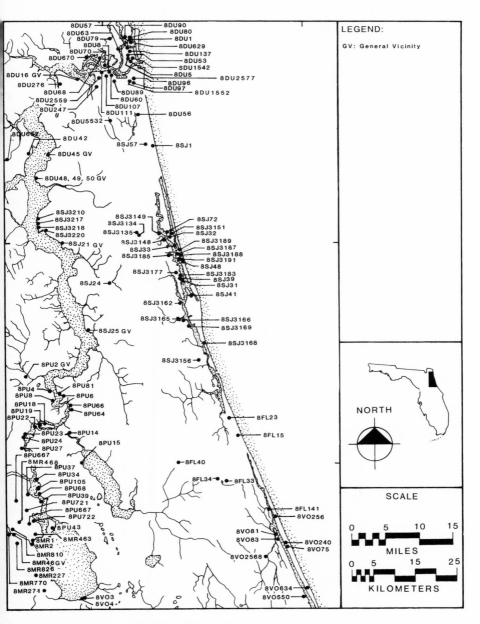

NORTH

SCALE

| 0 | 5 | 10 | 15 |

MILES

| 0 5 | 15 | 25 |

KILOMETERS

Map 4.3. Distribution of St. Johns II Period sites

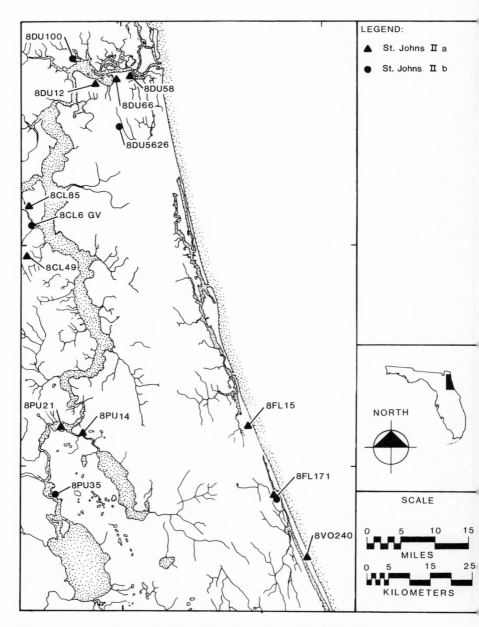

Map 4.4. Distribution of St. Johns IIa and St. Johns IIb Subperiod sites

Table 4.1. Prehistoric sites by period and subperiod

Period and subperiod	Number of sites	Length of (sub)period in centuries	Number of sites per century
St. Johns II unspecified	143	7.5	19.1
St. Johns IIb	5	2.5	2.0
St. Johns IIa	10	5.0	2.0
Total St. Johns II	158	7.5	21.1
St. Johns I unspecified	88	13.0	6.8
St. Johns Ib	14	5.0	2.8
St. Johns Ia	19	8.0	2.4
Total St. Johns I	121	13.0	9.3

times there was less need to live adjacent to coastal and riverine resources. The most reasonable implication of this fact is that St. Johns II people relied on an alternative food source.

The archaeological evidence for social organization during the St. Johns I and II periods, that is, before the time of European accounts, is not direct; rather, interpretation depends on certain assumptions. Complex social stratification at the chiefdom level was well documented by European observers in the sixteenth century; the relevant archaeological problem is to determine the evolution of such complexity over time. Population increase and reliance on domesticated crops are generally regarded to occur in association with complex social organization, and there is little doubt that these two factors increased in northeast Florida before European contact.

Other archaeological markers of social stratification are mainly derived from excavations of burial sites (Thunen and Ashley 1995, Mitchem in press). In these archaeological contexts it is clear that certain individuals received preferential treatment, as evidenced by the type of burial offerings, presumably a reflection of status. In the earliest part of the St. Johns I Period, grave offerings are rare in burial mounds, and it would appear that all people were buried in mounds. After about A.D. 100, a distinctive complex of burial artifacts appears in mounds associated with burials; these items are found in similar contexts at sites throughout the eastern United

States and are recognized as part of the Hopewellian trade network that transmitted not only exotic goods but also an associated agricultural technology and distinctive ideology. For the first time in the archaeological record of the St. Johns region, such foreign materials as galena, mica, copper, quartz, cut animal jaws, ear spools, animal effigies, and plummets appear in burial mound contexts (Milanich 1994:260–262). It is generally accepted that the presence of these high-status items in association with the burials of certain individuals was an indicator of differential social rank.

The St. Johns II Period, A.D. 800–1500

By St. Johns II times, beginning around A.D. 800, foreign ceramics of non-utilitarian design are common in burial mounds, mounds become larger, and it appears that only a few individuals are accorded the privilege of mound burial. Outside of the St. Johns culture area, particularly in the northern interior and Gulf Coast of Florida, the ceremonial expressions of this time period, which are recognized archaeologically as part of the Weeden Island culture, are more fully developed. It is apparent when comparing the large culture areas of the Florida peninsula that the St. Johns region is an area of little cultural change. One likely reason for this is that the soils, being largely marine sands, do not support a highly productive agriculture; the sociological and ideological traits associated with the agricultural complex would not have had much adaptive value. As will be noted in chapter 5, European accounts attest to food shortages during certain parts of the year when fresh or stored crops were not available. Squash and corn were present in St. Johns II times, a conclusion based not only on clay effigies (Milanich 1994:265) but also on corncob-marked ceramics as well as cucurbit seeds and rind from the Hontoon Island site (Newsome 1987). Cucurbits (squash, gourd, pumpkin) are native to Florida and have been found in archaeological deposits since Paleo Indian times (Milanich 1994:264). It is also possible that the St. Johns region, being somewhat more distant from the source of these cultural innovations, did not receive the full effect of intensive cultural contact and change.

By St. Johns IIb times, beginning around A.D. 1050, the southeast United States experienced the emergence of a dominant culture, termed the Mississippian culture (Smith 1990). Comparable in complexity and organization to any North American tribe but less developed than the kingdoms of the Aztecs and the Incas, Mississippian cultures were based on an agricultural subsistence. It is this cultural manifestation that was encountered, recorded to some extent, and largely decimated by Europeans in the sixteenth century in Florida. Represented in northeast Florida by the major ceremonial centers of Shields Mound and Grant Mound in Duval County, Mount Royal in Putnam County, and Thursby Mound in Volusia County, Mississippian culture is characterized by large pyramidal temple mounds more than 4 meters in height situated in town complexes usually exhibiting a central plaza surrounded by additional mounds and dwellings. Of the four northeast Florida Mississippian mound complex sites, Mount Royal is the largest, exhibiting a "causeway" of parallel ridges extending more than 800 yards to a small lake. Thursby Mound may have had a similar feature extending toward the St. Johns River. Shields and Grant mounds seem less exotic in their structure and content, and may represent local, not regional, centers. They are also likely older in age, demonstrating the development of Mississippian culture rather than its classic expression (Thunen and Ashley 1995:6–8). All of the major Mississippian Period mounds in northeast Florida are along the St. Johns River and consist, at least in part, of freshwater shells. The number and architectural complexity of these Mississippian mound sites is minor compared with the Gulf Coast and Panhandle areas of Florida—no northeast Florida Mississippian mounds are accompanied by planned complexes of associated mounds—and it appears that many aspects of mound construction and use carried forward from St. Johns I times (Thunen and Ashley 1995:6).

5

Patterns of European Contact and Colonization, 1500–1600

From an ecological perspective, the "discovery" of the American continents can be viewed as part of the biological expansion of Europe and, inadvertently, Africa. Native American people and cultures were not the only casualty of the new contact between the hemispheres. Human populations, communities, and adaptations were replaced by their European correlates, and the changes wrought upon the land were equally profound. From this point forward, the narrative and analysis must contend with a new source of change. The complex of elements available for introduction into the northeast Florida human ecological system from the sixteenth century to the present is global in its scope and scale. Much of the remaining discussion will concern the source and effect of introduced technology, social organization, and ideology as well as plant and animal species. Soon after the first European sighting of the Florida peninsula, it became apparent that the cultural and biological adaptations to the northeast Florida environment that had proved so successful and persistent over the previous 5,000 years were obsolete.

Exploration and Discovery, 1500–1562

Although the initial European encounter with Caribbean islands of North America was accidental, in the sense of finding something that had not been sought, it was a deliberate event in European development. In the context of fifteenth-century Europe, seafaring and the successes in exploration, conquest, and settlement were aspects of the great cultural awakening from the Middle Ages. The Renaissance provided a technology, a social organization, and an ideology that were absent even 50 years earlier.

In the opinion of Quinn (Cumming, Skelton, and Quinn 1972:13–14;

Quinn 1977:77–107), two technologies were crucial in the European expansion to the New World: weapons and seafaring. Reaching the Americas or, perhaps more accurately, even conceiving that a trans-Atlantic voyage was possible, depended on advances in shipbuilding and rigging, expanded knowledge of Atlantic islands and currents, and new developments in navigation, particularly methods of dead reckoning and celestial navigation to determine position (Parry 1974). Edged weapons, swords, knives, spears, and the like had long been in the European arsenal, and long-range weapons had recently become effective in the form of longbows, crossbows, side arms and cannon. The fact that cannon could now be carried aboard vessels meant that war could be waged effectively from a distance, and the military technology of Europeans compared to Native Americans was overwhelming.

In terms of social organization, Europeans arrived with a highly developed social hierarchy; perhaps even overly developed in the case of the Spanish. Their administrative and bureaucratic skills provided the means to maintain a disciplined extension of royal authority and control reaching to the most routine matters of the most remote frontier settlements. For the French, the Dutch, and the English, the organization was commercial rather than political. In every case, however, the primary purpose of European contact was exploitation; the profitable exchange of goods and the exploitation of natural resources were the main motivations for settlement (Quinn 1977:103).

In the commercial model, contracts with private corporations granted rights of property along with permission to produce and export goods. In the political model, the contracts were with individuals who were granted positions of authority over certain regions along with certain property rights not reserved by the crown. Expeditions were led and corporations formed by the upper class; social status and political status were well correlated. Nonetheless, there was much greater possibility for one to advance socially and economically in the expanding settlement of the Americas than in Europe, and recruits for new expeditions were easy to find.

Ideologically, Europeans arrived in the New World with a new knowledge of their historical role as representatives of a "superior" civilization. The classical texts of the Greeks and Romans had only recently been resurrected from the Arabs, from whom the Europeans also obtained astronomical theories and observations important in navigation (Parry 1966). Their new intellectualism, based largely on objective and secular scientific principles, was the foundation for rapid developments in the fifteenth century in geography, astronomy, and technology, which fueled expansion.

At the same time, to be European was to be Christian. And, more important, to be non-Christian was to be inferior. By 1450, the Spanish and Portuguese had developed and refined the practice of conquest on the west and north coasts of Africa (McAlister 1984:41–69), and the dominance of European organization and ideology had only recently been won from the Mongol states. The Crusades, as Crosby notes (1986:58), were the first massive attempts to permanently extend European power outside the boundaries of the continent. Christian righteousness in the face of pagan ideology was a driving force in the European legitimization of conquest. By the time of the voyage of Columbus, Europe had fully rationalized the subjugation of non-Western cultures in the name of God.

As knowledge of the people encountered in the New World and their treatment at the hands of the explorers and conquerors spread through the political and religious systems of Europe, the rights and status of non-Christians were widely debated. It was important to determine:

> whether the Indians were rational beings, or more like beasts of the field as indicated by their cannibalism, idolatry, and other vices. If they were rational beings, could they with justice be deprived of their lands and freedom? If they were utterly barbarous—inferior by nature according to Aristotelian doctrine—justification for their conquest might be found in the Christian duty of raising them to a higher plane of human dignity. (Haring 1947:8–9)

The official attitude during the first several decades of conquest is well illustrated by the *Requerimiento* of 1514. It ordered all Indians who encountered a Spanish expedition to agree to become Christians or else be killed or enslaved. Of course, as Quinn observed, few Indians understood the concept of Christianity, let alone the language in which the *Requerimiento* was read to them: "It was a manifesto to the explorers rather than to the Amerindians that forceable conversion of the native peoples was the first duty of a Spaniard in America" (Quinn 1977:98).

The best-known and most effective criticism of the Spanish policy of subjugation was that of Bartholomé de Las Casas. Las Casas knew firsthand the atrocities inflicted upon the native people of the Americas, having served on the expedition of Diego Velásquez to Cuba in 1511–1512 and having been in the American colonies regularly for the following 35 years. His vigorous efforts to convince the crown and the Catholic Church that Indians were free persons who should not be used in any way against their will struck at the very heart of the Spanish *encomienda* system. The economic arrangement of encomienda depended upon rights of property granted by the crown to individuals and included grants of lands as well as the *repartimiento,* an associated right to the forced labor of Indians upon such lands.

Throughout the first half of the sixteenth century, the conquistadores, the Church, and the Spanish crown fought for their respective views of the enforced labor of Indians. Without the indigenous peoples, the rich mineral resources of the New World grants were unexploitable, and the conquest and settlement would have no economic foundation. The papal bull of Pope Paul III in 1537 declared that Indians were rational beings capable of becoming Christians. This pronouncement was followed by promulgation of the New Laws of Charles V in 1542 confirming the free legal status of Indians and weakening the encomienda system by prohibiting future grants and making existing grants uninheritable. Response in the colonies was violent and it was not until the early 1600s that the practical effects of legal freedom were experienced by Indians (Haring 1947:42–74). By this time the Caribbean islands had been essentially depopulated, the most accessible deposits of gold and silver ores had been exhausted, and the Indian societies throughout the Americas had suffered the social, cultural, and biological effects of European dominance.

Besides the crucial question of forced labor, the Spanish encomienda system that had served the conquest of North Africa and the Americas so well carried an implicit new view of the relation between people and land: personal and private right of ownership, authority, and inheritance. While there were similarities in the hierarchical social organization of Spaniards and American Indians and a correspondence in the recognition of the authority inherent in high social status, these systems differed fundamentally in their views of property.

For native societies in Florida and the rest of the Southeast, access to land was controlled by the theocratic hierarchy; ownership of land was corporate or communal, rather than personal. For the Spanish, an absolute property right flowed from the crown by right of conquest to the conquistadores and later settlers, regardless of previously existing Indian rights (Haring 1947:259). The privileges of ownership allowed full conveyance of property rights to others, and a clear recognition that such rights extended to natural resources and products of the land. The imposition of a European land-tenure system upon an undeveloped and undivided landscape concentrated authority and power among the wealthy Spanish upper class, and encouraged the exploitation of the land as a means of producing additional wealth. In Florida, as throughout the Americas, the Spanish emphasis was on export production rather than settlement, on exploitation rather than development.

The early Europeanization of the American landscape was supported by the superior technology, effective social organization, and legitimizing ideology of the Spaniards, but a factor of even greater importance was the European biological baggage, the portable Old World ecosystem, that accompanied the first explorers and settlers. European contact constituted a massive biological exchange (Crosby 1972), both deliberate and unwitting, that introduced not simply new plant and animal species but rather an entire human ecological complex consisting of animals for food, transportation, and labor, domesticated grains, fruits, root crops, vegetables, and all of the associated plant and animal pests, vermin, weeds, parasites and commensal species that depended on them. For the Native American populations the deadliest invaders were the disease pathogens: Their transport to the New World was unavoidable but unintended; their spread across the continents was rapid; and their consequences were fatal.

To understand the role of disease, it is necessary to know the size of the indigenous population of North America before European contact. For nearly half a century, anthropologists and historians have relied on the estimate of James M. Mooney (1928) of approximately one million people. This assessment has been critically reviewed by Henry Dobyns. He charges not only that such a low estimate directly impacts in a negative way the interpretations of social scientists about New World civilizations and cultures (1966) but also that the devastating effects of European-introduced diseases are diminished by assuming a comparatively small precontact population (1983). Francis Jennings (1975) develops the corollary argument that the standard scholarly view of New World aboriginal cultures directly affects the estimates of population size: "Proponents of the concept of savagery stipulate . . . that large populations are impossible in savage societies. It follows that if aboriginal populations can be shown to have been large, they could not have been savage. A logical approach may thus be made into the whole question of the nature of aboriginal society and culture through the gate of numbers" (Jennings 1975:16).

Even though there are few reliable data on which to base estimates of protohistoric population in northeast Florida, the Timucua tribe of this region is used by Dobyns as a case study of the effects of disease on population in eastern North America (1983:147–294). Estimates of Mooney (1928), Swanton (1946), Goggin (1952), Tebeau (1971), Covington (1975), and Deagan (1978) cited in Dobyns (1983:table 20) range from 5,000 to 20,000 people, the most common estimate being the 13,000 originally given by Mooney in 1928. All estimates, it is noted, are for time periods after 1560. Dobyns argues that a series of epidemics, introduced by European explorers and beginning as early as 1513, decimated successive portions of much larger initial populations, estimated to have been in excess of 720,000 people in 1519. Between 1519 and 1617, Dobyns postulates eight episodes of native depopulation caused by epidemics; three of these are estimated to have reduced the population by 50 percent, and all resulted in a 10 percent or greater loss. Critical review of Dobyns's population estimates (Henige 1986a, 1986b summarized in Weber 1992:382, and Hann 1996:260) reveals fundamental flaws of fact and assumption.

In the poorly documented protohistoric period, 1512–1562, from the time of first recorded contact by Ponce de León to the time of the first detailed accounts by the French at Fort Caroline, Dobyns estimates population to have declined from some 722,000 to about 150,000, a loss of nearly 80 percent. Dobyns's postulated epidemics of 1513–1514 (disease unidentified—malaria?), 1519 (smallpox), 1528 (gastrointestinal infection), 1535–1538 (disease unknown), 1545–1548 (bubonic plague), 1549 (typhus), 1550 (mumps), and 1559 (influenza) are not well accepted by scholars. These are diseases that are known to have been present in the New Spain colonies of the Americas, but it is not clear that they spread through Florida, a region characterized by scattered and somewhat sparse population distribution (Hann 1996:291) not conducive to the transmission of European "urban" pathogens.

The first recorded official instance of European contact with Indians of the Florida peninsula is the landfall of Juan Ponce de León along the northeast coast of Florida on April 2, 1513. Ponce is believed to have landed somewhere between Daytona Beach and the mouth of the St. Johns River. Morison (1974:507) puts the landing at Daytona Beach, some 50 miles south of St. Augustine, but St. Augustine is the more popular choice (Tebeau 1980:19). Previous European contacts are likely to have occurred but are undocumented. The famous Cantino map of 1502 depicts the Florida peninsula. It is possible that slave-raiding parties had already gone ashore in the peninsula, judging by the hostile receptions Ponce and later explorers received (Sauer 1971:27). His landing in a longboat resulted in a brief battle; after returning to the ship for a day, the sailors sailed south and took on water and wood, perhaps at Jupiter Inlet on the southeast coast (Morison 1974:510).

Taking a month to sail against the northward-flowing Gulf Stream, Ponce's next landing in south Florida was the scene of another battle, in which a Spaniard was killed. Rounding the Florida Keys, the fleet entered the Gulf of Mexico on June 3, 1502, and reached safe harbor perhaps as far north as Charlotte Harbor in the territory of Carlos, the powerful chief of the Calusa tribe. Amazingly, an Indian who spoke Spanish appeared and served as interpreter. Nevertheless, after a short interlude, Carlos mounted an attack of archers in 80 canoes, and Ponce quit the Florida mainland (Morison 1974:511). The existence of an Indian among the Calusa who spoke Spanish strongly suggests previous and perhaps extensive European contact. There is also the possibility that the language could have been learned in Cuba, to which island the Calusa are known to have navigated fairly regularly in oceangoing canoes. In either case, the extent of contact necessary to have learned a foreign language is probably sufficient also for the transmission of a new disease, or perhaps a host of diseases.

Between the 1513 "discovery" of Florida and the crucial *entrada* of Hernando de Soto beginning in 1539, at least seven episodes of European contact with natives of La Florida are recorded, including Ponce's attempted return to Charlotte Harbor in 1521 to establish a permanent colony. In no case is the historical record sufficiently detailed to determine whether natives were suffering or had suffered from epidemic diseases, but in at least two instances it is documented that members of the ship's crew were sick at the time of contact (Smith 1987:55). It is very likely that there were additional contacts either not recorded or not yet discovered in archival documents, as ships routinely put ashore for water and wood, and there was a lucrative slave trade in the Caribbean as well. In addition, it was common practice to take along a few natives, willing or not, to serve as interpreters and guides for groups not yet contacted. Their degree of interaction with Europeans probably afforded the best possibilities for contagion of Old World pathogens.

Following the unsuccessful attempts of Ponce de León at Charlotte Harbor in 1521, Lucas Vásquez de Ayllón on the Atlantic coast in 1526, and Pánfilo de Narváez on the Gulf Coast at Apalachee in 1528, the king of Spain granted the title of *adelantado* of Florida to Hernando de Soto (Milanich and Hudson 1993:29). De Soto was a veteran of the conquests, having accompanied Francisco Pizarro to Peru and become wealthy in the process (Hoffman 1993). His dream was to repeat his accumulation of fame and fortune, this time in the southeast United States.

The particular means by which the Spanish crown granted rights of exploration, settlement, and spoils to explorers such as de Soto is helpful in explaining the nature of contact during this important episode in Europeanization. In the crown's view, its own legal claim to the territory to be explored had been firmly established. This right existed in the context of political competition among European monarchies for portions of the New World over which they would rule; as the Spanish clergy and crown debated the niceties of whether Native Americans were fully human, there was no consideration of whether they possessed a legal property right to the lands they occupied. De Soto's royal orders of April and May 1537

> gave him authority to conquer, pacify, and settle whatever he wished within the ample limits of Florida. . . . The crown share of revenues was specified, in particular, the gold, silver, precious stones, and pearls found. If these were gained in the usual manner in battle, on entering towns, or by trade with the Indians the Crown was to have a fifth. If they were taken from graves, sepulchres, temples, places of religious ceremonies, or buried in a private or public place the Crown was to get half. (Sauer 1971:158)

As de Soto and his expedition of 600 traversed the spine of the Florida peninsula, it is unlikely they reached the extremity of northeast Florida; certainly they did not see the St. Johns River (Milanich and Hudson 1993:186–210). The secondary psychological and epidemiological effects of the expedition were felt throughout the southeastern United States, but it does not appear from French and Spanish accounts of the early 1560s that the tribes of northeast Florida had been severely reduced in population within the previous two decades (Hann 1996:35). It is not necessary here to recount the many episodes of contact between Indians and Europeans along the de Soto route; three contemporary accounts and an additional later account are readily available (Clayton, Knight, and Moore 1993), and a recent synthesis has combined archaeological, ethnographic, and historic evidence to provide a detailed narrative (Hudson 1997). Here we are more interested in the judgment of de Soto by his contemporaries and by later historians to understand how the Spaniards' view of Native Americans determined the nature of the two peoples' interaction.

Gonzalo Fernández de Oviedo y Valdés, author of the contemporary standard history of the first half century of Spain in the New World, reports the account of one of the members of the expedition as to the reasons porters, women, and chiefs were so frequently captured: "The [porters] were additional slaves and servants to carry things, the women were taken to serve and satisfy their carnal pleasures, the chiefs were detained to keep their subjects quiet. Neither the governor nor any one else knew where they were headed other than to find a land so rich as to satisfy their desires and to discover the great secrets which the governor said he knew" (quoted in Sauer 1971:179). Sauer himself is even less complimentary:

> De Soto landed at Tampa equipped with collars and chains to be used on gangs of captives. His tactics were to attack settlements, or if he

was received hospitably, to provoke hostility. He had learned in Panama that seizure of a cacique would ensure compliance of the subjects, and followed the same practice in the north. . . . It is apparent that he was only looking for loot as he had in Panama, Nicaragua, and Peru. In those countries the persons of rulers, their houses, and temples yielded large and quick booty; the robbing of graves a steadier and continuing profit. In the stubborn and stupid belief that Indians elsewhere had accumulated such treasures De Soto wandered up and down the coast plain seeking out the towns where important chiefs lived. (1971:179–180)

During the first four months of the four-year expedition, the Spanish army tested its strategy among the Tocobaga, Western Timucua, and Apalachee Indians of Florida. Before arriving at the first winter camp in Apalachee in what is now Tallahassee, the expedition experienced several violent contacts with Indians, captured hundreds of men and women, occupied villages and towns, and otherwise exposed the leaders and people of three separate chiefdoms to disease agents. These illnesses were likely transmitted by blood contact, sexual relations, airborne germs, and probably animals that traveled with the army. There is no disputing the devastating effects of the European diseases on southeastern tribes in the sixteenth century; the problem is one of timing. The question is, were the chiefdoms of Florida and the rest of the Southeast encountered in 1539–1543 already severely depopulated as a result of unrecorded epidemics of the previous half century, or were the first serious effects of epidemics felt following de Soto and the settlements of the French and Spanish in northeast Florida in the early 1560s?

It is probably not possible to answer this question in detail, although Smith (1987) has developed some useful archaeological measurements of depopulation that complement the less direct documentary evidence. Now that depopulation has been identified as an issue with broad implications for historians, anthropologists, and archaeologists, the subject will likely receive more attention. The population estimates of Dobyns, 10 to 20 times higher than previously published, and the implied loss of up to 80 percent of the population before 1565 have been rejected. Important future research questions are the geographic range, number, timing, identity, and fatality of various epidemics.

Besides pathogens and their ecologically aggressive European hosts, a variety of animal and plant species were introduced to the southeast United States and the Florida peninsula during the period of exploration by various expeditions and other means. The success of these species was determined primarily by whether there was a suitable ecological niche, i.e., whether competing indigenous species allowed the foreign species' survival and whether physical conditions such as temperature, moisture, and soils were suitable. In general, Old World species encountered a very fertile ground indeed in the New World. It is instructive to remember that the explorers outfitted their expeditions primarily with weapons rather than farm implements. Their goal was to live off what they could take rather than what they could produce. Nonetheless, the economic foundation of the Europeans was pastoralism and agriculture rather than hunting and gathering, and certain parts of their domesticated food complex were introduced early.

The mammalian fauna of North America before European contact was significantly different from that of the Old World. Not only were wild species fewer in number and smaller than their European counterparts, but there were also few domesticated animals. No beasts of burden served the American natives; there were no animals tended for milk or fur, and the only domestic food animals were a small variety of dog and the turkey, neither of which had a great impact on the landscape outside the limits of settlements. As a result, there were no artificially maintained pastures, although naturally occurring grasslands and savannas did occur. Although there were cultivated and abandoned fields for corn, the American landscape first viewed by Europeans had not been transformed to support animal herds, as their own homelands had been for several millennia.

The portable support system of the explorers relied upon a complex of animals; on the second voyage of Columbus in 1493, horses, dogs, pigs, cattle, chickens, sheep, and goats were introduced to the Caribbean islands. For the explorers and expeditions two species were most important—the pig and the horse.

The sixteenth-century pig bore little resemblance to the farm animal we know today; if anything, it is closest to the wild razorback, known now as a game animal and recognized for its fierceness and adaptability. Pigs had two characteristics important to explorers: They were self-sufficient and they were prolific. Pigs are long lived yet breed within a year. Two large litters can be produced annually (Davis and Dent 1968:76), and their rate of increase is unmatched by any other domesticated animal. It was a common practice in the sixteenth century for mariners to drop off a pair of pigs on a remote island to provide food for later shipwrecked sailors. Pigs are very efficient at producing food for humans; approximately 20 percent of the energy they consume is converted to edible meat, in contrast to some 5 percent for cattle. They require absolutely no care and thrive in mixed and varied environments rather than requiring maintenance of pastures. As early as 1514 Diego de Velázquez estimated the number of pigs on the island of Cuba at 30,000, less than a quarter century after the first voyage of Columbus (Sauer 1966:189). De Soto brought 13 pigs to Florida in 1539, and these increased in number to 700 by the time the expedition reached the Mississippi River three years later (Crosby 1972:78). It would be reasonable to assume that some pigs escaped from de Soto's herds; given their omnivorous and fecund habits, it is also likely that pigs competed directly with Florida Indians for the products of their fields and gardens. Pigs' grubbing quickly reduces vegetation, uproots seedlings, and reduces the ability of oaks and other seed trees to reproduce. In a short time forest diversity is reduced as undergrowth is replaced by grass (Davis and Dent 1968:76).

Horses are a different sort of domesticate. They require special feed or pasture and do not breed either as rapidly or as readily as swine. Nonetheless, their impact on the native population was dramatic. Horses were not a source of food, except in extreme need; rather, they served as an instrument of conquest (Graham 1949). The Spaniards and Portuguese who made up the early expeditions were the finest horsemen of Europe riding the finest horses of Europe; for Iberian nobility and soldiers, horses were an integral cultural element. Although horses served to transport equipment and supplies, the preferred animal for this purpose was man. More important, horses provided a vast military advantage to the conquistador, not only in allowing swift travel and communication but also in facilitating the slaughter of pedestrian enemies. As Bartolomé de Las Casas noted, one horseman could skewer 2,000 Indians in an hour (cited in Crosby 1972:81). It is unlikely that feral horses entered the Southeast landscape from the early expeditions as pigs might have. Horses were not only highly regarded by the Spanish; they were too important to lose. The death of a horse was noted as seriously as the death of a soldier. Nor was the open and mixed forest of the Southeast suitable habitat for horses to survive in the absence of human care.

It is also recorded that de Soto brought mules and bloodhounds ashore in Florida (Swanton 1979:38). To this list it would be reasonable to add rats and mice, although these may well have already reached the mainland either by other expeditions or shipwrecks. Rats, of course, are vectors of typhus and bubonic plague and, when unchecked by domestic or natural predators, can multiply in such numbers as to constitute a plague in themselves. The classic ecological case is Bermuda, where rats spread to every part of the isolated island complex shortly after their introduction by their European shipmates and threatened the colony's very survival (Crosby

1972:97). There is no direct record of the associated insects, animal parasites, and weeds that were inadvertently introduced during the period of exploration and conquest, but it is likely that scores and perhaps hundreds of such species were well established in Florida by the end of the sixteenth century, as the pace of introduction and change began to increase dramatically after 1560.

French and Spanish Colonization, 1562–1600

The year 1562 marks the beginning of permanent European presence in Florida, starting with the French at the mouth of the St. Johns River and continuing three years later with the Spanish at St. Augustine. Suddenly, the documentary record of the southeast environment and its people becomes rich in comparison to the previous 50 years of explorations and expeditions.

Spain's repeated attempts in the first half of the sixteenth century to control La Florida had all met with failure (Milanich and Milbrath 1989, Weber 1992:30–59). To a large degree, this situation must be blamed on the lack of commitment and ability to establish a permanent colony. Following upon her fabulous success in appropriating the vast gold and silver treasures of the Caribbean islands, Mexico, and Peru, Spain's model of occupation of the New World was based on exploitation and subjugation. Despite the crown's mentions of settlement in the successive charters to Ponce de León, Narváez, Ayllón, de Soto, and Tristan de Luna y Arellano, these expeditions came more prepared for conquest than cultivation. Spanish interest in La Florida continued high, however, as the region played an important role in the larger theatre of European geopolitics.

Ponce de León's discovery of the Gulf Stream on his first voyage was the beginning of what came to be known as the Carrera de las Indias, "the life line of the Indies" (Sauer 1971:274–76), the northern maritime route from the Caribbean principal port of Havana to Spain. Treasure laden fleets would assemble in Havana and then navigate the dangerous Straits of Florida between the peninsula and the Bahamas to follow the steady five-knot current northward along the coast as far as South Carolina before bearing east for the trans-Atlantic leg of the voyage (map 5.1).

Like Spain, France claimed a religious justification for its New World enterprise; it was, however, no coincidence that the French Protestant settlement at the mouth of the St. Johns River was situated in one of the most crucial segments of the risky Spanish treasure route. Whereas French corsairs and privateers had initially preyed on Spanish fleets off the Iberian peninsula, they advanced their threat across the Atlantic to the mouth of the Gulf Stream in midcentury. As King Philip II of Spain failed in his at-

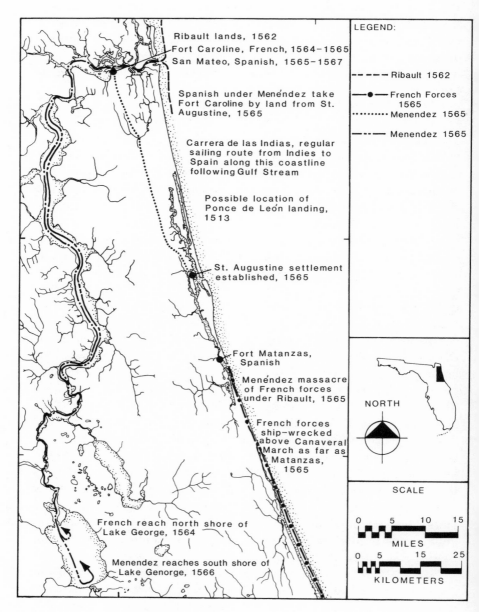

Map 5.1. Routes of discovery and exploration

tempt to establish a protective coastal settlement in present-day South Carolina, the French pressed their advantage by first building a small fort at the same location and then establishing a more permanent settlement in northeast Florida at the mouth of the St. Johns River. Fort Caroline, built in 1564 east of what is now Jacksonville, commanded the most strategic port on the Florida coast. The following year the settlement was populated with colonists under the leadership of René Goulaine de Laudonnière (fig. 5.1), and in the process, a rich and valuable record of the Florida Indians was documented.

The French decision to settle at Fort Caroline was political, religious, and economic. During the first half of the sixteenth century, France was torn by religious and civil wars between a Catholic majority and a Protestant minority. The Protestant Huguenot enterprise in Florida, implemented by the Protestant admiral Gaspard de Coligny, had the blessing of the young King Charles IX. Coligny sought not only to establish a Protestant settlement in Florida but also, and more important, to control for France the crucial

Fig. 5.1. Fort Caroline constructed by the French at the mouth of the St. Johns River, de Bry engraving 10 years after the painting by Le Moyne; published in 1591. Florida Photographic Archives.

treasure fleet route that rode the Gulf Stream northward along the Florida coast. By the mid-sixteenth century vast amounts of gold, silver, emeralds, pearls, and lesser commodities were leaving Spanish New World ports for Spain. The value is difficult to determine but was so large as to completely dominate the economy of Europe throughout the sixteenth century.

By the middle of the century the supply of riches seemed so inexhaustible, and the rate of spending was so great, that most treasure shipments were appropriated before they arrived (Haring 1964:169). Around 1560 the government share of annual Spanish imports of gold and silver came to about 2 million pesos; at its peak in 1600 the figure reached almost 7 million pesos per year (Gibson, 1966:104). To this total must be added the larger portion remaining in the private market, a significant proportion of undocumented contraband, production lost in shipwrecks, and the amount lost to pirates and corsairs. A threat to the Carrera de las Indias was a threat to the economic survival of Spain (map 5.2).

It is not clear to what extent previous sporadic contact had affected the people of northeast Florida before Jean Ribault's 1562 landing at the mouth of the St. Johns. If there had been serious depopulation, it is not apparent in the French accounts. The first record by Ribault and his small army upon arriving is full of delight, not only of the new land and its inhabitants but very likely also at the pleasure of disembarking after two and one-half months at sea (fig. 5.2). Ribault's account, written in England immediately following his return from America, was published in an English translation in 1563; no original French version is known to have existed (Connor 1927). After describing his peaceful and pleasant interaction with the Timucuan Indians, led by Saturiwa, near the mouth of the St. Johns, he turned his attention to the surrounding land:

> [we] enterd and veued the cuntry therabowte, which is the fairest, frutefullest and plesantest of all the worlde, habonding in honney, veneson, wildfoule, forrestes, woodes of all sortes, palme trees, cipers, ceders, bayes, the hiest, greatest and fairest vynes in all the wourld with grapes accordingly, which naturally and withowt mans helpe and tryming growe to the top of okes and other trees that be of a wonderfull greatnes and height. And the sight of the faire medowes is a pleasure not able to be expressed with tonge, . . . and to be shorte it is a thing inspeakable, the comodities that be sene there and shalbe founde more and more in this incomperable lande, never as yet broken with plowe irons, bringing fourthe all thinges according to his first nature, whereof the eternall God endued yt. (Ribaut 1927:72–73)

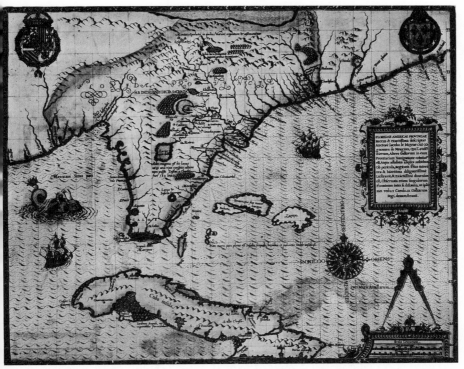

Map 5.2. The Le Moyne map of Florida, as engraved by de Bry, published in 1591. Florida Photographic Archives.

Ribault also recorded important observations on the Indians themselves:

> They be all naked and of a goodly stature, mighty, faire and aswell shapen and proportioned of bodye as any people in all the worlde, very gentill, curtious and of a good nature.
>
> The most parte of them cover their raynes and pryvie partes with faire hartes skins, paynted cunyngly with sondry collours, and the fore parte of there bodye and armes paynted with pretye devised workes of azure, redd, and black, so well and so properly don as the best paynter of Europe could not amend yt. The wemen have there bodies covered with a certen herbe like unto moste, whereof the cedertrees and all other trees be alwaies covered. The men for pleasure do allwayes tryme themselves therwith, after sundry fasshions. They be of tawny collour, hawke nosed and of a pleasaunt countenaunce. (Ribaut 1927:69)

Fig. 5.2. The de Bry engraving entitled *The French Arrive in Florida*, 1591. Florida Photographic Archives.

There is no clue in the account of the 1562 encounter as to whether the Indians Ribault was writing about had suffered from epidemic diseases. Dobyns has postulated a population decrease of nearly 80 percent between 1513 and 1565, that is, from an estimated original 722,000 people to approximately 150,000 (1983:292). This estimate implies that over the course of two and one-half generations, i.e., within the living memory of some survivors, a stable and adapted cultural system would have lost four of every five individuals. It is difficult to imagine, if Dobyns is correct, how labor responsibilities as well as social status and roles would have been reallocated to maintain a successful agricultural adaptation in the face of such losses. The image presented by Ribault is of an attractive people successful at agriculture and organized in a stratified social structure:

> About there howses they laboure and till there ground, sowing there fildes with a grayn called Mahis, wherof the[y] make there meale, and in there gardens the[y] plant beans, gourdes, cowekcumbers, citrons, peasen, and many other simples and rootes unknon unto us. There spades and mattockes be of wood, so well and fyttely made as ys possible, which they make with certen stones, oister shelles, and mus-

telles, wherwith the[y] make also ther bowes and smale lances, and cutt and pullishe all sortes of woodes that they employe abowt there buldinges and necessarye use. (Ribaut 1927:73–74)

On the last day at the St. Johns, Ribault took final stock of the people and the land, with particular reference to gold, copper, turquoise, and other valuables:

The scituation is under the elevation of xxx [30] degrees, a good clymate, helthfull, of good temperaunce, marvelous pleasaunt, the people gentill and of a good and amyable loving nature, which willingly will obaye, ye, be content to serve those that shall with gentilnes and humanytie go aboute to alure them as yt [is] nedefull for all those that shalbe sent thither hereafter so to do, and as I have chardged those of oures that be lefte there to do, to thende that by these meanes they may ask and learn of them where the[y] take there gould, copper, turquises, and other thinges yet unknown unto us, by reason of the shortnes of tyme we soiurned there; for if any rude and rigorious meanes shuldbe used towardes this people, they would flye hither and thither through the woodes and forestes and abandon there habitations and cuntrye. (Ribaut 1927:82–83)

Several items in this first informative account of the region are of interest. Ribault devoted considerable attention to the navigability of the St. Johns. As in all the river and estuary entrances and inlets along the Florida east coast, a shallow sandbar either prevents or jeopardizes the passage of vessels, depending on their draft. While the St. Johns offers a slightly deeper entrance than St. Augustine Inlet, its bar was thought to be too shallow for Ribault's small oceangoing vessels, and the party anchored a few leagues offshore, entering the mouth by three smaller boats. For more than three centuries the vagaries of the bars at the entrances of St. Johns, St. Augustine, and Matanzas would continue to have great military, strategic, and economic importance.

Within the river itself Ribault commented several times on the abundance of fish, describing the river as "boylling and roring through the multytute of all sortes of fishes" (1927:66). At nearly every meeting the Indians presented Ribault's party with fish, which they captured by means of weirs, "so well and cunyngly sett together, after the fashion of a labirinthe or maze, with so manny tourns and crokes, as yt is impossible to do yt with more cunning or industrye" (1927:71). It is clear that the Timucuans possessed no items of forged metal, although they were supplied some by Ribault; they did have items of beaten and polished copper, as had prehistoric people centuries earlier. Ribault the seaman was impressed by the canoes (fig. 5.3), "which boates they make but of one pece of a tree working yt hollowe so cunnyngly and fyttely, that they put in one of these thus shapen boates or rather great troughes, xv [15] or xx [20] persons, and go therwith verry swiftly. They that rowe stand upright having there owers short, made after the fashyon of a peele" (1927:80–81).

A wide variety of foodstuffs is mentioned, indicating a mixed subsistence that includes crops of maize, beans, and squash as well as game and gathered foods from all local environments (fig. 5.4). It is interesting that Ribault refers to wild swine and citrons; both of these are Old World domesticates and were no doubt previously introduced, either accidentally by shipwreck or intentionally as a ready food source for emergencies. In general, food seems to have been abundant, and in the joyous and excited opinion of the French, the Indians appeared to be as healthy as their bountiful environment.

After raising a stone monument engraved with the arms of the king of France (fig. 5.5), the French sailed northward along the Sea Island coast, arriving in mid-May at the site of present-day Port Royal, South Carolina, and established the small fortification of Charlesfort. Leaving a small garrison of men and promising to return within six months with supplies and reinforcements, Ribault sailed back to France with both ships, only to find his country in the throes of civil war. He escaped to England, where he composed his account and was subsequently imprisoned, unable to return to New France until 1564. In the meantime, the small force at Charlesfort, without contact for two years, having run out of food, and having failed to plant crops or otherwise ensure their survival, saw a return voyage as their only salvation. They constructed a small makeshift vessel and set sail for France. After a desperate voyage they were picked up by an English ship, by which means the English learned of the French settlement (Lorant 1965:9).

The French effort in Florida was renewed in 1563 as Admiral Coligny arranged for another expedition as soon as the French religious war had been settled. Ribault was still imprisoned in England, so a force of three ships and 300 men under the command of de Laudonnière was sent out, arriving in Florida in 1564. They found the stone column left by Ribault at the mouth of the St. Johns and built a small fortification with the assistance of the still-friendly Chief Saturiwa, naming it Fort Caroline after King Charles. The sequence of events in Florida (and in Europe) concerning the French force in the heart of Spanish Florida is complex and need not be repeated in detail. Much of the difficulty of the French at Fort Caroline results from the same mistake that doomed the Port Royal colony: failure to

Fig. 5.3. The de Bry engraving *Storing Their Crops in the Public Granary*, 1591. Florida Photographic Archives.

Fig. 5.4. *Drying Meat, Fish and Other Food*, engraved by De Bry after the painting by Le Moyne; published in 1591. Florida Photographic Archives.

Fig. 5.5. *The Natives of Florida Worship the Column Erected by the Commander on his First Voyage*, de Bry, 1591. Florida Photographic Archives.

establish a source of food other than that which the Indians were willing to supply. It is clear, as it had been for every previous European attempt, that the intent was "new means of traffic and profit in strange lands" (Lorant 1965:10) rather than an enduring, self-sufficient colony.

Although the French were not prepared to feed themselves, they had made provisions to document their discoveries in Florida. The artist-cartographer Jacques Le Moyne de Morgues was engaged by Laudonnière to "map the seacoast and harbors, indicate the position of towns, [and] plot the depth and course of the rivers. In addition, I was to portray the dwellings of the natives and anything else in the land that was worthy of observation" (Le Moyne in Lorant 1965:36). All but one of Le Moyne's paintings, produced in the two decades following his escape from the Spanish destruction of Fort Caroline and his return to Europe, have been lost. Yet, because they were reproduced and published after his death by the French engraver and publisher Theodore de Bry, they form the foundation for one of the fullest depictions of a New World society and environment in this early period, and continue to provide a valuable record of Florida before it began to suffer the severe effects of European colonization.

The 41 engravings and the one surviving painting are a complex product of sixteenth-century European graphic art. The reliance on the images as accurate depictions of the people and land has been criticized as misleading, and these pieces must be regarded as part symbol and part depiction. It is clear from the comparison of the one existing Le Moyne painting and its corresponding de Bry engraving (as well as the comparison between John White's watercolors of Virginia and de Bry's engravings of them) that the engraver took only the most minor liberties in copying; the fundamental differences between the reality and the depiction must rest with Le Moyne. Nonetheless, there are many European as well as Central and South American elements in the de Bry Florida engravings (Sturtevant 1977). It is important to note that the paintings were completed by Le Moyne, not "from nature," but rather from memory over the next two decades, while the artist was living in London. It is likely that Le Moyne painted from sketches, as the depiction of uniquely New World plants and animals is so accurate as to allow the identification of species in many cases.

The first seven de Bry engravings are likely based on Ribault's written account, as Le Moyne was not present on the 1562 voyage. Plates 8 through 42 in de Bry's *Great and Small Voyages* depict events or situations Le Moyne may have observed personally. Le Moyne's accompanying narrative, as well as other accounts, documents a complex relationship between the French and the Indians, first with Chief Saturiwa, who controlled the region around the mouth of the St. Johns, and subsequently with other leaders such as Outina, an even more powerful chief ruling a tribe centered around Lake George to the south. Laudonnière quickly became entangled in the complexities of Indian alliances and competitions, and it is clear from the account that the two principal factors influencing his judgment were the search for gold and silver and the inability of the French to supply themselves with food. The greed, hunger, and political intrigue in which they became enmeshed led many of the French force to mutiny. At the same time, the remaining French were committed by Laudonnière to assisting Saturiwa in a battle with Outina. Of this period, spring and early summer 1565, Le Moyne wrote:

After some of us had already died of hunger and the rest were starved until we were nothing but skin and bones, Laudonnière called a general council to discuss means of returning to France. He had now given up hope of receiving the reinforcements for which we had been waiting eighteen months. The general council decided to refit our third ship as well as possible and to build up her sides with planking to increase her capacity. While this work was in progress, a number of French soldiers were sent along the coast to collect supplies. (Lorant 1965:68)

In August 1565, the failing French colony was visited by the Englishman John Hawkins, whose voyage was narrated by John Sparke. Sparke summarized the plight of the French and its cause:

> In which place they [the French], being two hundred men at their first coming, had in short space eaten all the maize they could buy of the inhabitants about them, and therefore were driven certain of them to serve a king of the Floridians against other his enemies for mill and other victuals, which having gotten, could not serve them, being so many, so long a time; but want came upon them in such sort that they were fain to gather acorns. . . . Notwithstanding the great want that the Frenchemen had, the ground doth yield victuals sufficient if they would have taken pains to get the same; but they, being soldiers, desired to live by the sweat of other men's brows. (Sparke 1565:390–391)

Sparke marveled at the richness of the land around the French fort: "The commodities of this land are more than are yet known to any man; for besides the land itself, whereof there is more than any king Christian is able to inhabit, it flourisheth with meadow, pasture-ground, with woods of cedar and cypress, and other sorts, as better cannot be in the world" (1565:392). Mentioning various species of trees, herbs, roots, mammals (including the unicorn, "a beast with one horn, which, coming to the river to drink, putteth the same into the water before he drinketh"), reptiles, fish, birds, and a variety of plant foods, Sparke concludes with a prophetic opinion.

> Here I have declared the estate of Florida and the commodities therein to this day known, which although it may seem unto some, by the means that the plenty of gold and silver is not so abundant as in other places, that the cost bestowed upon the same will not be able to quit the charges, yet am I of the opinion that, by that which I have seen in other islands of the Indians, . . . the increase of cattle only would raise profit sufficient for the same. . . . And surely I may this affirm, that the ground of the Indians for the breed of cattle is not in any point to be compared to this of Florida, which all year long is so green as any time in the summer with us. . . . (1565:395)

Hawkins generously traded a small vessel, a barentine of 50 tons, along with 20 barrels of meal and some beans ("for they had not above 10 days victuals left"), to the French so that they might make their way back home. However, their fate had already been determined by events in Europe, as within three weeks of Hawkins's departure both the Frenchman Ribault and the Spaniard Pedro Menéndez de Avilés reached the Florida fort—one to save it, the other to destroy it.

The French presence in Florida, although well documented, was short lived. In a complicated series of battles, escapes, surrenders, and killing, Pedro Menéndez effectively eliminated the French threat to the Spanish territory and its adjacent shipping route. Historians have devoted considerable attention to deploring or justifying the slaughter of the Huguenots at the hand of Menéndez, but there is wide agreement on his ability to accomplish the settlement and control of the Florida enterprise of King Philip II of Spain. The *asiento*, or grant, to Menéndez from the king differed significantly from previous charges. Menéndez was required to take 500 men, 100 of whom were to be farmers, the balance to include sailors and soldiers, stonecutters, carpenters, sawyers, smiths, barbers, locksmiths, and two priests. Within three years, 500 more would be taken to Florida, at least 100 of whom were to be married; the rest were to be farmers and workmen, "in order that the land may be cultivated with more ease." Menéndez pledged to bring more than a dozen priests for instruction in the Catholic faith, as well as 500 Negro slaves, "in order that the towns may be built and the land cultivated . . . and for planting sugar cane for the sugar mills that may be built, and for building the said sugar mills" (Connor 1923, Appendix D).

The king, as was customary, granted Menéndez the titles of adelantado as well as governor and captain-general and provided him the authority to give repartimientos and lands and estates "without prejudice to the Indians." In addition, he was to choose 25 square leagues for himself, also without prejudice to the Indians, but would not receive the mineral rights. The majority of the Florida endeavor was to be personally funded by Menéndez, although certain income was granted, including one-fifteenth of all income, mines of gold and silver, precious stones, pearls, and other products belonging to the crown. The endeavor was excused from excise and import taxes, and Menéndez was granted certain funds, ships, and the right to keep whatever might be captured for six years. Finally, the agreement concluded that if Menéndez should fail to accomplish his responsibilities, he would be punished for trespass against "the commands of his King and natural Master" (Connor 1923, Appendix D).

Menéndez had agreed to a substantial undertaking, largely at his own expense. Besides removing the French from the St. Johns, establishing a permanent settlement at St. Augustine, and beginning conversion of the natives in that region, the *adelantado* was expected to reconnoiter the coast between the Florida Keys and Newfoundland, and choose suitable locations for settlements. Two or three towns consisting of at least 100 inhabitants were to be developed within three years. In each place there would be "a large house of stone, mud or wood, according to the nature and character of the land, with its moat and drawbridge; the most substantial that can be built according to weather and circumstances, so that in case of need the residents may gather therein and shelter themselves from the perils which may beset them from Indians, corsairs or other people." He further pledged to bring to the towns 100 horses and mares, 200 calves, 400 swine, 400 sheep and some goats, and all the other cattle and livestock that might seem proper to him. Finally the crown was serious about permanent settlement in Florida.

History has judged Menéndez harshly for his massacre of the French at Matanzas under an agreement of surrender. To his credit, he did attempt to establish small outposts on the southeast and southwest coasts of the Florida peninsula, as well as in the Guale province of Georgia; a much larger settlement was placed at Santa Elena in South Carolina, but relations with the Indians proved difficult, and these initial attempts were soon abandoned. By the time Menéndez returned from a trip to Guale, the St. Augustine settlement had been burned by the Indians. The description of this event by Solís de Merás, Menéndez's brother-in-law and his principal biographer, is reminiscent of the de Bry engraving *Setting an Enemy's Town on Fire* (Lorant 1965:97). The account by de Merás suggests a war as much against the land as against the people:

> Very unsuccessful war can be waged against them, unless one goes to their villages in search of them, to cut down the plantings and burn the houses and take the canoes and destroy the fishways, which is all the property they have, so that they must leave the land. (Solís de Merás 1567:183–84)

By this time, according to de Merás, more than 100 Spanish soldiers had been killed by Indians at St. Augustine and San Mateo, the name the Spaniards had given Fort Caroline after ousting the French.

This event prompted Menéndez to develop his defenses in earnest. The Spaniards decided to move their fortification to a location near the entrance of the inlet at St. Augustine and completed an earthenwork structure in 10 days. As food and supplies were exhausted, the governor sailed for Havana to obtain assistance but was unsuccessful; fortunately food, supplies, and men and women arrived in time from Spain. This crisis was the first in what was to become a well-established pattern of much demand and little supply in the relationship between St. Augustine and the other Spanish settlements of the Indies.

Throughout the 200 years of the First Spanish Period, no reliable means of self-support could be established for St. Augustine. Under the Spanish colonial model, it was intended that natives provide a controlled labor force engaged in food production that could support the Spanish population. The means of control was to be the mission system, operated first by Jesuits, then later by Franciscans.

The reason for failure was primarily an environmental one, as was clearly recognized by Father Juan Rogel in reporting on the state of the Florida missions in 1570 (Brinton 1861). Much hope was placed on the native production of corn as a possible food surplus to exploit, but both the French and the Spanish in the middle 1560s soon exhausted the marginal surplus and found no means of increasing the supply. Rogel explained the reasons for his abandoning the Franciscan mission effort, which had finally been reduced to his sole presence among two remaining Indian families. As soon as the acorns ripened in late spring, he said, "They left me quite alone, all going to the forests, each one to his own quarter, and only met together for certain festivals, which occurred every two months, and this not always in the same spot" (Brinton 1861).

To persuade the natives to settle, he supplied iron spades and abundant seed corn at a location where there were 20 houses already built, but all the families there dispersed to a dozen different villages, leaving only two families behind. "For all this I did not despair," he wrote, "but labored in those two families to do what good I could, preaching and exhorting, assisting and making much of them." Not surprisingly, Father Rogel's subsequent threat to return to Spain unless his converts consented to "become sons of God by becoming enemies of the devil" was gratefully accepted. His final report to the adelantado offers rare contemporary insight into the relationship between land and people:

> To win any of the blind and wretched souls of these provinces, it is first requisite that the Indians be collected together in towns, and cultivate the land sufficiently to provide themselves with food for the whole year, . . . then let preaching be introduced. . . . to congregate them together thus is a work of time and difficulty . . . for two reasons: First, because they have been accustomed to this kind of life for thousands of years, and it would almost kill them to tear them rudely from it; and secondly, if they were willing, the nature of the soil would not permit it, as it is poor and barren and easily wears out; and they themselves say that it is for this reason that they live so scattered and wander so much. (Brinton 1861:329)

6

Patterns of European Settlement and International Dependence, 1575–1821

Native Subjugation, 1575–1600

For the balance of the 1560s, Menéndez devoted attention to solidifying the fledgling settlements and extending the explorations of his lieutenants: northward beyond Santa Elena, westward into the Gulf of Mexico, into the southeastern interior, and into the middle of the Florida peninsula by way of the St. Johns River, which was navigated as far as Lake George. These attempts had little permanent effect, except at St. Augustine itself. There, Menéndez issued orders of governance, and established a municipal council with the power to grant lots within the town and collect taxes. Outside the small community, San Mateo on the St. Johns was destroyed in revenge by the French privateer Dominique de Gourgues, assisted by the Indians, and Santa Elena in present-day South Carolina was abandoned by its inhabitants, who fled to St. Augustine. Menéndez died in 1574, and the St. Augustine settlement became a crown colony, supported, in theory at least, by a regular subsidy supplied by other colonial treasuries (Bushnell 1983:32–36).

The succeeding governor, Pedro Menéndez Marquéz, nephew of the first governor, reported to the king in 1578 that the escaped French were still among the Indians, of whom he said "I should much like to break the spirit of those Indians. . . . I intend to drive them from their lands, burn their villages, and teach them that we are going after them" (Connor 1930:81–83). In a letter of April 1579 to royal officials in Santo Domingo, Marquéz reported that he had successfully reduced the Indian threat. Like the Indian hostilities in which the French had taken part in the previous decade, the method was war against land as well as people:

I set about overrunning the country of the enemy who had done the damage in these provinces, and in forty-five leagues of their land which I overran, I burned nineteen villages, and some Indians were killed. . . . Great was the harm I did them in their food stores, for I burned a great quantity of maize and other supplies. . . . In this province of St. Augustine the people are peaceful, and although they were so previously, they are much more so now since they have seen the war I made on the other Indians. (Connor 1930:225)

Around this same time, the food supply of the Spanish settlement seemed more secure. Marquéz reports in the same February letter that over 1,500 bushels of corn had been harvested the previous year and that many fruits and vegetables were beginning to be produced, including figs, pomegranates, oranges, grapes, mulberries, beans, kidney beans, melons, pumpkins, lettuce, artichokes, onions, and garlic. Marquéz concluded, "If there were those who would farm the land, it is ready for it" (Connor 1930:227). By June of 1579, however, the governor had sent the message to the king that if the subsidy was not received by December he would request permission to leave the country, "for I have no doubt that it will perish, and I should not wish, after so many years of service, to suffer from a calamity like that which is expected" (Connor 1930:237). In October the Royal Council of the Indies advised the king that the subsidy should be increased.

By 1580 the Spanish inhabitants of St. Augustine had reduced the Indian threat and were no longer at risk of ambush while planting, tending gardens, collecting fruits, fishing, or gathering oysters. In 1586, however, the young town was destroyed in a raid by the Englishman Francis Drake, the fort and houses burned, the gardens trampled, and the fruit trees cut down (map 6.1). Drake's report that upon their arrival local Indians began to die in great numbers suggests an epidemic introduced by Drake's crew, many of whom had already died from fever (Dobyns 1983:276–277). By the last decade of the century, it appears that the Indian population was reduced sufficiently in relation to the slowly growing European population to pose little threat. In the 1590s the number of missionaries increased in response to peaceful overtures by a number of village leaders, and the Franciscan conversion effort began in earnest (Hann 1996:137–173). It eventually succeeded where the Jesuits had failed.

Despite the rebellion among the Guale north of St. Augustine in 1597 and the subsequent threat of King Philip III to abandon the Florida territory, the colony improved in stability through the early decades of the seventeenth century. Indian hostility was tempered as mission settlements extended throughout Timucuan territory and northward through the Guale

Map 6.1. St. Augustine, 1586, showing the attack of Drake and the defense of the town. Florida Photographic Archives.

sea island coastal settlements. It is possible that this new stability, 50 years in the making, was more a reflection of native depopulation than of subjugation.

By 1602 mission records show little evidence of the original vitality of the Salt Water and Fresh Water tribes. The remaining natives lived in settled mission villages, acculturated in the Catholic faith and the Spanish language. Total population at the four missions in the vicinity of St. Augustine was estimated at only 200 souls (Hann 1996:158). The population losses of 1612–1616 are dramatic and well documented. For the first time, accurate population records existed for Indians who had officially converted to the Christian faith. Of the 16,000 such souls recorded in all the Franciscan missions, 50 percent died of disease very likely introduced into new villages by friars (Hann 1996:174). The decade of the 1630s may have been the peak of Timucua population after contact. Some 50,000 Indians were reported to have been baptized or received some Christian instruction. This comparatively large number reflects an expansion of missions into the territory of the Western Timucua. By 1655, about 26,000 Indians were reported as Christians in Florida, indicating a great loss of Timucuan speakers especially. No comparable estimates exist for non-Christian Indians. Other serious epidemics are recorded for 1649–1650 and 1672.

As population declined, villages coalesced, often around missionized settlements (map 6.2), and the Franciscans' dual tasks of control and conversion were simplified. In addition, as the Indian labor force in northeast Florida became too small to produce an agricultural surplus to support the St. Augustine colony, the crown and the clergy turned their attention westward beyond the St. Johns and Suwannee Rivers to the fertile Apalachee province in the Panhandle.

In contrast to the useful documentary record surrounding Spanish and Indian activities at the mission settlements, there is little information about the rest of northeast Florida for the first part of the seventeenth century. It is clear that native populations were virtually extinct by 1763, when Spain ceded Florida to England. When Indians ceased to exist in parts of Florida not regularly visited by the Spanish is not well known. One useful account is that of Alvaro Mexia, a young Spanish soldier from the St. Augustine garrison, who traveled in 1605 south along the coast to the territory of the Ais Indians in south Florida (Higgs 1951). In his trip along the inland lagoons, bays, and streams between St. Augustine and the Bar of Ais (map 6.3), Mexia mentions no Indian settlements until reaching the town of Nocoroco on the Tomoka River, 40 miles south of St. Augustine. This town and all subsequent settlements were abandoned. In the short narrative there is no mention of meeting any Indians in the whole 140-mile distance.

Spanish Missionization, 1600–1650

Between 1600 and 1680, when the Timucua existed in sufficient numbers to support permanent village settlements beyond the town of St. Augustine, a uniquely Spanish pattern of control of aboriginal populations proved successful in northeast Florida. Florida Indians lacked the state-level social and political organizations that Spain was so successful in controlling in Peru and Mexico. Rather, regional chiefdoms engaged in complex and dynamic competition, changing allies and enemies over time as might suit their immediate interests. In addition, the lack of mineral wealth in Florida left Europeans with no economic incentive and no means to exert a strong control over native labor as they had in the gold and silver mines elsewhere in America. Thus, in Florida the means of control was less violent, religious rather than military, and was based on producing crops and converting souls rather than making coins and ingots.

Map 6.2. Map of the city and fort of St. Augustine, 1593(?), from a manuscript original in the Archives of the Indies. Florida Photographic Archives

The mission system had two tiers, the *doctrina* or permanent mission town with a church and one or more clergy in residence, and associated *visitas,* towns with churches but no resident priest. In addition to a permanent church structure, the *doctrina* included a *convento,* or priest's residence, as well as a kitchen where the priest's meals were prepared and food stored, a Christian cemetery (sometimes in the floor of the church), a plaza, possibly a council house or Indian public structure, and a number of Indian houses, sometimes arranged roughly in a town pattern. Excavations at the Santa Catalina de Guale mission site on Amelia Island revealed all of these components except Indian structures (Saunders 1993:40–41). Visitas were smaller in population, may have lacked a convento, and probably had a less formal church structure in which services were offered by visiting priests

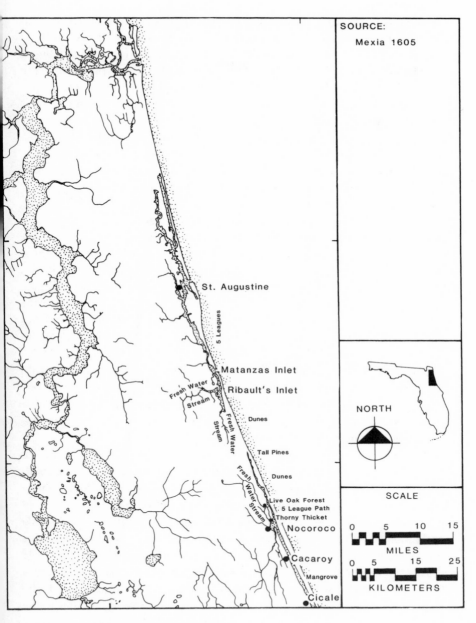

St. Augustine

5 Leagues

Matanzas Inlet

Fresh Water

Stream

Ribault's Inlet

Fresh Water Stream

Dunes

Tall Pines

Fresh Water Stream

Dunes

Live Oak Forest
5 League Path
Thorny Thicket

Nocoroco

Cacaroy

Mangrove

Cicale

NORTH

SCALE

```
0      5     10    15
```
MILES

```
0  5      15      25
```
KILOMETERS

Map 6.3. Derrotero of Alvaro Mexia, 1605

permanently stationed at a doctrina. Surrounding the town or village were agricultural fields of varying extent, depending upon the ability of the soils to support crops as well as the availability of Indians to cultivate them.

Missionization spread across the Florida peninsula for a century from its introduction at St. Augustine. First in the vicinity of the capital and north along the coast to Fort George Island, the principal mission effort was focused on the Salt Water Timucua. As native populations declined in this region, friars reached out to the inland tribes of the Western Timucua across the center of the peninsula and into north-central Florida. When Timucuan Indians, through depopulation and dissatisfaction, became unable to sat-isfy the demands for food production, labor, and tribute, friars expanded farther westward in the second half of the seventeenth century to the Apalachee in the area of present-day Tallahassee.

For the Saturiwa the two principal missions were Nombre de Dios at St. Augustine, serving mainly conscripted Indian laborers and families in the town, and San Juan del Puerto on Fort George Island near the mouth of the St. Johns River, serving Indians relocated from nearby abandoned villages. A smaller mission was established on the river at Tocoy west of St. Augus-tine, but it was short lived. For the Agua Dulce or Fresh Water Indians occupying the coast south of St. Augustine and the St. Johns River from Palatka southward, the principal churches in northeast Florida were San Sebastian south of St. Augustine and San Antonio de Anacapi on the St. Johns (Hann 1996) (map 6.4). These doctrinas were associated with outly-ing visitas in smaller villages, and in the case of San Juan del Puerto a few such locations are known as shown on the map. All mission locations are either on the coastal lagoons or the St. Johns River; no missions were lo-cated on the sandy interior marine terraces.

While agricultural productivity was relatively good in the provinces of Potano (near what is now Gainesville) and Apalachee (surrounding mod-ern Tallahassee), the same could not be said for the eastern Timucuan mis-sions. Part of the problem was the difference between European experi-ences and expectations on the one hand and the reality of the Florida environment on the other. Wheat, on which the Spaniards had depended for millennia, would not grow in east Florida. The climate was too cold during the winter and too wet and hot during the summer. A contemporary friar described the area of Guale and Timucua as "one hundred and fifty leagues of swampy, mosquito infested wilderness with extremes of heat and cold," and Bishop Calderón in the visitation of 1674 reported that "the soil is sand and therefore unproductive, no wheat grows and corn only sparsely at the cost of much labor" (quoted in Boniface 1971).

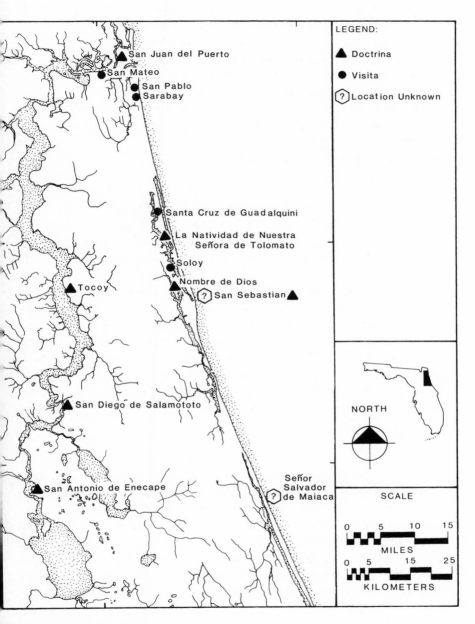

LEGEND:

▲ Doctrina

● Visita

⬡ Location Unknown

San Juan del Puerto

San Mateo

San Pablo
Sarabay

Santa Cruz de Guadalquini

La Natividad de Nuestra
Señora de Tolomato

Soloy

Tocoy

Nombre de Dios

San Sebastian

San Diego de Salamototo

San Antonio de Enecape

Señor
Salvador
de Maiaca

NORTH

SCALE

0   5   10   15
MILES

0   5   15   25
KILOMETERS

Map 6.4. Spanish missions

The only agricultural method suitable to such easily exhausted lands was slash and burn: Trees on forested tracts were girdled, left to die, and then burned to release their mineral nutrients to the porous sandy soils. As these new fields were planted and harvested, they reverted after a few years to their original infertile state, and new fields were cleared nearby. The effect on the landscape was to produce a pattern of "old fields" surrounding the mission villages, and when suitable nearby land was exhausted, it was often necessary to relocate the entire village and mission to an area that had not yet been cleared. The extent of such fields is not known, but the existence of these landscape features was recorded by British surveyors nearly a century later.

Florida Indians at the missions continued to produce the primary New World field crops: maize, beans, and squash, traditionally planted in the same mound rather than in separate fields. Garden plots and groves included fig and citrus trees, grapes, peaches, and yams. Fishing, gathering, hunting, and shellfish collecting continued to play an important role in the diet and the local economy.

By definition, the mission period lasted 140 years, from the time of the first Jesuit missionaries at the new St. Augustine settlement to the time of the destruction of the Spanish missions and villages by the British and their Creek Indian allies. John Hann has suggested four periods of missionization in Florida (Hann 1990). His second and third periods, lasting from 1587 to 1655, represent the greatest missionary activity; beyond this time, especially after 1680, the "missions' populations were killed, carried off, and otherwise dispersed to the points of the compass, creating a demographic vacuum" (1990:8).

Spanish Ranching and Defense, 1650–1763

While the mission towns relied on a form of garden agriculture that was a mixture of Indian and Spanish practices, the pattern of cattle ranching was much different. Ranches consisted of large land grants, including some land that had been previously cleared as well as natural savanna grasslands, and were distributed about the interior mainland between the Atlantic Coast and the St. Johns River and west of the river as well (map 6.5). Successful ranches were also established outside northeast Florida in the vicinity of present-day Alachua County among the Western Timucua and in the Panhandle of the state among the Apalachee Indians (Arnade 1961).

By mid-century, the Spanish enterprise in north Florida was still "at the mercy of war, weather, and disease" (Bushnell 1983:51). Epidemics of yellow fever in 1649 and smallpox soon thereafter took their toll among Span-

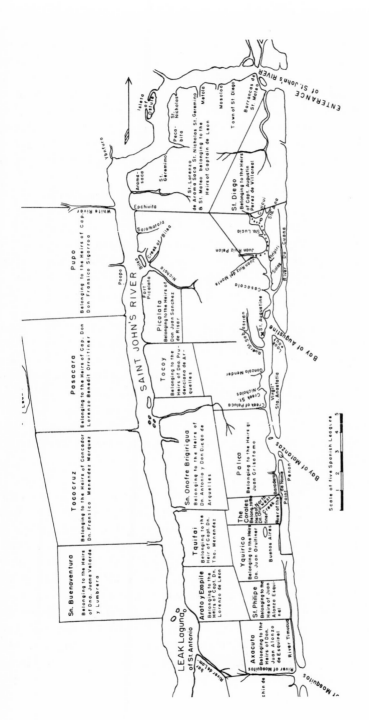

Map 6.5. First Spanish Period land grants (Covington 1961)

iards and Indians without discrimination. Out of 200 Timucuan Indians required to provide labor service in St. Augustine in one year, only 10 survived. Ranks of the military as well as the clergy were severely depleted. Franciscan missionaries in 1655 counted only 26,000 Christian Indians among all 38 Florida missions (Bushnell 1983). The following year a rebellion among the Timucuan chiefs, who had the sympathy of the Franciscan friars, added to the overall insecurity of the province and demonstrated to Spanish officials how precarious their control over the land and the people actually was.

An epidemic of measles in 1659 was reported to have taken 10,000 Indian lives; by the 1660s, Florida was a "hollow peninsula" (Bushnell 1983:53). The few remaining Indians in the interior of the state were situated in towns along the mission trail extending from Apalachee province in the Panhandle to St. Augustine. By the time of the 1696 trek of the shipwrecked Englishman Jonathan Dickinson, the number of Indian towns along the northeast Florida coast had been reduced to two (Dickinson 1699) (map 6.6).

As there were few draft animals in Florida, agricultural produce from fertile Apalachee province was transported to ports and sometimes all the way to St. Augustine on the backs of Indians, who were also pressed into service to operate the ferries across the Suwannee and St. Johns Rivers. The only other settlement in the province was at Spanish cattle ranches, where Indians as well as Africans provided the labor force (map 6.7).

Florida ranches were quite small in comparison to cattle operations in the Caribbean or in Mexico, where herds were numbered in tens of thousands. The largest Florida ranch was La Chua, situated on Paynes Prairie in present-day Alachua County; its herd was less than 1,000 head at the end of the seventeenth century. Within northeast Florida, ranches were even smaller, and were probably more diverse in their production. Based on recorded payments of a head tax on cattle at 10 percent, the number of cattle in northeast Florida was at least on the order of 1,000 head (Arnade 1961:9–10). Other agricultural products supplied to St. Augustine from the St. Johns River ranches were horses, mules, hogs, sheep, corn and beans (Boniface 1971:145). The ranch at Diego Plains (map 6.5), later known as Fort San Diego, relied on the vast natural savannas of northernmost St. Johns County to support its ranging herds. Citrus groves were also well established in the vicinity of St. Augustine in the first four decades of the eighteenth century, and there was even some export to northern ports such as New York and Philadelphia (Harman 1969:23).

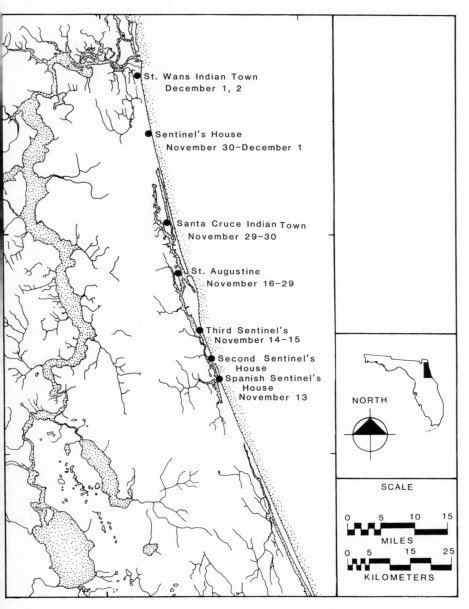

St. Wans Indian Town
December 1, 2

Sentinel's House
November 30–December 1

Santa Cruce Indian Town
November 29–30

St. Augustine
November 16–29

Third Sentinel's
November 14–15

Second Sentinel's
House
Spanish Sentinel's
House
November 13

NORTH

SCALE

0   5   10   15
MILES
0   5   15   25
KILOMETERS

Map 6.6. Jonathan Dickinson's journey, 1696 (after Dickinson 1699)

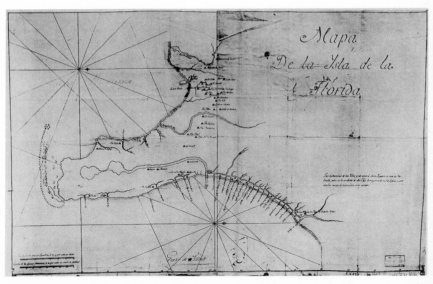

Map 6.7. *Mapa de la Isla de la Florida.* Florida in the period 1680–1700. Original in the Ministry of War, Madrid. Florida Photographic Archives.

The Florida range cow, not unlike the early Spanish pig, was an animal especially suited to the vagaries of colonial occupation. The breed introduced by the Spaniards was already well adapted to the humid and hot climate, the poor rangeland, and the fever tick. Descended from longhorned Castilian cattle by way of semi-wild herds in the Caribbean, the Spanish cattle were small, hardy, and required little attention. They were raised not only for beef, which was dried as jerky or salted, but also for tallow and hides. Oxen were also used as draft animals. Production of the ranches in the form of live animals as well as processed products found a market not only in St. Augustine, and to a lesser extent in smaller Florida towns, but also in other parts of the Spanish empire in Florida. Seventeenth-century cattle ranching produced one of the earliest Florida products available for export and developed the economic ties with other Spanish colonies that supplemented the meager and unreliable official *situado.* As Boniface shows (1971:table 3), hides, meat, and tallow from the ranches were the most important exports in the last quarter of the seventeenth century, but corn, beans, and pork were also shipped out.

The impact of Spanish ranching on local vegetation is not specifically recorded; however, it may be inferred on the basis of reports of Creek Indian ranching of the same type several decades later. Spanish ranches were large, at least on paper; those west of the St. Johns averaged 60 square miles, while the eastern ranches were much smaller (Boniface 1971:142). How many of the land grants were actually occupied or functioned as operating ranches is not known, so it is impossible to be specific about which local environments were affected or to what extent. It is likely, however, that lands were modified both by ranchers to improve grazing and by cattle, whose grazing maintained a grassy vegetation. Probably the most important means of creating and maintaining range was fire.

Burning the landscape was a common practice among Florida Indians before European contact. It served several purposes: to create or maintain clearings for fields and gardens, to improve browse for game animals like deer, and to drive game animals during communal hunts. Prehistoric Florida agriculturalists practiced a slash-and-burn method, using fire not only to clear trees but also to release into the topsoil nutrients stored in vegetation. Burning served ranchers in the same way, except that nutrients were not taken up by domesticated plants; rather, they supported a tender and temporarily luxuriant growth of native grass much preferable as browse over the perennial, rather tough wiregrass that formed the usual ground cover in the pine flatwoods.

Frequent burning in the southeast United States has another, more prolonged, environmental effect. It is now well known that the southern pine forest is a fire-adapted vegetation community, that is, fire is necessary for its continuation. The importance of fire in succession of natural communities was unrecognized earlier in this century (fig. 6.1), and fire was widely regarded as destructive rather than beneficial. As a result, fires were generally prevented or extinguished quickly when they did start, causing an unnatural accumulation of flammable litter on the forest floor.

This practice had two effects: If fire was eliminated for a sufficient period, the fire-adapted longleaf forests were replaced by hardwood forests, and, if fire did occur, it thrived on the store of branches, needles, dried leaves, and other vegetation on the ground, burning extremely hot and fast. Such an intense fire destroyed the crowns of the old pines that had shaded out hardwoods for so long and essentially eliminated the pine forest. Frequent burning, as would occur naturally as a result of lightning, acts to consume ground fuel several times a year and preclude fire on a scale that would destroy or permanently affect the pine forest.

It is likely that the land management practices of the Spanish ranchers and their Indian and African laborers resulted in a decrease in the extent and diversity of hardwood forests and an increase in the area of natural or artificial grasslands. How pine forests were affected would depend on whether they had been regularly burned in the past or were intentionally cleared by trunk girdling followed by burning. In most locales, the soils of

Fig. 6.1. Fire line right-of-way being cleared by Emergency Relief Labor, Duval County, 1933. Florida Photographic Archives.

the pine flatwoods are relatively infertile and sandy, better suited to pasture than to intensive cultivation. Surely the extent of such change was not dramatic, as British observers of northeast Florida after 1763 commented upon the extensive hardwood and pine forests still available for exploitation.

As if the difficulties presented by rebellious Timucuans, lack of money and commodities, and persistent disease were not enough, the Spanish colony in Florida, was, for the European powers, little more than a pawn in a game of colonial chess of two centuries' duration. That the tiny colony was virtually defenseless had been proved by Francis Drake's attack of 1586. In 1668, slightly less than a century later, another Englishman, the privateer Robert Searles, raided the city again, killing 60 civilians and plundering the buildings and the treasury. St. Augustine resolved to build a permanent fort, but it was not until 1696 that the Castillo de San Marcos, built of stone and large enough to hold the entire population, was largely complete (fig. 6.2).

English pressure continued. In 1670 a permanent British military and civilian presence was established at Charleston, in the region of the aban-

Fig. 6.2. Artist's idea of St. Augustine in 1671. Florida Photographic Archives.

doned Spanish settlement at Santa Elena. By 1690, the boundary between the encroaching British colony and the shrinking Spanish one had been settled as the St. Marys River, only 20 miles north of the St. Johns River; the once populous Guale province of the Georgia and South Carolina sea islands was under British control.

The stone fort at St. Augustine was a major undertaking for the small town (fig. 6.3); it was to be the strongest and largest fortification on the continent east of Vera Cruz in Mexico (Arnade 1959:2). Stonecutters and engineers were assigned from Havana, and the massive amount of labor was supplied largely by Indians, many from Apalachee province; local native populations were too decimated to meet the demand for labor. The fort was constructed of coquina, a lithified shell and sand mixture that hardened upon exposure to air. It was mined by cutting large blocks from a quarry on Anastasia Island, ferrying them across the river, and carrying them to the construction site in wagons. Not much use had been made of the stone until the building of the Castillo, but from that time forward coquina became an important natural resource for military, commercial,

Fig. 6.3. The Castillo de San Marco in St. Augustine. Florida Photographic Archives.

and residential construction (De Brahm 1773:205, Dickinson 1699:63, Forbes 1821:89).

The fort was barely finished when it met its first test, the siege of Governor James Moore of the Carolina British colony (Fairbanks 1858:131). Moore's forces advanced from the north, destroying the fortifications, towns and missions at the mouth of the St. Johns River and on Amelia Island; one force continued up the St. Johns and attacked St. Augustine from the west overland by way of the landing at Picolata. The naval force, led by Moore himself, entered the town through the inlet, finding the whole population and all available food inside the new stone fortification. The entire town, less a few stone buildings, was burned, but Moore's forces were compelled to retreat in the face of Spanish reinforcements arriving from Cuba (Arnade 1959).

Two years later another expedition organized by Moore destroyed the mission chain in Apalachee, depriving St. Augustine and the other Spanish settlements of a crucial source of food and labor (Hann 1988). By 1706 the La Chua ranch was burned and abandoned at the order of the Spanish governor. With this action, the effective boundaries of Spanish Florida extended little beyond the walls of the stone fort. The end of Queen Anne's

War in 1713 resulted in an unsteady and temporary peace, but British expansionism was to continue (Waterbury 1983).

Moore's raids signaled the end of the Timucua Indians; by 1725 it is reported that the remaining 15 men and 18 women moved close to the Castillo in St. Augustine. All but the chief died of disease within a short time (Deagan 1978:115). Between the 1730s and 1750s there is little information available on the Timucua population. In 1763, when the Spaniards withdrew to Cuba, they were accompanied by 89 Indians of various tribes. Only two are recorded as Timucua speakers, marking the end of the once great tribe of north Florida (Hann 1996:322–325).

From the beginning of the eighteenth century until the end of the First Spanish Period, the Florida settlement was beset by economic problems that were primarily structural in nature. There was little incentive or opportunity for growth associated with trade, as this sector was minutely regulated by Spain. All imported goods were required to be transported on licensed Spanish vessels and sold by licensed Spanish merchants. Foreign goods, vessels, and merchants were prohibited. It was frequently necessary for the Spanish governors in St. Augustine to ignore such prohibitions, particularly in times of dire need; as a result, there was frequent trade with British merchants both in northern ports and in St. Augustine. British goods were high in quality, readily available, and reasonably priced (TePaske 1964:71–72).

In addition, because there was no free market and little domestic production of trade items, Florida remained dependent on the situado, the supposedly annual grant for support in the form of supplies and money provided by other Spanish provinces on the King's order. By the beginning of the eighteenth century the Florida colony required some 81,000 pesos each year. The situado system was open to widespread abuse, not only at its source, where ample excuse could be found to delay or reduce the quantity and quality of the subsidy, but also at its destination, where much of the amount due had already been borrowed against at high rates of interest. Overall, goods as well as money were extremely scarce in Florida. The food portion of the situado was often rancid, spoiled, or infested and usually of inferior grade. Various reforms were attempted, but with little success.

In fact, the utter dependence of the Florida colony was so well established that when a vessel from St. Augustine loaded with pitch and tar arrived at Vera Cruz, Mexico, royal officials were "shocked and perplexed"; it was Florida's first export in nearly 200 years. The Mexican port had seen more than 10 million pesos leave for St. Augustine since 1570; no goods had ever before arrived in return, and customs officers were unwilling to forego the customary taxes. King Charles granted some tax relief in 1760, and hopes for the naval store industry of Florida were high. Unfortunately, Spain's tenure in Florida would be over three years later (TePaske 1964:77–107).

By 1740 fortifications had been constructed overland surrounding the town of St. Augustine, forts had been constructed on both sides of the St. Johns landing west of St. Augustine at Picolata and Pupo, the cattle ranch at Diego Plains had been fortified, and a stone fortification had been completed at Matanzas Inlet to guard the southern access to the town. General Oglethorpe's raids of 1740 (Anonymous 1742) and 1743 (Kimber 1744) into Spanish territory were largely unsuccessful, although Forts Picolata, Diego, and Pupo were captured and destroyed.

The British goal was eventually realized in February 1763, when Florida was ceded to England under the terms of the Treaty of Paris. By the last few years of the Spanish Period, the St. Augustine colony had been reduced to privateering near English ports to obtain food supplies; inhabitants had limited access to flour in early 1762, and some rice was captured later in the year; otherwise, subsistence depended upon fishing, gathering, and local cultivation (Harman 1969:73–74). Within one year virtually the entire population of St. Augustine and the surrounding territory, including the few remaining Florida Indians, had been evacuated to Cuba for resettlement.

Despite the protection it afforded to adjacent sea routes, the failure of the Spanish occupation in Florida has been convincingly blamed on the situado system:

It stifled initiative and was a factor preventing the rise of productive enterprises within the colony. Floridians inevitably looked to the subsidy or to aid from the outside to improve their lot. . . . Throughout the eighteenth century it was almost as if the colonists were afflicted with a kind of economic hypochondria, constantly complaining about their ills and suggesting many remedies but never able to grow better. Poverty and want characterized life in Florida and pervaded all aspects of life. (TePaske 1964:229)

British Colonial Grants, 1763–1784

It is infrequent in history that one culture in an environment is totally replaced by another in a short time, and even more unusual when both occupations are relatively well documented. The transfer of Florida from Spain to England affords a rare opportunity to compare essentially contemporaneous adaptations to the same environment as they were affected by different social, political, and ideological systems. In addition, after 20 years of British tenure, the territory was ceded back to Spain, and another opportunity is provided to compare the two systems.

As we have seen, the Spanish system was more corporate than individual. It was organized around the crown, represented by the military and the administrative officials, and around the church, represented primarily by the missionary clergy and to a lesser extent the parish priest in the city. Except for the highest officials, the private individual is relatively unknown from Spanish documentary sources. With the exception of a few privately operated cattle ranches across the state, there was little opportunity for a person to advance other than by appointment to an administrative or a military position.

In contrast, the British system, imposed upon the same landscape just vacated by the Spanish (map 6.8), was mainly entrepreneurial. As we shall see, British colonists accomplished in two decades what the Spaniards had failed to achieve in two centuries: economic growth based on the exploitation of natural resources within a system of colonial dependency. Spanish Florida had been dependent, to be sure, but its production was so limited that the relationship between the colony and the rest of the Spanish empire was rather one-sided. St. Augustine, at least during the First Spanish Period, protected first the treasure fleet route along the Florida coast, then the Florida territory; in exchange, Cuba, Mexico, and Spain supported the tiny settlement. British Florida embarked immediately upon the more familiar methods of dependency: grants of land and rights of production and distribution to private individuals; production of cash crop and natural resource exports; and large-scale land conversion and modification for intensive agriculture.

The British entrepreneurial system differed fundamentally from the Spanish feudal system. Great Britain, at the change of flags in Florida, had experienced nearly a half century of modernization characterized by the overthrow of the feudal system, an independent commercial class, a relatively weak religious order, and a free-market economy with capital available for investment. This transformation had set the stage for the Industrial Revolution, just beginning in the 1680s but soon to alter forever the economy and culture of Europe and the colonies.

The transfer of authority was an occasion for the departing Spaniards as well as the incoming British to take stock of the territory. By 1763, Spain had ruled northeast Florida for almost two centuries. The state of the territory at that time was a measure of the Spanish success or lack thereof. The

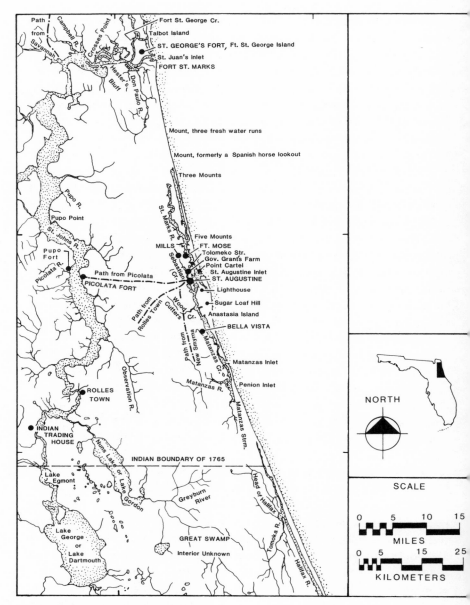

Map 6.8. British Period, 1763–1784

population was 3,046 persons, including the garrison. Of the total, 89 were Christian Indians in 15 families, 315 were slaves, and 95 were free blacks. There were around 300 residential and commercial buildings in St. Augustine, as well as a few public buildings, including the Castillo (Mowat 1943:9, Tebeau 1980:74). Improvements extended little beyond the town's limits. Virtually the entire population of Eastern Timucuan Indians had been decimated, and the missions had been destroyed or abandoned. Of course, the British themselves were partly responsible for the state of the Spanish settlement, having maintained a steady military pressure from the north for roughly a century, not to mention attacks by sea. The British acquired little more than land and water in 1763.

The new British territory, running roughly from the Mississippi River to the Atlantic Ocean on the north and including the entire Florida peninsula, was divided in October 1763 into two provinces at the Apalachicola River. West Florida was governed at first from Pensacola, then later from Mobile; St. Augustine, the only settlement in the province other than the tiny Fort St. Marks in the Panhandle, was the seat of East Florida. James Grant, a leading citizen in the South Carolina colony, was appointed governor but did not arrive in St. Augustine until August 1764. By the end of October, he had appointed His Majesty's Council for East Florida, composed mainly of prominent citizens of Georgia and South Carolina with experience in law, Indian affairs, medicine, plantation development, and surveying. Unlike the other, more prosperous and populated British colonies, East Florida had no general assembly or legislative body; Grant's power was substantial, although limited by the terms of his commission and regular oversight from London. And, like Spanish Florida, the British colony was supported by a subsidy to pay the salaries of officials and some expenses of government.

One of Grant's most important acts early in his rule was to establish the Indian boundary. In the vacuum left by the demise of the native Timucuans even before the British arrived, Lower Creek Indians, mainly from Georgia, began to occupy the interior lands west of the St. Johns River. In a congress with chiefs held at Picolata on the St. Johns and attended by chance by William Bartram, who left a famous account, the chiefs signed a treaty ceding a described territory running roughly from the St. Marys River on the north to a little above Lake George on the south. The ocean was the eastern boundary, and the western boundary was slightly west of the St. Johns River (Mowat 1943:22–23). In addition, the chiefs ceded to the British all the coast as far as the tide flowed. The territory inside the Indian boundary in northeast Florida measured roughly 2 million acres (Fairbanks

1974:153). Grant's strategy in dealing with Indians was to be most generous with his hospitality and presents. His purpose was to obtain clear title to lands so that grants could be made to those willing to populate the wilderness of East Florida. Considering the vastness of East Florida, the territory ceded by the Indians was minute, but it eventually proved more than the British could effectively manage.

The settlement policy for East Florida was determined by the British in the context of a vast colonial empire. Having received Canada and East Florida by virtue of the Treaty of Paris, Britain now controlled the entire eastern seaboard of North America as well as half the coast of the Gulf of Mexico. The British system recognized two competing strategies: to settle colonies that would comprise a market for British goods, or to develop colonies that would produce goods Britain must import. In selecting East Florida over Cuba in the Treaty of Paris, Britain made clear its preference for the first option, a continental rather than a sugar empire (Mowat 1943:5). Britain wanted to encourage the settlement of the new colonies in a balanced manner, providing incentives for settling the new vacant territories and impediments to the westward expansion of the older colonies, which had already been largely populated. In principle, it was advantageous to arrange emigration from overpopulated colonies to new ones, and the pool of potential settlers in many of the settlement schemes for East Florida was as vast as the British Empire itself.

Potential settlers from other colonies or from Europe held Florida in low esteem. This prejudice was overcome in two ways: first, by a comparatively generous and liberal land-granting policy and second, by an intensive public relations campaign in America and abroad. The descriptive literature of British East Florida in the first decade of the period surpasses in quantity and detail the entire documentary record compiled over two centuries of Spanish occupation.

Even before the British took over Florida, English readers had had access to a description of the territory, written by the king's geographer, Thomas Jeffreys, and entitled *A Description of the Spanish Islands and Settlements on the Coast of the West Indies* (Jeffreys 1762). Soon after the acquisition of Florida, William Roberts published his *Account of the First Discovery, and Natural History of Florida* (1763), which was followed several years later by William Stork's *Account of East-Florida* (Stork 1769). Stork served as a land agent for land grantees, and later editions of his work included portions of the journal of John Bartram, relating the journey taken with his more famous son, William, in 1765–1766.

William Bartram's return to the territory in 1774 resulted in the famous

Travels through North and South Carolina, Georgia, East and West Florida (1791). Bartram's *Travels* did not reach the public until after the end of the British tenure and did not influence the settlement of East Florida, but it serves as a valuable natural history produced by an acute observer (map 6.9). Bernard Romans's *Concise Natural History of East and West Florida* (1775) was also late in publication, but it provides another accurate and useful account. For the first time also, the cartographic record of northeast Florida becomes relatively detailed and widely available. The most important primary maps of this period are those of Romans and De Brahm (1770) (map 6.10).

The foundation of the British settlement scheme was the land grant system, whereby large tracts within the new territory could be transferred to private ownership, provided certain conditions were met. Between 1763 and 1773, grants of land could be obtained by two methods. The more common allowed grants of land in a township of 20,000 acres or less to be obtained by an Order of the Privy Council in London. Presentation of the Order in Council to the governor at St. Augustine authorized a survey to be undertaken and the grant to be issued in accordance with the conditions imposed by the Privy Council, namely:

The land was to be settled within ten years with one person for every hundred acres, subject to forfeiture of the whole if one-third was not settled within three years, or of those parts not settled at the end of ten years; that a quit rent of a halfpenny per acre was to be paid on half the land after five years, and on all after ten; and that mines of gold, silver, copper, lead, and coal were reserved to the King, as well as land needed for military and naval purposes (Mowat 1943:54).

The second method of obtaining a grant was known as "family right," or "king's bounty" in the case of inactive military personnel. The head of a family could receive 100 acres, along with 50 more acres for each additional family member, as well as up to 1,000 additional acres at five shillings per 50 acres, upon proof that he was able to cultivate it. Forfeiture could occur unless 3 acres out of 50 were cleared or developed within three years; however, proof of settlement of three acres in 50 resulted in transfer of permanent title. Quit rent of a half penny per acre was payable after two years (Mowat 1943:54–55).

The land grant system was somewhat more sensitive to the landscape than was an arbitrary land grid. For example, each grant was to be three times as broad as long, and the shorter side was to be on a river bank. This method guaranteed transportation access and maximized the number of

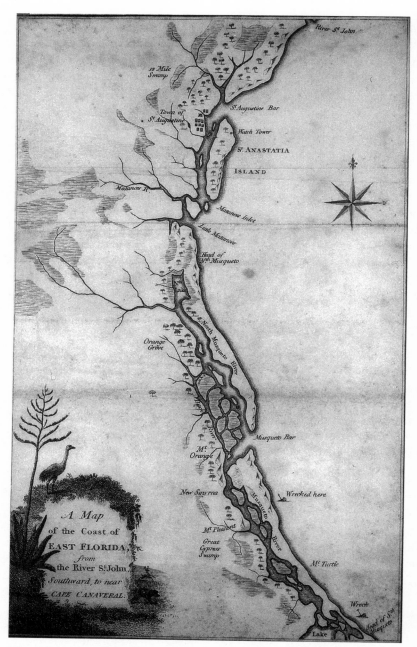

Map 6.9. *A Map of the East Coast of Florida*, by William Bartram, published in 1792 based on the travels during the British Period. Florida Photographic Archives.

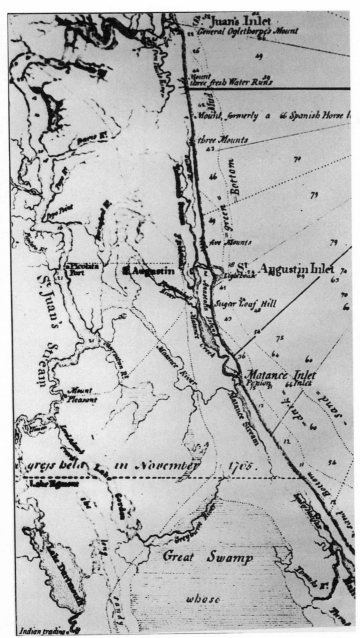

Map 6.10. Map of the General Surveys of East Florida (De Brahm 1770)

grants that could be situated on the rivers, along the banks of which the most desirable land would be found. Each grant would contain profitable as well as unprofitable lands, so that no settlement would be bound to fail because of poor land. At the same time, as much as possible of the ceded land within the territory could be granted quickly. It was the intent of the policy that when the entire territory had been granted, the townships would be surveyed internally and special lands set aside for public purposes. In addition, Anastasia Island, from which the coquina rock to build the Castillo had been mined, was not available except by special license from the king (Mowat 1943:55).

There were several weaknesses to the British land grant system; whether these were important factors in the eventual failure to settle the East Florida wilderness is not clear. First, this was a system that depended upon privately funded schemes that were large in scale and expensive. While there was a small subsidy for public officials and certain limited administrative responsibilities, there was no assistance other than land to grantees. The costs of establishing even a small settlement included transportation, slaves, buildings, tools, provisions, livestock, and the land survey. An initial investment of $2,500 was suggested by Bernard Romans as necessary for a single family (1775:130–133). Assuming a survey could be obtained promptly (seldom the case), it could be several years before sufficient improvements could be made to result in a marketable crop.

Because the scale of the investment was large, the grant system was effectively limited to the upper class and was largely speculative. Between 1764 and 1770 the Privy Council issued orders for 227 grants in East Florida totalling 2,856,000 acres. During the same period, the total number of grants for all of Nova Scotia, Quebec, New York, and West Florida was only 199. Much of the interest in Florida as an investment was caused by the glowing accounts appearing in England in the middle and late 1760s.

The vast majority of the grantees had never seen East Florida and never would. The typical absentee grantee was an "English nobleman or gentleman who fancied himself as the squire of broad American acres" (Mowat 1943:59). William Turnbull, grantee of the ill-fated settlement of Minorcans at New Smyrna, is a good example. Of the 300 or so petitioners, "thirteen were members of titled families, eleven were baronets or knights, sixteen were officers in the army, five officers in the navy; five were minor government officials, several were members of Parliament, four were doctors of medicine, and forty-nine were merchants" (Mowat 1943:59).

The difference between the nearly 3 million acres represented by Orders in Council and the actual settlement in Florida is dramatic. Only 121 Orders were presented to the governor; of these, 114 resulted in grants. By 1776, Governor Tonyn reported, only 16 had actually been settled. There were, in addition, people who obtained grants through family rights, and, of course, land for which title had been legally transferred could be divided and sold. In 1771, the hundred or so "planters" listed by De Brahm (1773) were mainly small farmers rather than operators of large plantations.

Those grants that were taken up depended primarily upon a land agent and an overseer for their operation. The land agent was the owner's representative in America and was responsible for managing the legal and practical affairs related to obtaining and developing the grant. Few land agents visited the tracts, preferring to conduct their business from Charleston or Savannah. The overseer was responsible for the day-to-day operation of the plantation; land clearing, drainage, planting, and the processing and shipping of agricultural products were under his charge. The plantation system in East Florida was critically dependent upon indentured servants and slaves to undertake the large-scale modifications of land that were necessary to bring the swamps, hammocks, and pine barrens into production.

The general self-sufficiency of the plantations was achieved within a few years and lasted at least until the large influx of Tory refugees during the American Revolution. The principal exports were indigo, naval stores, and lumber, although there was much experimentation and some production of sugar, cotton, silk, wine, rum, figs, raisins, cochineal, safflower, hides, tallow, pork, flour, corn, coffee, cocoa, molasses, honey, tobacco, rice, legumes and salt. Attempts to duplicate the important export crops of the more northern colonies—rice, cotton, and sugar—largely failed (Gray 1941:I,115).

The principal crop of the region, at least during the first decade of the British Period, was indigo, a crop already well developed in the Caribbean islands and the southern colonies of the mainland. The primary factors in determining whether Florida could compete with existing producers were quality of the dye and number of crops that could be harvested annually. Although falling short of Governor Tonyn's fabulous claims that Florida indigo surpassed any other ever exported to England and that it could be cut four times per year, the crop was a success on the plantations along the St. Johns. Cleared hammocks or drained and dried freshwater swamps provided the best land for indigo cultivation, but the plant also grew wild in great quantity. By 1769 the crop was ready to export and, because of its high quality, brought higher prices than did South Carolina indigo; however, the quantity was small, slightly over 6,000 pounds. The peak of East Florida production occurred in 1776, when 58,300 casks were exported.

Two years later the production was half that amount as the thin soils became exhausted and planters turned their attention to more lucrative naval stores and timber products (Gray 1941:I,295, Siebert 1929:67–68).

Exports of naval stores and timber during the British Period developed as a result of the Revolutionary War, when regular trade with the other southern colonies was interrupted and a bounty was placed on such products. According to a report by Francis Fatio in 1785, beginning in 1776 planters recognized a profitable market in forest products and abandoned the cultivation of indigo. By 1799, 25,000 barrels of tar, rosin, and turpentine were produced; in 1782 the amount was doubled. By 1783, 100,000 barrels annually were under contract, but the treaty of 1783 ending British rule eliminated the industry (Lockey 1949:479–480). The method of producing tar and pitch did not involve the large scale clearing of pine forests. Rather, turpentine was collected by removing some of the bark and in the exposed face of the tree cutting parallel diagonal grooves out of which the sap flowed into a container near the ground. The liquid was collected by slaves at the rate of about two barrels per day; 1,000 trees would yield about two and one-half barrels every two weeks (Gray 1941:I,159–160).

The size of cut timber exports also increased during the Revolution. In 1776 shipments out of East Florida included over 50,000 feet of pine boards and timber, nearly 87,000 oak staves, 7,600 pine staves, and nearly 53,000 feet of mahogany (the latter from the southern part of the Florida peninsula). The following year the corresponding figures were 553,000 feet of pine, 419,000 oak staves, and 124,500 cypress shingles. In 1778 these quantities declined slightly (Siebert 1929:67–69). During this three-year period of revolution in the American colonies, the influx of British loyalists into British East Florida more than tripled the population. The war created not only an increased demand for exports but also an increased labor force to produce them. Following the conclusion of the war, population and exports dropped again more or less to their previous levels (Mowat 1943:79).

A fairly detailed account of the nature of British settlement is provided by the claims of loyalists for compensation for their losses at the cession of East Florida to Spain in 1783 (Siebert 1929:II). While the large majority of claimants were owners of small plantations, several hundred acres on average, a good portrayal of the British plantation system is provided by the claim of John Moultrie. Moultrie was in East Florida throughout most of the two decades of British occupation and served as lieutenant governor following Governor Grant's departure in 1771. His complete holdings included 12 separate tracts of land in the province as well as a lot in St. Augustine. His plantation, Bella Vista, which served as his home, is a unique example of the gentleman's estate, the ideal to which the upper-class grantees aspired. Moultrie describes Bella Vista, four miles below St. Augustine on the Matanzas:

> His home and place of residence—a Stone mansion 52 by 42 feet lower Story rustic, upper Ionick, containing a rustick hall 44 feet long, Six arches supports the ceiling, a dining parlour; cov'd drawing room six bed chambers: two unfinish'd porticos: Offices and other necessary buildings for a hundred people besides Kitchen garden 10 acres fenced and laid out in pleasure gardens containing a bowling green: laid walks planted with many trees Olives dates oranges lemons limes citrons figs chaddock vines white Mulberry pomegranate peach and plumb banana pines &c. A park in good order about the house off [sic] about 30 acres with many pea fowls, Poland geese Pidgeons, bees &c—100 acres hard marsh; fish ponds stock'd with fresh water fish 300 acres of land well clear'd cultivated and well fenced . . . this Plantation contains a thousand acres. (Siebert 1929: II,239)

Among other Moultrie holdings was Rosetta, a more typical working plantation on the Tomoka River. It was described as follows:

> Rozetta a plantation situated on the tomoca river at the Musquito containing 2000 acres of which 1500 is good planting land both high and low—150 of the high land cleared fenced and planted 200 acres of rich tide land well dam'd and drained with between 3 & 4 miles of dikes and canals and two reserves of back water sufficient to flow over the low lands in the driest season. A neat dwelling house with 10 rooms, Kitchen pantry & Pidgeon house: a rice barn 50 by 30 feet a pounding rice machine Smith's shops, smoke houses, and negroe houses and a Kitchen garden. (Siebert 1929:II,239)

Among the other holdings Moultrie claimed: 1,500 acres five miles from St. Augustine containing pines and cypress with 25,000 trees boxed for turpentine; 1,000 acres, about 20 miles from St. Augustine, with a stone quarry and 50 cleared acres, 10 in orange groves; 1,500 acres near Rosetta, of which one-half was good, high land with sufficient water to flood the low land along with an orange grove; another tract of 2,500 acres near Rosetta, of which 1,000 were rice lands and the remainder pine and cypress; and a half-dozen other undeveloped tracts, not to mention a flatboat for moving produce in 50 barrel quantities to port. All Moultrie's holdings were undeveloped when he acquired them, although a witness testified that about 200 acres of the Bella Vista plantation were old field cleared by the Spaniards (Siebert 1929:II,245). Moultrie testified that he had about 100 slaves at Bella Vista who were occasionally used at the other plantations and that his turpentine lands were also used for cattle. At Rosetta there were 70 Negroes, about half of whom were workers who cultivated the tract in rice and indigo, for which it was ditched and dammed.

A more regional view of the extent of landscape modification during the British Period is provided by the other claims of loyalists who suffered losses of property upon the Spanish return (Siebert 1929,II). Claims were heard in London and in the Bahamas, but only the records of the former include details as to land type and improvements. Twenty-eight claims in London accounting for tracts of land other than city lots in St. Augustine totalled 123,312 acres acquired by grant or purchase. For many tracts, types and acreages of different kinds of land are noted, including portions cleared for crops as well as those ditched, diked, and drained for rice or indigo.

Of the total 123,000 acres so enumerated, about 53 percent is not described as to land type or improvements. Most such entries in the record are for grants that were never occupied or developed. The remaining 46.8 of the total sample are reported as follows: pineland, 29.7 percent; swampland, 10.5 percent; oak hammock, 3.1 percent; and savanna, 0.5 percent, all comprising unimproved lands. Only 2.4 percent or 2,927 acres are reported as cleared land, and just 0.6 percent or 852 acres are reported as diked and ditched. Although the British efforts to settle northeast Florida were much more extensive than those of the Spanish, it would appear from the available information that the 3 million or so acres ceded by the Indians had been little modified over the two decades of British occupation.

The plantation agriculture of British East Florida, based on slavery and indentured servitude, was an extensive and exploitative rather than an intensive and soil-conserving agriculture; labor was more highly valued than land (Gray 1941:II,448). Given an abundance of land and the degree to which successive harvests of such crops as indigo and rice exhausted the nutrients of the sandy coastal plain soils, it was economically more advantageous to abandon the land and move than to restore the soil fertility. This practice was, in concept, a continuation of the slash-and-burn, shifting cultivation practiced by the original Indian inhabitants and the Spanish in previous centuries. Whether production was for self-sufficiency or export, East Florida in the British Period never reached an intensity of settlement or scale of production comparable to other colonies on the North American continent or in the Caribbean. While Governor Grant reported at the beginning of the Revolution that unless new lands were ceded from the Indians there would be none available for new loyalists, this issue was a paper problem rather than a land problem. During the British Period (except for the temporary loyalist influx), population reached a level comparable to that of the Spanish at the 1763 change of rule, around 3,000 residents for St. Augustine and surrounding lands. Clearly the British adaptation produced greater exports than the Spanish; nonetheless, 20 years later the majority of major plantation attempts had failed.

The duration of British occupation is short from the point of view of social history as well as environmental history. As Mowat concludes: "Twenty years is no long time by which to judge a country. For East Florida, at least, the span was too short to produce a firm and reliant society, too short for the roots to take much hold of the soil" (1943:149). Yet while the contrasts between British and Spanish approaches to the land are pronounced, the results are similar: Neither system proved successful in permanently overcoming the obstacles imposed by the northeast Florida environment.

At the same time, both systems had in common the factor of dependence: Decisions that directly affected the well-being of the territory were made elsewhere. Spain's reason for the settlement's existence was military security; the purpose of the territory for England was to contribute to the commerce of the colonial empire. Northeast Florida was a relatively insignificant piece in an international game of several centuries' duration. It is clear that the environment presented specific opportunities as well as constraints for Spanish and British settlers alike. However, in view of the system of colonial dependency, in which policies and decisions were imposed from Europe, it would be false to conclude that the success or failure of this remote colony was fundamentally due to local environmental factors.

Spanish Land Grants, 1784–1821

The Treaty of Paris concluding the American Revolution returned Florida to Spain once again. The Second Spanish Period lasted 37 years and was marked by the continuing growth of American interest in Florida. By 1821 Florida would be an American territory. In the intervening period, Spain had little more success than the British in effectively settling the country; its strategy was to continue the grant policy, initiated by the English, that had served to distribute tracts of land to potential settlers.

Upon the arrival of the new governor, Vincente Manuel de Zéspedes, there had been little change since Spaniards last occupied the Castillo. He described the province in 1785 as in a state of "extreme decadence," its timber unexploited, riverbanks uncultivated, houses in ruins, plantations abandoned, roads overgrown, "and a general desolation reigning over the whole province" (Lockey 1949:570). A consummate optimist, the new governor expressed his hope of seeing the territory

> rise from its present decadence to a state of vigor and usefulness. Its fertile soil insures it; its luxuriant pastures promise it; its woods in copious variety announce it; its pitch, tar, turpentine and resin, easily extracted, acclaim it; its navigable rivers and the sea which bathes its coasts, abounding in fish of good quality, declare it; and above all, its commodious Bay of St. Marys, of which I shall send Your Excellency a description and map as soon as the engineer can draw it up, assures it. . . . In order to reap such considerable benefits, and reinfuse life into this languishing province, it is necessary for the royal clemency to deign to send adequate help in settlers and money as soon as possible. (Lockey 1949:571–572)

Zéspedes toured his new territory and reported to Spanish officials in 1787 that the population excluding the garrison was "only nine hundred white persons," and 490 slaves. Of the whites, 448 were Minorcans from the failed Turnbull colony at New Smyrna and 339 were Britons. There were 31 natives of Spain and 25 Canary Islanders, the latter relocated from Pensacola, who, Zéspedes reported, were so slothful as to be "nothing but a source of useless expense" (Whitaker 1931:55). Clearly, the first four years of Spanish reoccupation had resulted in little new settlement. The town of St. Augustine was also little changed, consisting of fewer than 300 houses, of which only 35 were in good repair (Tebeau 1980:90).

Zéspedes reported that the new territory was poverty-stricken, with the exception of the six or eight slave-owning English plantation owners; without a legal means to grant land ownership, he believed it unlikely that the inhabitants would exert themselves to improve their land or its production. Should the population be encouraged, however, the governor explained that trade could be established immediately in the production of "myrtle-wax, beeswax, honey, herbs and medicinal plants, oranges and their juice, salt fish, vegetables, and above all, pitch, tar, resin, turpentine, and spirits of turpentine." Zéspedes wrote:

> There is an inexhaustible supply of materials for these resinous substances, and I believe that, whenever there are hands, energy, and means for preparing them, there will prove to be such an abundance that in time it will suffice to provide the royal navy and even the merchant marine with these articles, to the total exclusion of those from the Baltic. (Whitaker 1931:51)

The following year, another Spanish official, José Salcedo, found the state of the province so hopeless as to be only worth ceding to the British. As chief of the department of war and treasury in the colonies, Salcedo was no disinterested observer. After a lengthy analysis, he concluded that the territory had only

> a few poor and useless fortifications which are very expensive to maintain; that what is called a port is only a very dangerous bar and the water is very shallow and of diminishing depth; that it is impossible to intercept or prevent contraband from it, or to carry on privateering; that its settlement contributes nothing to the propagation of the true religion or to aid in the retention and defense of the neighboring provinces; that its inhabitants are insignificant because of their quality and very small numbers; that they have no livestock; that its products and fruits do not deserve the least consideration; that it is not capable of any commerce whatever; that its possession by any other power would not cause anxiety; and finally that it is in every respect useless and troublesome to the state, and its retention is very expensive, very hazardous and very injurious. (Whitaker 1931:87)

Near the end of 1790, with the province still languishing, Luis Fatio, a resident of Spanish Florida who had remained in East Florida throughout the British occupation and was probably one of the most knowledgeable residents of the territory, reported to the new governor on which "products and fruits" were being and should be produced (Whitaker 1931:125–139). Although there was abundant timber—most important, pine, but also cypress, live oak, cedar, ash, and other oaks—the resource could not be taken advantage of for two reasons: lack of population and lack of reliable river access. St. Augustine remained the only inhabited port; the St. Marys and St. Johns Rivers supported no port facilities, and the bar at St. Augustine remained an impediment to commerce and navigation. Because the water was so shallow at the mouth of the inlet, only ships of shallow draft could enter the harbor; even then, Fatio reports, the winds and tides could cause undue delays, adding to the expense of shipping lumber which, he noted, was of small value and great bulk. Among other potential commodities were rice, corn, rye, tobacco, cotton, wheat, hemp, flax, indigo, sugarcane, syrup, rum, cattle, salt meat, hides, tallow, butter, fisheries, silkworms, olives, and olive oil. In late 1790 there was little production for trade; the items listed were either produced in the limited quantities necessary to satisfy the needs of the province itself or were not even in production at all.

The potentially valuable trade with Lower Creek Indians populating

Florida beyond the Indian boundary was poorly managed by the Spaniards, who had agreed to allow the British trading firm of Panton, Leslie and Company to continue to operate stores within the new territory in return for British support against the United States, which was eager to annex Florida (Coker and Watson 1986). Fatio reports that such trade resulted in exports of 150,000 deerskins annually from the region, much of which was arranged by the British company at its two posts on the St. Johns River, Spalding's Upper Store and Spalding's Lower Store. Spaniards in East Florida were initially prevented from obtaining goods from either the English or the Indians, being restricted to imports from Havana. Even though it later became clear that such trade was legal, the residents found they had no surplus of goods to offer in exchange. Four years later, in 1794, 13 prominent East Florida residents complained to King Charles IV that the Panton, Leslie monopoly dominated the commerce of the territory. "As concerns the Indians," they wrote, "it has been as if this province were still under the dominion of his Britannic Majesty. All the goods and other articles given them as presents are English; English also are those who trade with them and those who live in the stores that the said house has in this province (for all the other inhabitants are excluded from this trade. . .)" (Whitaker 1931:189). After a lengthy plea for permission to participate in the Indian trade, the residents offered their opinion on the prospects for the future of the colony:

> In vain does your royal clemency provide the means for increasing [immigration], and in vain has it granted permission to foreigners to settle in this province, for, as we see it, it is doubtful whether anyone will dare to come here now. The few who came here at the outset have withdrawn sadder but wiser and have told what happened to them, which reflects very little credit on our nation. (Whitaker 1931:195– 197)

The royal policy remained unchanged on the matter of Indian trade, but around this time a program of land grants was instituted that would lead to a resettlement of the region lasting beyond the establishment of the new American Territory in 1821. Throughout the Second Spanish Period considerable pressure was exerted at the northern border of East Florida by American settlers who wanted to expand into the mostly vacant region. Early in the period, in 1793, the crown authorized the governor to grant land on condition there was either complete settlement of the land or some public improvement. A second royal order 10 years later quickened the pace of land granting; in 1809 and 1815 grants were authorized as concessions for military service (Vignoles 1823). By the latter date, most Spanish East Floridians recognized that it was simply a matter of time before their region became an American territory, and many land grants were made for the primary purpose of ensuring property rights that would be honored by the next government (Tebeau 1980:103). Every acre legally granted to a Spaniard before annexation was an acre that the American government could not sell to new settlers.

Such grants covered much of northeast Florida; Vignoles (1823) recorded their distribution as filling the neck of land between the St. Marys and St. Johns Rivers from the Atlantic Coast to the King's Road at Cowford; on both sides of the St. Johns River as far as its head; on Dunn's Lake and Haw Creek and upon most other tributaries of the St. Johns; along each branch of the North River north of St. Augustine; on the San Diego Plains; throughout Twelve Mile Swamp; and all choice lands south of St. Augustine to the Tomoka River east of the main road and beside the banks of all the small watercourses. Additional grants extended farther south beyond the region of interest here. Vignoles summarized the granted area as follows: "the peninsula from the head of St. John's River, and between the right bank of that stream and the Atlantic Ocean" (1823:147).

The granted land north of the St. Johns River was reported by Vignoles to be in cultivation; whether this was also true of the remainder of the province is not stated. A reasonable idea of the distribution of grants that actually represented working farmsteads or plantations is available, however. Article VIII of the Adams-Onis Treaty between Spain and the United States, proclaimed by President John Adams in February 1821, provided that any grant made before January 24, 1818, would be ratified and confirmed if the original conditions of the grant had been met. Grants made after that date were declared and agreed to be null and void (Forbes 1821:212). Each land grant was reviewed by a commission; those that had been "taken up," i.e., settled as far as their grant stipulations required, were confirmed and the grantee's ownership honored. These tracts are readily recognizable today because their property boundaries superseded the township and section surveys that began several decades later, interrupting the regular square grids of the township and range system. The distribution of tracts interrupting the township surveys is shown in map 6.11.

The lands most desired for grants can be assumed to be those that had actually been settled. The pattern is not unlike what was observed in the British Period, although somewhat more extensive: along the banks of the St. Johns, along most other navigable waterways including coastal lagoons and rivers, and along the rich hardwood hammocks inland from the coastal

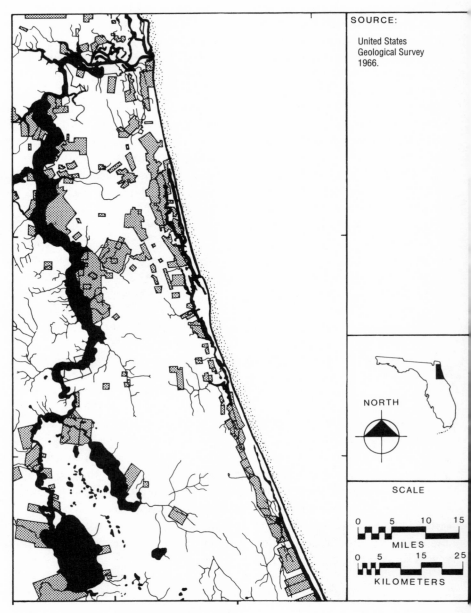

SOURCE:

United States
Geological Survey
1966.

NORTH

SCALE

0   5   10   15

MILES

0   5   15   25

KILOMETERS

Map 6.11. Second Spanish Period land grants

strand. The extent of occupation and land modification represented by the Second Spanish Period grants is complicated to determine. British grants had been recognized by the Spanish crown, and these carried through to the Territorial government. Thus, some of the more successful British plantations such as Fort George Island, Moultrie's Bella Vista, and Mount Oswald had been well established and operating for some 50 years, although with some interruptions. The majority of the Spanish grants, however, were smaller in scale; most were less than 640 acres in total, of which only a portion would be cleared and worked, usually by a single family with a few slaves. Despite the large total number of grants, more than 1,000, the population was estimated by Vignoles at the end of the Second Spanish Period as only 5,000 for all of East Florida (1823:42). Settlement was neither intensive nor extensive. Vignoles offered the following explanation and characterization:

> The general characteristic of this portion of the peninsula is flat, and unprepossessing: but there are upon it many fertile tracts which will, when the hand of industry is judicially applied yield profitable returns. It is remarkable that this part of the new country, which had once made large advances in the path of civilization, should have so retrograted and have become in many parts as great a wilderness as in its primitive state: the withering influence of the old system of Spanish government perhaps occasioned this, by hitherto casting its blight around, and for forty years impeding the natural advantages of the country from being improved, by those willing and capable of the task. (Vignoles 1823:66)

Despite the large number of grants, many were, as during the British Period, mainly on paper, and Vignoles observed during his travels of 1821 and 1822 that the territory was nearly empty. Between St. Augustine and Tomoka, near the coast, he noted the plantations of Hernandez, Perpall, and Pellicer as "good"; that of Bulow farther south was just beginning to be developed. On the St. Johns River from the mouth to Lake George no single settlement warranted his comment; rather the region seemed abandoned:

> The number of settlements that once adorned the banks of St. John's river have disappeared, in consequence of the Indian wars and other causes before alluded to; and in sailing up that majestic stream an air of stillness impresses the beholder with the idea that he is navigating the waters of an uninhabited and new country. (Vignoles 1823:69–70)

Another observer of the same year, John Eatton Le Conte, intent on discovering the source of the St. Johns, described the settlement on the river between Lake George and the mouth as "a few habitations and vestiges of many more that have long been deserted, sad monuments of the folly and visionary extravagance of the English" (Le Conte 1822). Although the land was unpopulated, that is not to say it was unchanged. Virtually every observer commented on the ruins and remains of the English plantations. Canals, old fields in second growth, groves and exotic trees were among the more common landscape features.

The character of the forests had also changed somewhat by this time owing to timber cutting. The primary valuable species were live oak and pine. The low, massive, curving branches and forks of the live oak were so valuable for the frames of large warships that the trees had been completely eliminated from all parts of the territory from which they could be transported. Vignoles noted that live oak was no longer to be found on the St. Johns or any of its tributaries. A few small stands remained on the Diego Plains and along the North River, but these could not be transported if cut (Vignoles 1823:70). Le Conte confirms, noting that the live oak "have long ago disappeared, and can only now be recognized as having once existed there, by the indestructible quality of their remains" (Le Conte 1822:28).

Relations with the Indians, so carefully cultivated and controlled by the British governors between 1763 and 1783, were potentially dangerous for the subsequent Spanish government. In a complicated series of economic and political arrangements with the Spanish crown, the British trading concerns of Panton, Leslie Company and John Forbes Company as well as various Creek Indian leaders, Spain relied on the English to maintain the Indian trade along with the general peace. The English-Creek alliance had been strong throughout the late seventeenth and eighteenth centuries; with the decimation of Florida's original tribes in the early 1700s, Creek bands slowly began to occupy the peninsula, particularly around the Alachua Prairie and the old Apalachee province in the Panhandle. The St. Johns River continued to serve as an Indian boundary; through the early 1800s, while Creeks organized and coalesced into the early Seminole tribes, there were no Indian towns east of the river (Cline 1974).

The forts at Pupo and Picolata on the St. Johns west of St. Augustine had been abandoned during the British Period and were not reoccupied in the Second Spanish Period. In 1822 Vignoles described their remains:

A few miles above the mouth of Black creek stands the old block house of Picolati: nothing remains of it except two of the shattered walls, through which loop holes and meutrieres are pierced: it stands

on a low bluff and half concealed by the luxuriant branches of surrounding trees, it reminds the visitor who views it from the river, of the
deserted castellated residence of some antient feudal lord. On the opposite or west side of the St. John's was fort Poppa, of which scarcely a
vestage remains. (Vignoles 1823:67)

West of the Indian boundary at the St. Johns, Seminole leaders and towns
had established their independent identity from the Creeks by 1804; as
British allies, Creeks fought against the Americans in Spanish territory during the War of 1812. Other minor incursions during the Second Spanish
Period as well as the Territorial Period, especially in the north along the
Georgia border, discouraged most settlers from entering the Florida peninsula, at least until the "Indian problem" was resolved.

Although the major events of what is now called the First Seminole War
(1835–1842) occurred in west and middle Florida, the eventual result was
the annexation of the entire peninsula as an American territory, the first
step on the road to statehood. On the pretext of protecting American interests against actions of the Seminoles and African-American escaped and
freed slaves who were part of their community (Klos 1995), General An-
drew Jackson waged undeclared war in West Florida, reducing the Spanish
forts at St. Marks and Apalachicola as well as the town of Pensacola to
American control. The repeated attempts of the United States to obtain
Florida, not always by the most honorable methods, finally culminated in
fair negotiations resulting in a treaty (Patrick 1954). The treaty of cession
between Spain and the United States was signed on February 22, 1819, but
flags were not transferred until more than two years later (Tebeau 1980:113–
114).

7

American Agriculture, Industry, and Tourism, 1821 to the Present

Territorial Plantations, 1821–1845

The Territorial Period was a time during which the United States government accomplished the conversion of a Spanish colony into an American state. Economic, political, and social features, distinctly American in nature, were imposed upon a territory that had been ruled from Europe for some three centuries. Natural and physical aspects of the landscape carried over their European flavor to the American settlement, and a number of Spanish subjects, mainly landowners and Minorcans, remained to become American citizens. During this 24-year period, for a variety of reasons, development was increasingly effective, yet progress was frequently marked by major setbacks, like Indian wars.

As at the beginning of the Territorial Period, there was a considerable amount of information about Florida available to the reading public. The anonymous narrative of the voyage of the ship *Two Friends* provided a fair description of the region just prior to the 1821 treaty, but it focused largely on the complicated and colorful political intrigue of Sir Gregor MacGregor and the invasion of Fernandina. James G. Forbes's *Sketches, Historical and Topographical, of the Floridas; More Particularly East Florida* is recognized as a useful source on the British occupation and has its greatest value in full and accurate descriptions of the geography. Appearing in the same year, William Simmons's *Notices of East Florida* contains a brief geographic description but was more highly valued for its section on the Seminole Indians. A good part of Dr. Simmons's first chapter is devoted to discussing the possible causes of yellow fever, which had struck St. Augustine the previous year. Charles Vignoles, author of *Observations upon the Floridas* (1823) was a trained surveyor and military engineer. His topographic and natural history descriptions were accurate; his book was a useful guide for visitors and immigrants. These two accounts have another trait in common with the many early British descriptions: They were intended, in varying degrees, to encourage tourism and settlement in the new territory. Such boosterism has been an important element in development in many parts of the country (Cronon 1991). The same could not be said, however, of John James Audubon's impressions of northeast Florida recorded during his visit of 1831. Spending time on the St. Johns as well as at several of the plantations and in St. Augustine, Audubon found the territory especially unattractive:

> St Augustine is the poorest hole in the Creation—The living very poor and very high—was it not for the fishes in the Bay and a few thousand of oranges that grow immediately around the Village, the people must undoubtedly abandon it or starve for they are all too leazy to work, or if they work at such price as puts it out of the question to employ them. The Country around nothing but bare sand Hills—hot one day cold another &c &c (Proby 1974:17)

During the Territorial Period (maps 7.1, 7.2), the plantation economy, begun by the British and continued by the Spanish, began to prosper, to the point of supporting a "plantation aristocracy." Among the more successful planters was Joseph M. Hernandez, a native of St. Augustine whose parents were among the Minorcans who fled the unsuccessful Turnbull colony at New Smyrna. Hernandez, a Spanish citizen, stayed on after the change of flags and converted to American citizenship. He owned and managed three plantations totaling 2,265 acres, all situated near the coast along the Matanzas River south of Pellicer Creek; they were named Bella Vista, Mala Compra, and St. Joseph's. Mala Compra was primarily a cotton plantation and served as the residence; St. Joseph's was dedicated to sugar; Bella Vista was eventually given to his daughter and her new husband to develop.

A good deal is known of the Hernandez plantations because of claims filed for compensation as a result of damage caused by Seminole Indians and American militia in 1835, 1836, and 1837 (U.S. House of Representatives 1844b). Mala Compra featured a dwelling of 1 1/2 stories, measuring 18 by 30 feet on a coquina stone foundation. The cotton house, a frame structure, was 40 by 20 feet, with a loft and two enclosed piazzas or porches, sufficient to hold 200,000 pounds of seed and 200 bales of ginned cotton. The kitchen building, detached from the house, was also 18 by 30

Map 7.1. Map of the Territory of Florida (Swift 1829)

Map 7.2. Map of Florida (Williams 1837a)

feet, 1 1/2 stories high, and on a stone foundation. The loft above was used for curing tobacco; the downstairs included two rooms that served as a kitchen and a washroom. A corn house, approximately the same size, was adjoined by a framed shed for horses and cattle. Smaller buildings included a framed privy, a driver's house of stone and plaster, two framed houses, 12 other post and wattle houses for slaves, and a fowl house. Other improvements included a cattle pen with a post-and-rail fence and a garden fenced with post and picket. The orange grove had approximately 1,500 trees in full production, and there was a variety of other types of fruit trees. Equipment included two horse-powered cotton gins and 24 foot gins, along with a full complement of handtools and animal-drawn implements. Animals included horses, cattle, oxen, hogs, pigeons, and bees.

St. Joseph's plantation had 200 acres in sugarcane, 200 acres of corn intermixed with sugarcane, 80 acres of hammock land in corn, 80 acres in peas, and 20 acres in potatoes by the middle 1830s. The sugar lands were heavily developed with a system of ditches including several large canals of four, five, and six feet in depth from 1/2 to 1 1/2 miles in length. The 200 acres were crossed with ditches two feet wide, two feet deep, and 35 feet apart for drainage. There was, in addition, a corresponding system of causeways, roads, and bridges. This tract, planted in ratoon or perennial as well as annual cane yielded 150,000 pounds of sugar, or approximately 750 pounds per acre. Sugar was valued at 10 cents per pound, for a crop yield of $75 per acre. The same land would produce 8,250 gallons of molasses, about 40 gallons per acre, having a value of 40 cents per gallon, or $16 per acre each harvest. The land planted to cane and corn yielded 2,000 bushels of corn or 10 bushels per acre; the 80 acres of hammock land in corn alone yielded 1,000 bushels or 12.5 bushels per acre. Potatoes were produced at 100 bushels per acre on 20 acres.

In lost crops, both in the field and in storage, Hernandez claimed some $60,000; of this, about one-third was sugar and molasses from the previous year's production. Another $40,000 was claimed in lost property and equipment, and the value of buildings and improvements destroyed was estimated to be about $35,500. Some measure of relative value is offered by a few of the items that have modern equivalents: an ox was worth $25, a cow $10; a skilled laborer at the plantation received $2.30 per day including board, a carpenter and a millwright $3.20 per day including board; and an engineer, responsible for overseeing the manufacture of the sugar mill machinery at the foundry and for 6 1/2 months of work at the plantation to install the mill and construct associated machinery, was paid $1,320. A rough estimate of the value ratio of 1837 to modern dollars might be on the order of 1 to 50. The production of St. Joseph's in a single year could be very roughly estimated at $40,000, around $2 million in modern currency.

By the end of 1835, the plantations of East Florida were in ruins, destroyed by Seminoles unwilling to submit to being relocated west of the Mississippi (fig. 7.1). The growing and unusually successful citrus industry developed in northeast Florida on Anastasia Island as well as along the St. Johns River was also destroyed in 1835, by a severe freeze rather than hostilities (Davis 1937). Yet again, the citizens of the territory retreated to the comparative safety of St. Augustine, and none of the productive sugar mills, of which there had been some two dozen total, were ever restored to production (Tebeau 1980:160). The citrus groves began to be replanted in the early 1840s, but an insect infestation known as purple scale spread rapidly following its accidental introduction from China. By the early 1850s all the groves around St. Augustine and most along the St. Johns as far south as Lake George were ruined. The industry did not fully recover until 1875, and by that time the commercial groves were restricted to warmer climates of the central part of the peninsula (Davis 1937). Despite the establishment of a network of Second Seminole War forts throughout the peninsula (maps 7.3, 7.4), Seminole Indians dominated the land, preventing any effective use. The Niles Register of February 27, 1836, reported:

> The whole of the country, south of St. Augustine, has been laid waste during the past week, and not a building of any value left standing. There is not a single house now remaining between this city and Cape Florida, a distance of 250 miles; all, all have been burnt to the ground. (quoted in Hanna and Hanna 1950:65)

In May 1840 an article in the St. Augustine *Florida Herald* presented this assessment:

> Those of us that remain, have been penned up in this little city for the last four and a half years by a few worthless outlaws. Our friends and neighbors one after another, have been hastened to mansions of the dead and he who is foolhardy enough to look beyond the gates of the city may be the next victim. (Hanna and Hanna 1950:117)

Major and minor skirmishes throughout the Florida territory were finally concluded in 1842 with a declaration of peace and an agreement by Seminole leaders to accept a temporary reservation in south Florida. Although the land was again secure, there was no great rush to reoccupy it. Once again, a system of land conveyance by the government was instituted; this time it was the Armed Occupation Act of 1842.

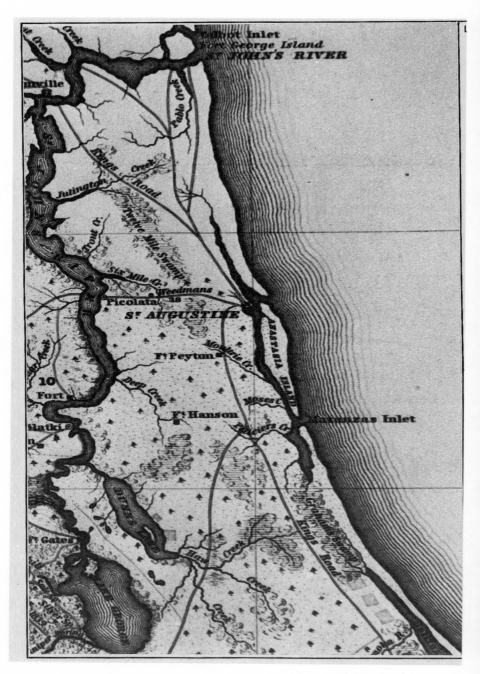

Map 7.3. Map of the Seat of War in Florida (MacKay and Blake 1839)

Map 7.4. The State of Florida (Bruff 1846)

Fig. 7.1. *The Ruins of the Sugar House*, by John Rogers Vinton, 1843. From the Collection of Sam and Robbie Vickers, The Museum of Arts and Sciences, Daytona Beach, Florida.

The confirmation or rejection of each Spanish land grant was a complicated and onerous task, but it had mostly been completed by the middle 1820s, although a few major cases endured in the courts for many years. Beginning in 1824 the official land surveys of the new territory were initiated by the establishment of the primary base and meridian lines. These intersected in Tallahassee and formed the axes of the grid from which all six-mile-square townships would be laid out consistent with the American rectangular system established in 1785.

Townships were measured north and south of the Tallahassee base line, and ranges were measured east and west of the Tallahassee meridian. Each six-mile-square township was further divided into 36 sections of one square mile or 640 acres each. Since all land not privately owned as a result of confirming a previous grant was public land, settlement of the Florida territory could make little progress until the federal government completed its subdivision and devised a means for conveying title to new private owners. Land sales began in East Florida out of an office in St. Augustine in 1827. The slow pace of development, as well as the large amount of land taken up by grants, is indicated by the fact that between then and 1845, when Florida achieved statehood, only 70,155 acres had been sold in all of East Florida; in West Florida, in contrast, nearly 800,000 acres were sold (Martin 1944, Tebeau 1980:124).

The Armed Occupation Act was a temporary free homestead law intended to encourage settlement of the frontier, thereby creating a buffer against Indian raids. The act stated that the Florida peninsula south of Township 9 (i.e., a line about 15 miles south of St. Augustine) was open to homesteading for those who would establish residency and farm the area. Homesteads of 160 acres, a quarter section, could be obtained by any head of family or single man over 18 years of age who would erect a habitable dwelling, cultivate five acres or more, and occupy the tract for five years.

Three hundred and seventy claims were filed at the St. Augustine office, but 87 of these were annulled for failure to comply with the provisions of the act. The remaining 283 claims amounted to 45,280 acres; however, the large majority of these were in central and south Florida at such locations as Lake Monroe, Ft. Pierce, St. Lucie River, Lake Worth, Merritt Island, Cape Canaveral, Indian River, Miami River, and Everglades (U.S. House of Representatives 1844a, Tebeau 1980:149). Clearly, even with the incentive of free land, settlements in northeast Florida were few during the Territorial Period.

During the latter part of the Second Spanish Period and continuing through the Territorial Period, the focus of settlement in northeast Florida shifted somewhat from St. Augustine northward toward Georgia. Fernandina, at the north end of Amelia Island, saw a brief florescence as a port having two attractive features, one natural and the other cultural. The bar at the mouth of St. Marys River was not only slightly deeper than that at St. Augustine, it was also somewhat more stable, notwithstanding the claim of Spanish Governor Zéspedes in 1785 that it was the deepest and easiest to enter between Mexico and New York (Lockey 1949:571). More important, because of the inability of the Spanish governor to control effectively that portion of the territory between the St. Johns and the Amelia Rivers, Fernandina became a free port of sorts, a port of call for privateers, smugglers, and slave traders seeking access to American markets across the Georgia border, where slave trading had been illegal since 1809.

The appeal of Fernandina and the St. Marys River area as a center for slave trading was somewhat diminished with the increased control that accompanied statehood, but the illegal trade continued along Florida's east coast until the Civil War. As the eastern terminus of the Florida Railroad connecting the Atlantic and the Gulf of Mexico at Cedar Key, Fernandina had good potential to become a transportation center, offering shippers an alternative route to sailing all the way around the peninsula. Later, the military and political actions of the Civil War prevented Fernandina's development from occurring, even though the railroad route was entirely finished before the outbreak of hostilities (Hanna and Hanna 1950:128–140).

Steamboats began to serve northeast Florida during territorial times, the first visit being that of the *George Washington* to Jacksonville in 1831. Because of the dangers and frustrations caused by the bar at the mouth of the St. Johns, as well as the limited passenger and cargo markets, service remained intermittent through the 1830s. Between 1840 and 1845, on average two steamboat companies provided connections between Charleston or Savannah and St. Johns landings (Jacksonville, Mandarin, Picolata, Palatka, Enterprise) or St. Augustine. From the middle 1850s to the establishment of the Civil War blockades, northeast Florida enjoyed regular and fairly reliable service by between five and eight vessels at any one time, providing transportation, shipping, and mail at least twice each week (Mueller 1962). For planters and settlers throughout east Florida, both above and below Lake George, steamboats provided essentially the only means of communication and transportation of goods and people. The road system was inadequate or nonexistent, and no railroads had yet penetrated the peninsula.

Also north of St. Augustine, the small community of Cowford, later to become Jacksonville, was developing during the Territorial Period. Situated at a convenient crossing point on the St. Johns River, where the King's Road had been constructed during the British Period, Cowford grew slowly from the time of its first settlers in 1816; by 1830 its population was only 100. Growth was slow during the next decade as a result of the Indian wars, reaching 600 residents by 1840. Jacksonville itself, incorporated in 1832, offered a somewhat more suitable ocean inlet than St. Augustine and a more stable political climate than Fernandina.

Regional Integration, 1845–1920

Statehood did not bring about dramatic changes in the northeast part of Florida. Some of the planters who had lost everything during the Second Seminole War were compensated by the U.S. government (U.S. House of Representatives 1843, 1844b). Joseph M. Hernandez was one of the few to receive money, probably because of his military and political stature; with it he rebuilt St. Josephs and Bella Vista.

Slavery had been established in Florida under British rule from 1763 to 1783, but Spanish Florida before and after British occupation served as a haven for runaway slaves until the Territorial Period. Slave trading flourished in Florida as an American territory as well as a state, and slave labor supported Florida plantations not only in northeast Florida but to an even greater degree in Middle and West Florida. Florida entered, and left, the Union on the side of the slave states, but being primarily a coastal-oriented state was brought rapidly and effectively under the control of U.S. naval blockades.

By middle 1862 federal forces occupied and controlled the East Coast towns of St. Augustine (fig. 7.2), Fernandina, and St. Johns Bluff, as well as the territory between the coast and the St. Johns River. Jacksonville was occupied four times by northern forces, between March 1862 and July 1864. The plantation economy of northeast Florida, which depended so fundamentally on slave labor, was essentially destroyed by the Union occupation. The military offered refuge as well as transportation to runaway slaves, and thousands of slave families made their way to Jacksonville and Fernandina, where many black men enlisted in the Union army (Shafer 1995).

As it had so often since the First Spanish Period, the western bank of the St. Johns River served as a boundary between territory under the control of

Fig. 7.2. St. Augustine, December 11, 1864. Residence converted to Post Quartermaster's building. Florida Photographic Archives.

the prevailing government and land occupied by a hostile power. While federal naval ships and army troops controlled the peninsula's coast, Confederate forces held the interior, relying on overland transportation routes to supply produce, troops, and imports to the other southern states (Hanna and Hanna 1950:141–156). By April 1865, with the surrender of General Robert E. Lee at Appomattox, Jacksonville was a ruined town. Most able-bodied men had long left to fight elsewhere in the South; families loyal to the Confederacy abandoned the Union-occupied town for the interior of the peninsula. According to one estimate, the population of Jacksonville had been reduced to 20 men. Many of the houses and buildings had been destroyed, including every sawmill in town save one. Food was scarce; there was no ferry across the river; the lumber and logging business had ceased; there were no steamboats on the river; and the single railroad had been partially dismantled (Gold 1929:153, Proctor 1963) (map 7.5).

Destruction was not restricted to Jacksonville; federal gunboats had navigated 200 miles up the St. Johns River, raiding and burning settlements. At the end of the war, Florida's economic strength had been exhausted by the blockade and occupation; its business activity had no access to outside markets and had degenerated or disappeared (Davis 1913:171, 217).

Post–Civil War development in northeast Florida followed a pattern that was to prove more successful than any previous attempt in populating the region and increasing the size as well as the stability of the economy: the introduction of tourism. At first, Florida's climate was promoted as a healthful attraction, particularly for those in poor health. As early as 1823 Vignoles had recommended St. Augustine as a winter haven for the ill:

> The fashion of sending invalids from the north, on an expensive journey to the south of France and Italy, may perhaps be superseded, if the physicians could be induced to recommend a winter at St. Augustine to their patients, who would thus, instead of being removed, perhaps to die in a foreign climate, be near their friends and within a few days' sail of their homes: admitting for one instant that the summer months are unhealthy, no one can doubt the salubrity of the rest of the year. The geniality of the climate, the beauty of the orange groves, the vicinity of the ocean, and the quietude of the place, would contribute greatly towards the restoration of health to consumptive persons. (Vignoles 1823:111–112)

It is unlikely that many heeded Vignoles's advice during the periods of territoriality, early statehood or the Civil War. However, another call for

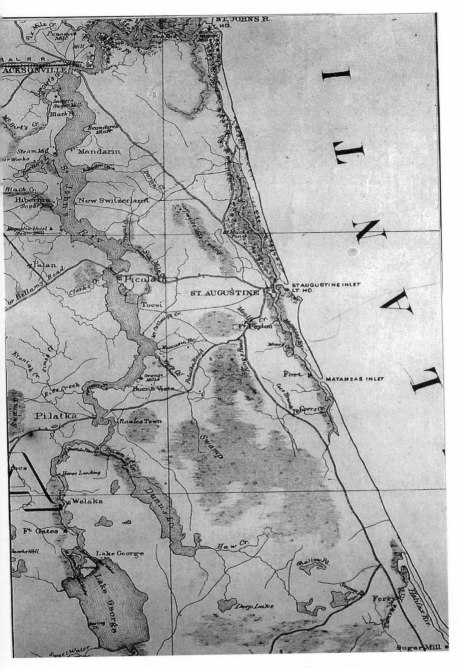

Map 7.5. Northern part of Florida (U.S. Coast Survey Office 1864)

making St. Augustine a health resort was published soon after the war. Daniel G. Brinton's *A Guide-Book of Florida and the South for Tourists, Invalids and Emigrants* (1869) was styled after the well-known Baedeker travel books then guiding so many tourists through Europe. It offered comments on how to pack, gave steamship and rail routes from the Northeast, provided the history, geography and descriptions of the regions of Florida then open to tourists, and, finally, gave advice to invalids. Transportation routes and the growth of settlement are represented by map 7.6.

Quoting a contemporary medical authority, Sir James Clark, M.D., ("It would be difficult to point out the chronic complaint, or even the disordered state of health which is not benefitted by a timely and judicious change of climate"), Brinton introduced the major ailments that would improve after Florida travel: Most important was consumption (tuberculosis), followed by bronchitis, rheumatism, dyspepsia, nervous and mental exhaustion, old age, and infertility.

Although Brinton was more famous for his accomplishments in archaeology and anthropology later in life, he was, at the time of writing his guidebook, a practicing physician and had served as surgeon-in-chief in the Union army. As might be inferred from the descriptions of diseases and supposed efficacy of the suggested cure, medicine had not yet recognized the cause of many major ailments. Citing the danger of "swamp miasm" or miasma, "an invisible poisonous exhalation, into which the traveler ventures at his peril," Brinton recommended that October to May was the safe season for Southern travel. Miasma was, in fact, the misunderstood cause of yellow fever, an acute infectious viral disease for which the mosquito *Aedes aegypti* is the vector. This connection was not proven until the first part of the twentieth century, and miasma was frequently commented upon by northeast Florida visitors.

The narrator of the voyage of the *Two Friends* explained that the action of the sun upon decayed plants "produces putridity, creating the miasmata so fatally and widely destructive" in the Carolinas and Georgia. The author noted that the "destructive vapour" did not exist in East Florida (Anonymous 1819:156); however, an epidemic struck St. Augustine two years later (Vignoles 1823:110), as well as Jacksonville in 1857 (Brinton 1869:58) and 1888. Writing in 1844, Edward C. Anderson, Master of the U.S. steamer *General Taylor*, offered the opinion that the St. Johns River would never be "thickly peopled," at least not until the heavy vegetation had been cleared away. "Even then," he wrote, "the rays of a hot sun acting upon the moist land left bare by the removal of the forests will produce miasma worse than poison" (Anderson 1844:19). Between August and December of 1857,

Map 7.6. Colton's New Township Map of the State of Florida (Colton 1870)

5,000 cases of yellow fever were recorded in Jacksonville, causing 400 deaths (Gold 1929:175).

For consumptives Brinton recommended "Courage," particularly as an antidote to the "Giant Despair, who is still as ready as ever to pounce on unwary travelers, especially on wet days, alone in dull country taverns, with nothing to think of but themselves and their own aches and pains" (Brinton 1869:131). And one of the best ways to occupy one's mind was in collecting, Brinton observed, recommending "bugs, and butterflies, and mosses, and fossils, and flowers, and Indian curiosities, and species of woods, and birds' eggs, and skins, and minerals" whose pursuit and subsequent arrangement would provide exercise and interest. Nature, in Florida, had distributed "boundless attractions in the animal, the vegetable, and the mineral worlds, the study of which has ever something soothing and rejuvenating" (1869:131).

The once abundant wildlife appears to have declined in number by 1857, the time of Brinton's visit. For example, William Bartram in 1774 remarked upon the abundance of alligators on the St. Johns between the mouth of the river and Picolata (Bartram 1791:85, 94, 115). In 1822, William Haynes Simmons reported that the "alligators are uncommonly numerous in the St. Johns, being to be met with, on a warm day, at every hundred yards, basking or reposing on its rushy banks" (Simmons 1822:28). In 1831, on his tour of the river, John James Audubon remarked that the alligators were "extremely abundant." The naturalist noted: "A rifle bullet was now and then sent through the eye of one of the largest, which with a tremendous splash of its tail, expired" (Proby 1974:316). He goes on to recount the killing of two large alligators in as many days, for use as a model, but neither could be recovered from the river. Shooting alligators was common sport. As Edward C. Anderson wrote in 1844, "We amused ourselves by shooting alligators as we ran along the banks" (Anderson 1844:17). By 1857, Brinton reported that alligators "were now scarce in the lower St. John" (1869:50). Finally, writing of his tour of the river in 1879, George Barbour stated that alligators are very rare north of Lake George, and explains why:

> Alligators are quite wise in their generation, know the universal propensity of mankind to kill something, and are aware of their own very tempting qualities as a target when exposed to a boat-load of travelers, of whom the masculine members are nearly all armed with deadly weapons; so they do not offer any very extended opportunity to study their physiognomies, but always rush for deep water, the principal impression they convey being that of a scurrying, splashing monster

with a great tail curled upward, plunging head-foremost into the water. Above Lake Monroe, in the savanna region, alligators are very plentiful and not shy, but below Lake George they are very rare, and none are seen from the steamers. (Barbour 1882:111)

By the 1920s visitors wishing to see an alligator resorted to the Alligator Farm tourist attraction at St. Augustine (Graham 1983:203).

The Florida of the Spanish and the British, for all its failure to develop and for all its disadvantages so apparent before the Civil War, had suddenly achieved the respectability of antiquity and wilderness. Although there had been changes to the environment of northeast Florida over the centuries, to the Northern traveler and the Southern promoter it offered the attractions of quaint old St. Augustine (fig. 7.3) with its coquina Spanish architecture, as well as the unspoiled St. Johns River, now served by steamboats on a daily schedule. Railroads, steamship lines and hotels began to promote the tourist image of Florida aggressively in guidebooks, travel accounts, and pamphlets (map 7.7). One of the more successful was prepared by the Southern poet Sidney Lanier under contract with the Great Atlantic Coastline Railroad Company in 1875 (Lanier 1875:xii). During the previous winter, Lanier observed, between 15,000 and 20,000 tourists visited the state; of these, 6,000 to 10,000 visited St. Augustine (1875:9,64). Some measure of the relative importance of tourism is gained by comparing the number of tourists to the census population of St. Johns County, of which St. Augustine is the seat: 2,618 in 1870 and 4,535 in 1880 (Dietrich 1978). During the season, tourists outnumbered residents two or three to one.

For the convalescing tourist suffering from consumption, Lanier recommended not a brief visit but a whole winter's stay. Various treatments were suggested, including small but "regular doses of whisky administered at intervals of from an hour to an hour and a half through each entire day from sleep to sleep," and avoiding getting wet, cold, or tired in the slightest degree (1875:213–215). Besides the climate of the region, however, Florida's natural productions were again recommended as an interesting and potentially lucrative diversion:

You may, if you like that sort of woods-life, kill alligators and sell their teeth, . . . or shoot herons, and collect their plumes for market—an occupation by which at least one invalid, of whom I have heard, has managed to support himself; or you might get a contract with some of the numerous colleges in the country to supply their cabinets with stuffed birds, or fish, or botanical specimens, from Florida. Of

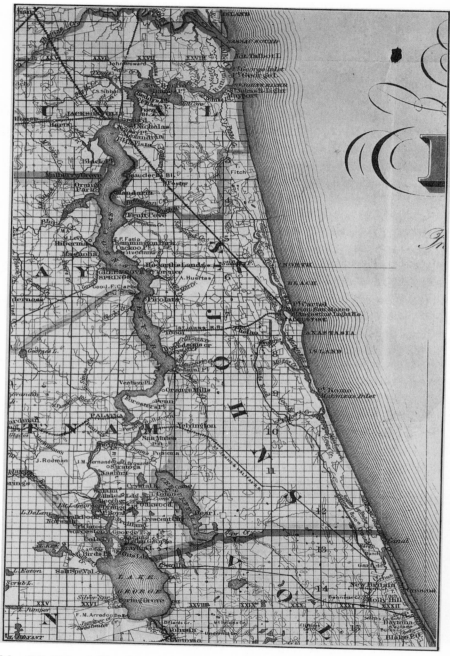

Map 7.7. Colton's New Sectional Map of the Eastern Portion of Florida (Colton 1883)

Fig. 7.3. St. Augustine city gate and bridge, March 16, 1871. Florida Photographic Archives.

course, if you have means which preclude the necessity of doing these things for support, you can do them for pleasure, and in applying yourself to the study of science you will soon cease to wither under that true consumptive sense that life is done with you and that you have nothing left but to die. (1875:216–217)

By 1885 the region was beginning to achieve the sort of solid growth that had eluded a succession of governments for more than three centuries. Rail lines had been completed connecting Jacksonville with Fernandina to the north, St. Augustine to the south, and Lake City and points beyond toward the west (fig. 7.4). Steamboat transportation, with Jacksonville as its southern focus, was well developed and connected points on the St. Johns River (Fort George Island, Mayport, Mandarin, Green Cove Springs, Crescent

Fig. 7.4. Bird's-eye view of Jacksonville, 1878. Florida Photographic Archives.

City, Palatka, Spring Garden, and others) with Savannah, Charleston, and ultimately New York (map 7.8). According to a report of the Duval County commissioners, 74 vessels engaged in St. Johns River commerce (fig. 7.5), totaling 8,168 registered tonnage and representing an annual commerce of more than $2 million, claimed to be the largest tonnage in any local inland waterway south of the Hudson River. Shipments in 1885 included 37,000 bales of cotton, 68 million board feet of lumber, and 316,000 crates of fruit and vegetables (Gold 1929:187). In the next decade, the federal government was persuaded to undertake improvements at the St. Johns bar, constructing a permanent jetty and maintaining a deeper permanent channel; by the early 1900s, the control depth was established at 24 feet, finally opening Jacksonville and northeast Florida to international trade.

The level of tourism promoted by authors like Vignoles, Barbour, and Lanier, although helpful to the development of St. Augustine, was minor in comparison to what was to occur in the last decade of the nineteenth century. By the middle 1880s, St. Augustine had successfully captured a share of the wealthy Northeast tourist trade, which had traditionally wintered in the Mediterranean.

Fig. 7.5. Steamship *Okahumkee* on the St. Johns River, Palatka. Florida Photographic Archives.

One such visitor of 1884, Henry M. Flagler, was to transform the face of Florida, beginning with St. Augustine. Cofounder of Standard Oil with John D. Rockefeller, Flagler had already achieved astounding success in his first career and was at the time of his Florida enterprise one of the wealthiest and most powerful men in America. His dream was to develop the Florida east coast, from St. Augustine to Key West, in a tripartite scheme of railroads, hotels, and land developments. Flagler's rail line, the Florida East Coast Railway, bridged the St. Johns River at Jacksonville, and by the time of the opening of the opulent Hotel Ponce de Leon in St. Augustine (fig. 7.6) in 1888, wealthy New Yorkers could reach the new resort in their private railroad cars in 35 hours (map 7.9). Society avoided the town in

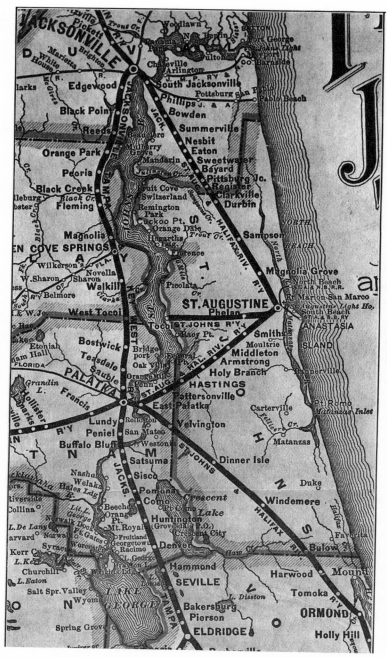

Map 7.8. "Standard Guide" Map of the State of Florida (Jacksonville, Tampa, and Key West System and East Coast Line 1891)

1889 because of a yellow fever scare, but 1890 witnessed the Vanderbilts, the Rockefellers, the Whitneys, and President Grover Cleveland among northeast Florida's winter guests (Graham 1983).

Rail transportation was viewed as the engine that could drive Florida's growing economy. The state of Florida offered rights of way to railroad companies at favorable rates along with alternating square mile sections of public lands for every length of track successfully built. The railroad companies, obtaining their lands virtually without cost and providing transportation to them, opened great opportunities for speculative residential development, attractive to Northern tourists, who would decide to return for good. In addition, train routes through the region, previously served only by waterborne transportation, opened up new interior areas for agricultural production (fig. 7.7); not only could produce be grown in newly farmed, unexhausted soils; it could also be shipped to the resort hotels and, more important, to eastern and northern markets by rail. The interior flatwoods swamps were drained and cleared between the Atlantic Coast and the St. Johns in the last part of the nineteenth century, and to the present they continue to provide winter vegetables, especially potatoes, for the nation (Dow 1983).

Fig. 7.6. Ponce de Leon Hotel, St. Augustine. Florida Photographic Archives.

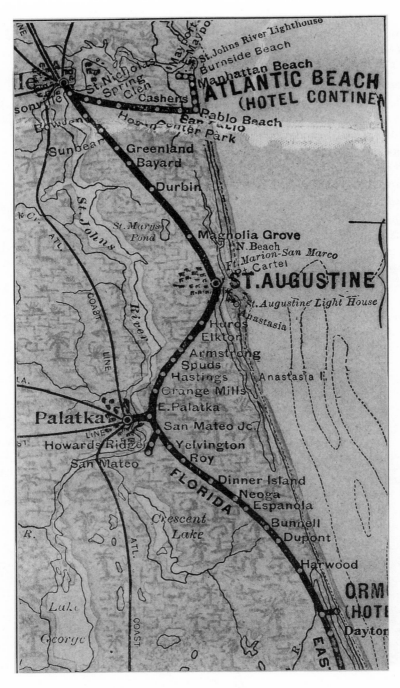

Map 7.9. Florida East Coast Railway (Florida East Coast Railway 1911)

Fig. 7.7. Excursion train in the 1880s of the Jacksonville, St. Augustine and Halifax River Railway, a precedessor of Florida East Coast Railway. Florida Photographic Archives.

The elegant years of St. Augustine tourism were few in number as Flagler pushed his railroad empire ever southward with major resorts in Ormond and then Palm Beach, culminating in the opening of the Key West Extension in 1912 (Akin 1988). The depression of 1893, the severe freeze of 1894–1895, and the development of Palm Beach as the new winter home of the very wealthy had contributed to the end of St. Augustine's hope of sustained economic success by the turn of the century (fig. 7.8). Nonetheless, by this time the town had grown out of its quaint antiquarianism and had in some sections acquired the amenities and services of a modern twentieth-century city.

Few travelers failed to comment on the vast expanse of the northeast Florida pine barren, actually a continuation of the great Southern pine forest blanketing the coastal plain of the southeast United States. In northeast Florida pine flatwoods are the predominant vegetation, covering the entire area except along the St. Johns River and other bodies of water such as the Atlantic Ocean and coastal lagoons (map 1.11). By the turn of the

Fig. 7.8. Charlotte Street, St. Augustine, 1900s. Florida Photographic Archives.

century, little use had been made of the pine forests for settlement, although the commercial value of the virgin timber had often been regarded as a resource of which the Spanish or the British should have taken advantage, and the tall, straight pines had been occasionally used for ships' masts and spars.

It was not until the late nineteenth century, however, that the uncut pine forest began to be exploited on a major scale (fig. 7.9). Water-driven saw-mills had been established during the British Period and a small quantity of wood exported. Through the middle of the nineteenth century the most valuable wood was live oak for fabricating the curved structural members of large wooden ships. Live oak was so strategically important that, upon Florida's becoming a territory in 1821, all live oak was reserved for the U.S. government. It was difficult, however, to implement such control in the vast unpopulated peninsula, and much live oak was cut without permission.

As shipbuilding practices came to rely more on iron and eventually steel for framing, the importance of live oak diminished rapidly, and pine and cypress became the major commercial forest products. It would not be an exaggeration to say that north Florida was developed on the foundation of the lumber industry. A water-powered mill was built on Six Mile Creek

Fig. 7.9. First harvest of the longleaf pine forest near DeLand, April 1915. Florida Photographic Archives.

near Jacksonville in 1819, and the first steam sawmill was established on Trout Creek in 1829; these were pit mills rather than circular mills, cutting wood with long, straight blades instead of revolving circular blades. During the next few decades the lumber industry grew rapidly. By the mid-1850s there were a dozen or so mills near Jacksonville, including a circular mill at Pottsburg Creek. The young industry was limited by restrictions on transportation; the bar at the mouth of the St. Johns would not admit vessels with over 10 feet of draft, and rail lines did not exist that could bring the products to Northern markets. Union occupation of Jacksonville and the coastal section brought manufacturing and shipping to a standstill, and the lumber industry was not rebuilt until after 1867 (Campbell 1932).

The construction of rail lines by lumber companies helped transport logs to the mills and lumber from the mills to the local market. Much of the production was consumed locally in the construction of buildings during the rapid growth of Jacksonville in the 1870s and 1880s. Between 1860 and 1890 the population of Duval County increased more than five-fold, from 5,074 to 26,800 persons (Dietrich 1978); Jacksonville was the fastest-growing city in the state, and the virgin timber of the pine barrens supported its construction boom. The larger market for wood products, however, was national and international, and it became clear in the 1880s that the unreliable and dangerous entrance at St. Johns bar seriously restricted the region's ability to participate competitively. Following a dredging project begun in

1880, additional shipping lines added Jacksonville to their routes; limited federal funds to make further improvements were appropriated in 1884 and 1886, but the project was not finished until the early 1900s (Martin 1972:151, Gold 1929:187).

Between 1879 and 1899, Florida lumber production increased more than three times, from 247 to 790 million board feet. From 1909 to 1929 the state's annual production exceeded one billion board feet more years than not (fig. 7.10) (Campbell 1932: table 14). In Jacksonville at the turn of the century, the single largest producer, Cummer Lumber Company, was capable of producing 36 million board feet of pine lumber annually. Principal products were railroad ties, construction timber, and lumber. Before production began to decline in 1909 ties from northeast Florida were used in maintenance and expansion of the principal railroads of the eastern states as far north as Maine, as well as construction of lines in Cuba and for the Panama Canal. Sawed timber was exported to Spain, England, and the Caribbean through Jacksonville (fig. 7.11).

In addition to sawed and finished wood, the extensive pine forests supported a naval stores industry that led the nation in production between 1905 and 1923. In fact, the center of naval stores production moved continually southward—from North Carolina in 1850, to South Carolina in 1880, to Georgia in 1890, and finally to Florida—as the vast Southern coastal pine forest was gradually depleted (Campbell 1933:table 1). Florida's prominence was due as much to lack of competition as to the fact that the state's pine forests had not yet been cut down or exhausted by sap collection. The growth of this industry, like that of sawed timber, depended upon transportation routes to markets.

Between 1850 and 1890 Florida accounted for 5 percent or less of the national production; between 1890 and 1900 the proportion increased 13 times, from less than three to more than 30 percent, and continued to increase to a peak of more than half the national production in 1910 (Campbell 1933:table 2). Most of the turpentine and rosin from northeast Florida's rapidly diminishing pine forests was destined for foreign markets; at its peak Florida was supplying roughly one-third of the world's demand for naval stores products (1933:18–19).

The Modern Landscape, 1920 to the Present

By 1932 the northeast Florida pine forest had been completely cut over. In the entire state only three stands of virgin timber remained, all in the southern part of the peninsula. The depressed timber industry anticipated using saw-log timber that had been ignored in the cutting of the virgin forest, as

Fig. 7.10. Centuries-old cypress tree prepared for harvest by girdling the trunk at the base, 1910s. Florida Photographic Archives.

Fig. 7.11. Mill and docks of the Wilson Cypress Company on the St. Johns River in Jacksonville, one of the largest cypress mills in the United States. Florida Photographic Archives.

well as tracts of second growth, "which, although understocked because of over-cutting, destructive turpentining, and fire, still support about one-third of a crop of timber." An industry leader observed, "Most of the present pine operations of any consequence will be liquidated within a five-year period" (Campbell 1932:79). A survey of timber operators throughout the state revealed that none replanted any of their timber tracts, nor did any make use of the state or federal forest service to advise them. The value of such advice would have been questionable because the role of fire in maintaining viable stands of pine flatwoods was not understood, and legislation had been passed preventing destructive fires (Campbell 1932:74–80).

Timber continues to be important regionally; however, production is for pulp products like corrugated board, kraft paper, and other pine-based products. While vast tracts are managed for timber, the rotation is short-term, and the monoculture slash pine crops are usually clear-cut in harvesting.

Since the 1920s or so Florida's development has been based on roads rather than rails. Few parts of northeast Florida remain inaccessible, and no parts can be termed wilderness. The mark of people upon the landscape continues its inexorable spread in extent and intensity. Florida remains one of the fastest growing states in the country, and northeast Florida continues to attract its share of new residents and visitors each year. As a result, Flagler County, with its planned community of Palm Coast, is one of the most rapidly developing counties in the United States. Many parts of northeast Florida exhibit little if any of the original character that distinguished the region for its more than four centuries of Euro-American occupation. The solutions to challenges imposed by local environmental opportunities and constraints are not those which have been locally developed and found successful. It would be difficult to distinguish a northeast Florida apartment complex, residential community, strip development, shopping mall, modern highway, or new business district from its counterpart in any other part of the southeast United States.

8

Into the Future

This review of 18,000 years of environmental history in northeast Florida began with the rather general charge of exploring how people and environment interact, that is, how people affect the environment and what the effects of nature are on human beings. Two related questions have been posed: What is the character of the environment without human disturbance, and what is the proper role of people in the environment?

Population as a Measure of Adaptive Success

In ecological terms, the success of an adaptation is the extent to which it supports the population growth of the species under consideration. To what extent is it valid to assess the local adaptations of various cultures of northeast Florida in terms of population? Do the population data generally reflect the relative success of the various successive cultural adaptations that are documented in the historical record, or might the population data suggest important changes in environmental relations that would correspond to periods of rapid growth or decline? Estimates for the population of northeast Florida are summarized in tables 8.1 and 8.2. Figures are provided every decade or so from 1595 to 1990. Because of differences between the shape of the study area and the sizes of the different areas for which population figures are defined, it is best not to rely too closely on minor differences; rather, the tables are intended to indicate broad trends over nearly four centuries.

There is no accurate measure of Native American population at the time of European contact, estimates for northeast Florida ranging from 13,000 to 722,000. Indian populations began to decline dramatically owing to

Table 8.1. Colonial population

Date A.D.	Population	Comment
1500	150,000?+	Aboriginal population estimates from 13,000 to 722,000, no Europeans

All following estimates of European population only

1595	175	
1600	275	St. Augustine
1607	400	300 to 500 in and around St. Augustine
1610	450	
1620	450	
1638	538	
1640	575	
1650	588	
1660	725	
1670	725	
1680	988	
1690	1,175	
1700	912	
1710	800	
1720	925	
1730	1,350	
1740	1,325	
1750	1,700	
1761	2,750	End of First Spanish occupation
1770	2,800	Estimates of 2,600 and 3,000
1780	11,000	of which 8,000 British Loyalist influx
1784	2,187	of which 1,181 scheduled to leave
1785	891	Beginning of Second Spanish occupation
1786	1,703	Including garrison and outlying areas
1793	1,729	Including garrison of 438 soldiers
1797	1,592	Including outlying areas
1811	1,400	Including outlying areas
1815	2,238	Including outlying areas
1821		Territorial period begins

Notes: Aboriginal population estimates after Dobyns (1983); European population estimates after Dunkle (1958). Totals are not comparable as some estimates are for the City of St. Augustine, others include various ill-defined outlying areas, others are unclear as to whether the garrison is included or excluded.

Table 8.2. Territorial and state population

Date A.D.	Regional population	State population	Annual % increase region	Comment
1830	4,508	34,730	—	St. Johns & Duval Counties
1840	6,850	54,477	5.2	
1850	7,751	87,445	1.3	Add part of Putnam County
1860	12,738	140,424	6.4	Add part of Clay County
1870	20,458	187,748	6.1	
1880	33,065	269,493	6.2	
1890	51,852	391,422	5.7	
1900	66,174	528,542	2.8	
1910	107,583	752,619	6.3	
1920	149,232	968,470	3.9	Add all of Flagler County
1930	201,600	1,468,211	3.5	
1940	258,329	1,897,414	2.8	
1950	370,332	2,771,305	4.3	
1960	541,758	4,951,560	4.6	
1970	632,395	6,789,443	1.7	
1980	750,820	9,747,197	1.9	
1990	956,557	12,938,071	2.7	

Notes: From county census data organized in Dietrich (1978) and Bureau of Economic and Business Research (1985, 1996). Figures are not precise for the defined study area because the study area boundaries do not correspond to county boundaries. Regional figures are derived by combining whole county populations for Clay, Duval, Flagler, Putnam, and St. Johns, omitting Lake and Marion.

disease, slavery, warfare, forced labor, and a variety of other factors. There are little primary data on northeast Florida aboriginal populations; it is clear, however, that whatever the initial population the Timucua were virtually extinct by 1700. The record of decline is fairly detailed, and to attribute the extinction to environmental causes would mean omitting important factors such as warfare, disease, and slavery or including so much in the concept "environment" as to explain everything, hence nothing.

The European population increased slowly in absolute value during the First Spanish Period, from 175 in 1595 to 1,000 around 1725, an increase of only 825 people in 130 years. Just before the British assumed ownership in 1763, the population increased to 2,750. For the next 20 years, excepting an influx of British loyalists during the American Revolutionary War, the population remained roughly the same, 3,000 or less. Few British subjects remained in Florida during the Second Spanish Period. Only 891 residents were recorded in 1785. Between that year and 1815, the Spanish population increased to 2,238 people. For 300 years of colonial occupation the population of northeast Florida never exceeded 3,000, except during a brief wartime period, and the region never achieved a population density of even one person per square mile.

Once Florida became an American territory its population began to grow rapidly in absolute numbers. For a century the annual rate of increase was greater than 5 percent in 8 out of 10 decades. At this rate, the population doubles approximately every 14 years. The slowest growth occurred during the decade of the Seminole Indian Wars, when virtually all settlements outside of St. Augustine were abandoned and destroyed.

It is difficult to conclude that annual rate of population growth or population increase in numbers is an accurate reflection of adaptive success. In the case of northeast Florida, populations were so small that minor increases yielded significant rates of growth. It would seem more reasonable to compare population densities to some standard. For example, excluding aboriginal population, density never reached one person per square mile within the 5,000 square mile region until 1835 or so. Yet, by 1930 density had reached 40 persons per square mile and was increasing 10 persons per square mile every year.

It appears from the population records as well as from what is known of the social and economic conditions of the region from historical accounts that northeast Florida failed to realize its potential during the colonial periods. The environments that would have supported the economic and population growth of the nineteenth century were available to the Spanish and the British, but the colonial and American occupations contrasted dramatically in the ways they were able to exploit those environmental opportunities. Some of the difference may be attributable to changes in technology, an explanation consistent with the materialist notion that technology acts as the interface between people and environment. For example, northeast Florida possessed vast and valuable pine forest resources that had always been available to support naval stores and timber industries, but neither the Spanish nor the British were able to develop a viable export. Surely this is due in part to lack of transportation to markets caused by an inability to control the shoaling and shifting bar at the mouth of the St. Johns.

However, there were other factors that were not environmental. Spanish regulations prohibited foreign vessels or traders in the territory, so opportunities to develop markets outside the region were extremely limited. The British exported forest products, but their goods were competitive only during the anomalous period of the Revolutionary War, when supplies from other Southern ports such as Charleston and Savannah became scarce. In fact, it was not until railroads penetrated northeast Florida after the Civil War and until the more northern stands of original pine in the Carolinas and Georgia had been exhausted that Florida developed its forest industry.

The Fallacy of Pristine Environment

In assessing the environmental history and future of northeast Florida, it is necessary to consider the concept of the pristine environment unaffected by human disturbance. This concept is appealing on two levels. First, it is obvious that people have been responsible for environmental degradation of many types, particularly since the beginning of the industrial revolution. It is more than academic speculation to wonder about the character of nature without the disturbing effects of people; it is more likely wishful thinking. Second, the environment without people is sometimes regarded as an ideal to be pursued. As people have the ability to consciously control environments, often through government management of large landscapes, one common management goal is to re-create an unspoiled environment, to reestablish a pristine wilderness.

However, as the history of northeast Florida demonstrates, no environment without people could ever be re-created. A prehuman environment would consist of many plant and animal species that are extinct; it would depend upon ranges and patterns of temperature and precipitation that do not exist; it would require elimination of nonindigenous flora and fauna; and it would consist of associations of species in community relationships without modern analogues. The pristine environment is a false concept that provides a means for wishing that environmental problems would disappear rather than a basis for understanding how they may be solved. By now in the history of the earth all environments are human environments; it would be difficult to find an ecosystem that is not affected by global warming, sea level rise, ocean pollution, or ozone depletion. Not only are environments as they are because humans have played some role in making them that way, but the process of human effect upon environmental systems will increase rather than decrease in the future.

Environmental history does not reveal even a typical or standard landscape for a region like northeast Florida. The landscape of more than 6,000 years ago was a function of rapidly rising sea level, a shoreline with no lagoons or barrier islands, a subsurface aquifer that was a sink rather than a source for water, and an assemblage of plant and animal species adapted to these conditions in associations that have no modern equivalents.

The landscape of the Timucuan Indians was relatively stable compared with that of the previous 10,000 years or so. Human effects were not dramatic, but presumably they were pervasive; at the time of European contact, the Indian population of the region was probably more than 150,000, a level not reached again until the early twentieth century. Descriptions of the environment in the early sixteenth century convey a rich and bountiful landscape, but one that was cultivated where soils were suitable. The European introduction of foreign plants, animals, and microbes changed the environment of northeast Florida so fundamentally that its precontact condition could never be reestablished; eliminating nonindigenous species would be impossible. The current environment of northeast Florida is as much European as it is Floridian. Virtually all domesticated species have their origins outside of the region; the result is a modern Euro-American ecosystem that becomes more and more unlike any environment that ever existed in Florida before the sixteenth century.

A fundamental characteristic of the ideal or pristine environment is that it is in equilibrium, that is, environmental change occurs but is kept within regular limits by self-regulating feedback relationships. There is little evidence in the environmental history of northeast Florida to support such a concept. Rather, equilibrium might well be the state of the environment that is studied at only one point in time. Certainly there are different scales of environmental change: The global climatic cycle related to glaciation has a period on the order of tens of thousands of years, while the shorter cycles of tides, droughts, floods, and severe storms are measured in months and decades. Nonetheless, the northeast Florida environment does not show that environmental change has a tendency toward an average or equilibrious condition. There does not appear to be an environmental ideal, except perhaps in the minds of people; rather, the environment exhibits constant change from human-induced as well as nonhuman factors. At any point in time the state of the environment is a function not only of the factors then in operation but also those factors that have operated in the past, left their mark, and no longer are present. The current state of the northeast Florida environment, the result of long-term, specific evolution, is a snapshot of a continuously changing complex rather than an approximation of an ideal.

There is a final fallacy inherent in the concept of a pristine environment, namely, that it is possible for local environments to exist unaffected by human actions elsewhere. It has long been recognized that environments, like other systems, consist of interrelated components and that change in one component affects others. One important factor in defining such an ecosystem is scale: How large must the system be to include the most important elements? Now it is clear that human activity is affecting the environment of our planet. Global warming, acid rain, ozone depletion, oceanic pollution, possible sea level rise and similar events now render the question of pristine environments moot.

Effects of People on Environments

For the last 500 years and possibly longer, the relation between the people of northeast Florida and the environment of the region has been subject to various degrees of outside control. This factor is often given insufficient weight in considering how people and environments interact at the local level. Many anthropological studies that have adopted an environmental or ecological approach have focused on relatively isolated and sometimes nonindustrial societies. The working concept of a human ecosystem has largely implied a group of people who make local decisions about their local environment. As the present review has shown, from the first incident of European contact continuing through the annexation of the Florida peninsula by the United States, fundamental decisions about the relationship between land and people were made in Europe. Florida settlements were maintained for specific geopolitical and economic purposes that had little to do with whether particular local adaptations were successful or not.

The very existence of the Spanish St. Augustine colony as well as the outlying associated missions and cattle ranches depended primarily on the need to protect the Atlantic Coast shipping routes. Investment by the Spanish crown was generally limited to only what was necessary to keep the Florida colony barely able to defend itself from English or French attack. As for the residents and soldiers, there was little incentive or ability to improve local means of support. Private land ownership was difficult to accomplish, and taxes on production as well as restrictions on trade and shipping were prohibitive. Agricultural and natural commodities like crops, livestock, timber, and other potential exports remained undeveloped throughout the First Spanish Period, not so much because of the absence of natural resources but rather the lack of capital, materials, facilities, and transportation; in two centuries Spain failed to construct a passable road through northeast Florida.

During the British Period as well as the Second Spanish Period the basis for fundamentally changing the unsettled landscape was the land grant system. As we have seen, even this crucial relationship between land and people was governed from Europe; British grants were made mostly to members of the upper class, who would never see their property. Subsequent Spanish grants were somewhat more successful in promoting agricultural production and settlement, yet trade and transportation were so severely restricted by the government that only a few planters in the entire province could arrange an export trade.

As part of the United States, northeast Florida was still fundamentally affected by outside factors, some international in scale. The Seminole Indian Wars as well as the Civil War led to virtual abandonment of the region; the local adaptation had failed, but not for environmental reasons. When northeast Florida finally became a functional part of the United States, linked by reliable transportation and communication facilities, its regional development was founded on the exploitation of the vast stands of pine forest that had not previously been cut. Its markets were international, and the economic factors driving the exhaustion of the forests were largely beyond local control. The tourist industry depended upon promoting and taking advantage of local environmental values such as a pleasant climate and unspoiled rivers but required continued inputs of people and money from other parts of the country for its success.

Effects of Environment on People

The environment provides opportunities and constraints according to the technologies available at the time. When new technologies are developed, resources can present opportunities not previously available as the value and accessibility of resources is altered. Similarly, environmental change resulting from both natural and human factors is constantly shifting the character and location of potential resources. As noted, the relationship between environment and people is more direct at lower levels of technology; fewer means are available to manipulate the environment to overcome limitations or exploit opportunities. During the prehistoric period, the character of adaptation appears fundamentally dependent upon environmental factors: Strategies dependent upon such resources as Late Pleistocene megafauna or shellfish in the St. Johns River and in lagoons behind the coastal barrier islands are dependent upon major environmental changes that are beyond human control. The nature of the human ecological relationship is that people can respond to take advantage of resources not previously available and in so doing will change the economic, social, and ideological aspects of their culture. This is a powerful analytical and explanatory scheme for the prehistoric period for two reasons. First, in the absence of written records the reconstruction of culture history will be general rather than specific; second, for societies with limited technological abilities, the relationship between nature and culture will be quite direct.

In the Spanish and British colonial periods, these two factors are different. Documentary sources allow a more detailed reconstruction of what happened in northeast Florida as well as an understanding of what decisions were made outside of the region. European technologies such as sailing vessels, written communication, metal tools and weapons, draft animals, domesticated plants, and wheeled vehicles would be expected to have opened vast opportunities to the new settlers in this previously unexploited environment. Instead, the colonial pattern was one of stagnation and failure for almost three centuries. The notions that limitations will be overcome and opportunities will be exploited when technology is available do not hold true in northeast Florida in the colonial period. Rather, the effect of environment was not as important as the effect of people outside the region. The complicated external factors of markets, competition, warfare, politics, and control dominated the adaptations in northeast Florida during the colonial period. This development is not entirely unexpected, as external control is the defining trait of colonial dependency, but it is important to recognize the comparatively lesser importance of local environmental factors in Spanish and British colonial culture.

For most of the nineteenth century, as part of an American territory and state, northeast Florida was still largely affected by external events; destruction of outlying settlements during the Seminole Indian and Civil wars was the result of national policies and actions, and the ability to develop an economic foundation for growth depended on such external factors as railroad network development, availability of capital, and competitiveness in foreign and national markets. Nonetheless, such resources as thousands of square miles of virgin pine forest and the natural harbor and transportation corridor afforded by the St. Johns River once the shallow bar was controlled were eventually exploited.

Conscious Adaptation

Our current technological ability to transform virtually any natural landscape into a completely cultural one—to turn a coastal wetland into a condominium or an inland forest into an airport—diminishes the importance of the relationship between people and land. All but the most fundamental environmental constraints may now be overcome by technological "solutions." Environmental opportunities are tempered in importance by the centralization of our distribution systems; it is unusual that locally produced commodities of any type are locally consumed. In general, people and environment are not closely related. People know little of local environments, spending most of their time in air-conditioned offices, homes, and automobiles. And people have little idea of the direct effects of their actions on environments, either local or distant.

At the same time, the impact of human actions upon environments is becoming more pronounced, and the reciprocal relationship comprises a potential feedback mechanism of a serious nature. As we introduce hazardous man-made substances into our ecosystems, so they find their way into our food and water supplies. As our production of hydrocarbons contributes to global warming, so our coastal cities and landscapes are threatened by sea level rise. As we drive increasing numbers of species toward extinction by harvesting or by destruction of habitat, so we reduce the quantity, diversity, and reliability of the animal and plant populations on which we depend. In short, we have lost sight of the ways that ecosystems support us, and we threaten our own success as a species by undermining these systems.

The northeast Florida environment that amazed the European explorers is gone and will never exist again. The population densities before 1900 of fewer than 10 people per square mile are equivalent to a modern population increase of five years or less. Between 1980 and 1990 some 200,000 people were added to the region: homes, cars, roads, workplaces, shops, public facilities, and infrastructure for more than 50 additional people each day. Over the next three decades, through the year 2020, the population is projected to increase by roughly 125 people per day. Spatially, the figures suggest that, on average, each square mile of northeast Florida received 40 new people in the previous decade and would be projected to receive nearly 100 more people between 1900 and 2020 (Purdum, Anderson, and Krafft 1988). Pressure to convert agricultural, forest, and natural land uses to residential and commercial uses will continue to increase in the future; as the amount of undeveloped land diminishes, its development value will increase, as will the cost of public control or protection.

Of course, population is not evenly distributed throughout northeast Florida, and certain parts of the region would receive most of the development associated with population growth. Much of the current environmental planning in the state now occurs as a result of the Florida Land and Water Management Act, Chapter 380, Florida Statutes. This comprehensive law established 10 regional planning councils around the state. The Northeast Florida Regional Planning Council's fundamental goals and policies were set out in the Northeast Florida Comprehensive Regional Policy Plan of July 1, 1987; the plan was evaluated in 1990, and amendments were adopted in 1991 (Northeast Florida Regional Planning Council 1987, 1990, 1991).

The plan specifies a number of environmental concerns for northeast Florida, which planners and regulators should take into consideration when making land use decisions. Broad categories include inland water resources, coastal and marine resources, natural systems and recreational land, land use, public facilities, agriculture, and tourism. The current nature of such resources is a function of the region's natural and historical development and depends in large measure on how they have been exploited and managed in the past. Their future management will hinge in part upon understanding their history, which has been an important component.

Another institution that is playing an increasingly important role in environmental management of the region is the St. Johns Water Management District. Florida's five water management districts have statutory responsibility to manage water resources in the state and have been granted taxing authority. The St. Johns district has instituted a comprehensive land acquisition program to carry out their mission of flood control, water storage, water management, and preservation of wetlands, streams, and lakes (St. Johns Water Management District 1998:1). Ecosystem management and habitat restoration are beginning to form the basis for management of the large tracts under control of the water management district as well as other state and federal land managers.

Perhaps the main weakness of environmental history as a policy tool is its immense scope; a comprehensive history of the land has no precise beginning in time, and its understanding requires at least some knowledge of many different fields of study. This study has explored in some detail a single region, and clearly more work would be useful. An environmental history of the entire state would help inform planning at the state and multiregional level. It would potentially have the added benefit of educating Florida's immigrant residents, who account for most of the current population growth, about the history of their local regions. Most of them have no personal, family, or traditional knowledge of the land or its people and have little understanding of environmental relationships, historical or modern.

In addition, detailed study of the past 50 years of northeast Florida environmental history, the period not covered in this study, would help account for many of the landscape modifications now evident in the region. The processes of deliberate environmental change in the last half century are readily recognized: they are essentially the capabilities of the fossil-fuel-driven machinery that we see in use every day. Dredges, draglines, bulldozers, graders, paving equipment, pumps, and other such devices impose the will of the planners, managers, and developers upon the landscape at an unrelenting pace.

The means of studying landscape change in the past half century are more productive than those for earlier periods. Much of the construction is still visible and functional, and it occurred within the memory of some local residents. Also, for the time period beginning around World War II, the use of aerial photography by such agencies as the Soil Conservation Service, Coast and Geodetic Survey, Forest Service, and Department of Transportation has provided comprehensive and accurate coverage of the landscape in a sequence of pictures, not unlike time-lapse photography, for more than half a century. Satellite imagery is approaching its third decade of coverage of the globe and offers the added ability to study land use and environmental change by means of sophisticated electronic analysis of remote sensing data.

One particular environmental process that requires additional study is sea level rise. The environmental importance of sea level change in modifying the landscape as well as influencing cultural adaptation has been amply demonstrated in the case of northeast Florida. Transgression of the shoreline a distance of 100 kilometers, coastal formation of the barrier island and lagoon system, and drowning of the St. Johns basin through aquifer discharge are all related to the postglacial sea level rise and stabilization.

As sea level continues to rise and its rate of rise increases with global warming, these effects will have important consequences for northeast Florida and elsewhere. It is estimated that sea level is currently rising about one foot per century; in northeast Florida, according to the Regional Planning Council, this phenomenon results in some 36 feet per decade of shoreline transgression or erosion. As such rates increase, the current practices of attempting to stop erosion, replenish eroded beaches, and stabilize the shoreline will become even more costly and yet less effective.

It is important to understand in more detail the relationships among sea level, piezometric surface, and water table. If our environmental reconstruction is correct, the flooding of the St. Johns River Basin around 5,000 years ago must have been a sudden event, in geological time. Because the artesian flow of a spring is a step function, that is, it is either on or off, there would have been little warning that the river basin was about to double in size; if such an event were to occur in modern times, there would be little effective means of controlling or ameliorating such artesian flow. The more prudent response is to determine whether such an event would occur in a region as a result of sea level rise and to plan land uses accordingly. Similarly, potential rates of sea level rise should be locally correlated to distances of shoreline transgression, and appropriate land uses ought to be planned. Such erosion is most likely to occur during storm or hurricane events and will occur suddenly rather than gradually. Finally, the effect of sea level rise on the relationship between water supply and saltwater intrusion should be determined. Substantial cones of depression resulting from industrial and agricultural pumping of freshwater from the aquifer already exist; their configuration may be influenced by a rising sea level.

If climate is indeed warming as a result of increased use of fossil fuels, and if, as appears likely, efforts to curtail these trends are unsuccessful, it will be necessary to plan for the resulting environmental changes. The effect of increased average temperature on precipitation should be studied. If the warmer climate is to be a wetter climate, the local water table and associated wetlands may be affected. The northeast Florida environmental history has shown that distribution of plant and animal species is directly related to climate. What species in or near northeast Florida are at the extreme of their range? Would increased temperature and precipitation cause certain plants or animals to be less or more successful in their local adaptation? Would plant associations change appreciably? Would the normal tolerances of agricultural crops be exceeded? What other plants would be better suited to a future climate and soil conditions?

Questions like these are easily posed once we begin to think of environments as constantly changing. Environmental history will be a useful and valuable planning tool if it can simply force us to recognize that we must foresee and accommodate rather than react in surprise to environmental change. We should attempt to understand local processes of change as well as local effects of past change, and with that new knowledge predict future environmental change and plan accordingly.

Florida's environmental protection and growth management laws are among the strongest in the United States. Their interpretation, implementation, and enforcement depends upon an informed government and public that are knowledgeable about local environments and the potential effects of proposed actions.

If we are to be effective in managing environments, that is, in determining the potential effects of our actions and making conscious decisions with knowledge of their implications, we must have a thorough understanding of the ways the environment works. We must understand how it formed and how it functions, how it has been modified, and how it will change in the future. Once we recognize the undeniable relationship between people and environment, it is our responsibility to learn the history of the environment so that we can guide its future.

References

Akin, Edward N. 1988. *Flagler, Rockefeller Partner and Florida Baron*. Kent, Ohio: Kent State University Press.

Anderson, David G., and Kenneth E. Sassaman. 1996. *The Paleoindian and Early Archaic Southeast*. Tuscaloosa: University of Alabama Press.

Anderson, Edward C. 1844. "The Diary of Master Edward C. Anderson, United States Navy." Pp. 13–68 in *Florida Territory in 1844*, edited, with foreword, afterword, and critical apparatus by W. Stanley Hoole. Tuscaloosa: University of Alabama Press.

Anonymous [James Killpatrick]. 1742. *An Impartial Account of the Late Expedition Against St. Augustine Under General Oglethorpe*. A facsimile reproduction of the 1742 edition, with an introduction and indexes by Aileen Moore Topping. Gainesville: University of Florida Press, 1978.

Anonymous. 1819. *Narrative of a Voyage to the Spanish Main in the Ship "Two Friends."* A facsimile reproduction of the 1819 edition, with an introduction and index by John W. Griffin. Gainesville: University of Florida Press, 1978.

Arnade, Charles W. 1959. *The Siege of St. Augustine in 1702*. Gainesville: University of Florida Press.

―――. 1961. "Cattle Raising in Spanish Florida, 1513–1763." *Agricultural History* 35, no. 3: 3–11.

Barbour, George M. 1882. *Florida for Tourists, Invalids, and Settlers*. A facsimile reproduction of the 1882 edition, with an introduction by Emmett B. Peter, Jr. Gainesville: University of Florida Press, 1964.

Barry, R. G. 1983. "Late-Pleistocene Climatology." In Wright, ed., 1983, q.v., vol. 1, pp. 390–407.

Bartram, John. 1769. "A Journal Kept by John Bartram of Philadelphia, Botanist to His Majesty for the Floridas; upon a Journey from St. Augustine up the River St. John's as far as the Lakes." In William Stork, *An account of East-Florida, with a Journal, kept by John Bartram of Philadelphia*. 3d ed. London: W. Nicoll.

Bartram, William. 1791. *Travels Through North & South Carolina, Georgia, East & West Florida.* Reprint, edited and with notes by Mark van Doren. New York: Dover Books, 1955.

Bermes, B. J., G. W. Leve, and G. R. Tarver. 1963. *Geology and Ground-water Resources of Flagler, Putnam, and St. Johns Counties, Florida.* Florida Geological Survey Report of Investigations no. 32, Tallahassee: Florida Geological Survey.

Bloom, Arthur L. 1983a. "Sea Level and Coastal Changes." In Wright, ed., 1983, q.v., vol. 2, pp. 42–51.

———. 1983b. "Sea Level and Coastal Morphology of the United States through the Late Wisconsin Glacial Maximum." In Wright, ed., 1983, q.v., vol. 2, pp. 215–29.

Bond, Stanley C., Jr. 1992. "Archaeological Excavations at 8SJ42, The Crescent Beach Site, St. Johns County, Florida." *Florida Anthropologist* 45, no. 2: 148–61.

Boniface, Brian G. 1971. "A Historical Geography of Spanish Florida, Circa 1700." M.A. thesis, University of Georgia.

Borremans, Nina. 1989. "The Paleoindian Period. Draft Historic Context for Florida Comprehensive Historic Preservation Plan." MS. Tallahassee: Florida Division of Historical Resources.

Botkin, Daniel B. 1990. *Discordant Harmonies, A New Ecology for the Twenty-first Century.* New York: Oxford University Press.

Bradley, James T. 1972. "Climate of Florida. Climatography of the United States." No. 60–68. U.S. Department of Commerce, National Oceanic and Atmospheric Administration. Silver Spring, Md.: Environmental Data Service.

Brinton, Daniel G. 1861. "Rogel's Account of the Florida Mission (1569–1570)." *The Historical Magazine and Notes and Queries Concerning the Antiquities, History, and Biography of America* 5: 327–30.

———. 1869. *A Guide-Book of Florida and The South, for Tourists, Invalids and Emigrants, with a Map of the St. Johns River.* A facsimile reproduction of the 1869 edition, with an introduction and indexes by William M. Goza. Gainesville: University of Florida Press, 1978.

Brooks, H. Kelly. 1981. Geologic map of Florida. Cooperative Extension Service, Institute of Food and Agricultural Sciences, University of Florida.

Bruff, J. Goldsborough. 1846. State of Florida. Bureau of Topographical Engineers.

Bullen, Adelaide K., and Ripley P. Bullen. 1961. "The Summer Haven Site, St. Johns County, Florida." *Florida Anthropologist* 21, no. 1: 14–16.

Bullen, Ripley P. 1959. "The Transitional Period of Florida." *Southeastern Archaeological Conference Newsletter* 6: 43–62.

———. 1972. "The Orange Period of Peninsular Florida." Pp. 9–33 in *Fiber-tempered Pottery in Southeastern United States and Northern Colombia: Its Origins, Context, and Significance,* edited by Ripley P. Bullen and James B. Stoltman. Florida Anthropological Society Publications 6. Gainesville: Florida Anthropological Society.

Bureau of Economic and Business Research. 1985. *Florida Statistical Abstract 1985.* Gainesville: University Press of Florida.

————. 1996. *Florida Statistical Abstract 1996.* Gainesville: University of Florida.

Bushnell, Amy. 1983. "The Noble and Loyal City." Pp. 27–55 in *The Oldest City,* edited by Jean Parker Waterbury. St. Augustine: St. Augustine Historical Society.

Campbell, A. Stuart. 1932. "Studies in Forestry Resources in Florida II. The Lumber Industry." University of Florida, economic series 1, no. 4. Gainesville: Bureau of Economic and Business Research.

————. 1933. "Studies in Forestry Resources in Florida III. The Naval Stores Industry." University of Florida, economic series 1(5). Gainesville: Bureau of Economic and Business Research.

Clark, J. A. 1981. "Comment on 'Late Wisconsin and Holocene Tectonic Stability of the United States Mid-Atlantic Coastal Region.'" *Geology* 9: 348.

Clark, J. A., and C. S. Lingle. 1979. "Predicted Relative Sea-level Changes (18,000 Years B.P. to Present) Caused by Late-Glacial Retreat of the Antarctic Ice Sheet." *Quaternary Research* 9: 265–87.

Clausen, Carl J., H. K. Brooks, and A. B. Wesolowsky. 1975. *Florida Spring Confirmed as 10,000 Year Old Early Man Site.* Florida Anthropological Society Publications 7.

Clausen, Carl J., A. D. Cohen, C. Emiliani, J. A. Holman, and J. J. Stipp. 1979. "Little Salt Spring: A Unique Underwater Site." *Science* 203: 609–14.

Clayton, Lawrence A., Vernon James Knight, Jr., and Edward C. Moore, eds. 1993. *The DeSoto Chronicles, The Expedition of Hernando de Soto to North America in 1539–1543.* 2 vols. Tuscaloosa: University of Alabama Press.

Clench, W. J., and R. D. Turner. 1956. "Freshwater Mollusks of Alabama, Georgia, and Florida from the Escambia to the Suwannee River." *Bulletin of the Florida State Museum, Biological Sciences* 1, no. 3: 97–239.

Cline, Howard F. 1974. *Provisional Historical Gazeteer with Locational Notes on Florida Colonial Communities, 1700–1823.* Florida Indians II. New York: Garland Publishing.

Cohen, M. M. 1836. *Notices of Florida and the Campaigns.* A facsimile reproduction of the 1836 edition, with an introduction by O. Z. Tyler, Jr. Gainesville: University of Florida Press, 1964.

Coker, William S., and Thomas D. Watson. 1986. *Indian Traders of the Southeastern Spanish Borderlands: Panton, Leslie & Company and John Forbes & Company, 1783–1847.* Pensacola: University of West Florida Press.

Colton, G. W. & C. B. & Co. 1870. New township map of the state of Florida. New York: G. W. & C. B. Colton & Co.

————. 1883. New sectional map of the eastern portion of Florida. New York: G. W. & C. B. Colton & Co.

Connery, J. H. 1932. "Recent Find of Mammoth Remains in the Quaternary of Florida Together with Arrowheads." *Science,* n.s. 75: 516.

Connor, Jeanette Thurber. 1927. Preface. In Ribaut, 1927, q.v.

———. 1930. *Colonial Records of Spanish Florida*, vol. 2, *1577–1580*. Publications of the Florida State Historical Society 5.

———, trans. 1923. *Pedro Menéndez de Avilés, Memorial by Gonzalo Solís de Merás*. A facsimile reproduction of the 1923 edition, with a new introduction by Lyle N. McAlister. Gainesville: University of Florida Press, 1964.

Cooke, C. W. 1939. "Scenery of Florida Interpreted by a Geologist." Florida Geological Survey. *Geological Bulletin 17*.

———. 1945. "The Geology of Florida." Florida Geological Survey. *Geological Bulletin 29*.

Covington, James W. 1961. *The British Meet the Seminoles*. Contributions of the Florida State Museum, Social Sciences 7. Gainesville: University Press of Florida.

———. 1975. "Relations between the Eastern Timucuan Indians and the French and Spanish, 1564–1567." In *Four Centuries of Southern Indians*, edited by Charles M. Hudson. Athens: University of Georgia Press.

Cronon, William. 1983. *Changes in the Land, Indians, Colonists, and the Ecology of New England*. New York: Hill and Wang.

———. 1991. *Nature's Metropolis, Chicago and the Great West*. New York: W. W. Norton & Co.

Crosby, Alfred W. 1972. *The Columbian Exchange: Biological and Cultural Consequences of 1492*. Westport, Conn.: Greenwood Press.

———. 1986. *Ecological Imperialism: The Biological Expansion of Europe, 900–1900*. New York: Cambridge University Press.

Cumbaa, Stephen L. 1977. "A Reconsideration of Freshwater Shellfish Exploitation in the Florida Archaic." *Florida Anthropologist* 29: 49–59.

Cumming, W. P., R. A. Skelton, and D. B. Quinn. 1972. *The Discovery of North America*. New York: American Heritage Press.

Daniel, Randolph, and Michael Wisenbaker. 1987. *Harney Flats: A Florida Paleo-Indian Site*. Amityville, N.Y.: Baywood Publishing.

Davis, Jefferson. 1856. State of Florida. Bureau of Topographical Engineers. Prepared by order of Jefferson Davis, U.S. Secretary of War.

Davis, John H. 1967. General map of natural vegetation of Florida. Institute of Food and Agricultural Sciences. Gainesville: University of Florida.

Davis, Margaret Bryan. 1983. "Holocene Vegetational History of the Eastern United States." In Wright, ed., 1983, q.v., vol. 2, pp. 166–81.

Davis, P. D. C., and A. A. Dent. 1968. *Animals that Changed the World*. New York: Crowell-Collier Press.

Davis, T. Frederick. 1937. "Early Orange Culture in Florida and the Epochal Cold of 1835." *Florida Historical Quarterly* 15, no. 4: 232–41.

Davis, William Watson. 1913. *The Civil War and Reconstruction in Florida*. A facsimile reproduction of the 1913 edition, with a new introduction by Fletcher M. Green. Gainesville: University of Florida Press, 1964.

Deagan, Kathleen A. 1978. "Cultures in Transition: Fusion and Assimilation among the Eastern Timucua." Pp. 89–119 in *Tacachale: Essays on the Indians of Florida and Southeastern Georgia during the Historic Period*, edited by J. T. Milanich and S. Proctor. Gainesville: University of Florida Press.

De Brahm, William. 1770. Map of the general surveys of East Florida, 1766–1770. In De Brahm 1773, q.v.

———. 1773. *Report of the General Survey of the Southern District of North America*. Reprint, edited and with an introduction by Louis De Vorsey, Jr. Columbia: University of South Carolina Press, 1971.

Delcourt, P. A. 1980. "Goshen Springs: Late Quaternary Vegetation Record for Southern Alabama." *Ecology* 61: 371–86.

Dickinson, Jonathan. 1699. *Jonathan Dickinson's Journal or, God's Protecting Providence*. Edited by Evangeline Walker Andrews and Charles McLean Andrews, with a foreword and new introduction by Leonard W. Labaree. Stuart: Florida Classics Library, 1981.

Dietrich, T. Stanton. 1978. *The Urbanization of Florida's Population: An Historical Perspective of County Growth 1830–1970*. Gainesville: Bureau of Economic and Business Research, University of Florida.

Dobyns, Henry F. 1966. "Estimating Aboriginal American Population: An Appraisal of Techniques with a New Hemispheric Estimate." *Current Anthropology* 7: 395–416.

———. 1983. *Their Numbers Become Thinned: Native Population Dynamics in Eastern North America*. Knoxville: University of Tennessee Press.

Doehring, Fred, Iver W. Duedall, and John M. Williams. 1994. *Florida Hurricanes and Tropical Storms, 1871–1993: An Historical Survey*. Division of Marine and Environmental Systems, technical paper 71. Gainesville: Florida Sea Grant Program.

Doran, Glen H., and David N. Dickel. 1988. "Multidisciplinary Investigations at the Windover Site." Pp. 263–89 in *Wet Site Archaeology*, edited by Barbara Purdy. Caldwell, N.J.: Telford Press.

Dow, Robert N., Jr. 1983. "Yesterday and the Day Before, 1913 to the Present." Pp. 211–42 in *The Oldest City*, edited by Jean Parker Waterbury. St. Augustine: St. Augustine Historical Society.

Dunbar, James S., and Ben I. Waller. 1983. "A Distribution Analysis of the Clovis/ Suwannee Paleo-Indian Sites of Florida—A Geographic Approach." *Florida Anthropologist* 36, nos. 1–2: 18–30.

Dunkel, John R. 1958. "Population Change as an Element in the Historical Geography of St. Augustine." *Florida Historical Quarterly* 37, no. 1: 3–32.

Fairbanks, Charles H. 1974. *Ethnohistorical Report on the Florida Indians*. Florida Indians III: A Garland Series American Indian Ethnohistory. New York: Garland Publishing.

Fairbanks, George R. 1858. *The History and Antiquities of the City of St. Augustine, Florida*. A facsimile reproduction of the 1858 edition, with an introduction and index by Michael V. Gannon. Gainesville: University of Florida Press, 1975.

Fairbridge, Rhodes W. 1961. "Eustatic Changes in Sea Level." Pp. 99–185 in *Phys-*

ics and Chemistry of the Earth, edited by L. H. Ahrens et al., vol. 4. New York: Pergamon Press.

Ferguson, G. E., C. W. Lingham, S. K. Love, and R. O. Vernon. 1947. *Springs of Florida*. Florida Geological Survey. Geological Bulletin 31.

Fernald, Edward A., and Donald J. Patton, eds. 1984. *Water Resources Atlas of Florida*. Institute of Science and Public Affairs. Tallahassee: Florida State University.

Fernández de Oviedo y Valdés, Gonzalo. 1959. *Natural History of the West Indies*. Translated and edited by Sterling A. Stoudamire. Chapel Hill: University of North Carolina Press.

Flint, Richard Foster. 1971. *Glacial and Quaternary Geology*. New York: John Wiley and Sons.

Florida Bureau of Geology. 1978. Environmental Geology Series, Jacksonville Sheet, 1:250,000, map series no. 89. Tallahassee: Department of Natural Resources.

———. 1979. Environmental Geology Series, Daytona Beach Sheet, 1:250,000, map series no. 93. Tallahassee: Department of Natural Resources.

Florida Division of State Planning. 1975. *Florida General Soils Atlas with Interpretations*. Florida Department of Administration. Tallahassee: Division of State Planning.

Florida East Coast Railway. 1911. Florida East Coast Railway, Jacksonville via St. Augustine, Ormond, Palm Beach, and Miami to Key West and Havana.

Forbes, James Grant. 1821. *Sketches, Historical and Topographical, of the Floridas; More Particularly of East Florida*. A facsimile reproduction of the 1821 edition, with an introduction by James W. Covington. Gainesville: University of Florida Press, 1964.

General Land Office. 1911. State of Florida. Compiled from the official records of the General Land Office and other sources, under the direction of I. P. Berthrong. Department of the Interior.

Gibson, Charles. 1966. *Spain in America*. New York: Harper and Row.

Goggin, John M. 1952. *Space and Time Perspective in Northern St. Johns Archeology, Florida*. Yale University Publications in Anthropology 47.

Gold, Pleasant Daniel. 1929. *History of Duval County Including Early History of East Florida*. St. Augustine: The Record Company.

Graham, R. B. Cunninghame. 1949. *The Horses of the Conquest*. Norman: University of Oklahoma Press.

Graham, Thomas. 1983. "The Flagler Era." Pp. 181–210 in *The Oldest City*, edited by Jean Parker Waterbury. St. Augustine: St. Augustine Historical Society.

Gray, Lewis C. 1941. *History of Agriculture in the Southern United States to 1860*. Carnegie Institution of Washington, publication no. 430. Reprint, New York: Peter Smith.

Griffin, John W., and James J. Miller. 1978. Merritt Island National Wildlife Refuge Cultural Resource Assessment. Report. National Park Service, Atlanta.

Griffin, John W., and Hale G. Smith. 1954. "The Cotten Site: An Archaeological

Site of Early Ceramic Times in Volusia County, Florida." *Florida State University Studies* 16: 27–59.

Hann, John H. 1988. *Apalachee, the Land Between the Rivers.* Gainesville: University Press of Florida.

———. 1990. "Summary Guide to Spanish Florida Missions and Visitas with Churches in the Sixteenth and Seventeenth Centuries." *The Americas* 46, no. 4.

———. 1996. *A History of the Timucua Indians and Missions.* Gainesville: University Press of Florida.

Hanna, Alfred Jackson, and Kathryn Abbey Hanna. 1950. *Florida's Golden Sands.* Indianapolis: Bobbs-Merrill.

Haring, C. H. 1947. *The Spanish Empire in America.* New York: Oxford University Press.

———. 1964. *Trade and Navigation Between Spain and the Indies.* Gloucester, Mass.: Peter Smith.

Harman, Joyce Elizabeth. 1969. *Trade and Privateering in Spanish Florida, 1762–1763.* St. Augustine: St. Augustine Historical Society.

Harper, Roland M. 1914. "Geography and Vegetation of Northern Florida." Sixth annual report. Tallahassee: Florida Geological Survey.

Hawks, J. M. 1887. *East Coast of Florida.* Lynn, Mass.: Lewis and Winship.

Healy, Henry G. 1975. Terraces and Shorelines of Florida. Map series no. 71, Florida Bureau of Geology. Tallahassee: Department of Natural Resources.

Henige, David. 1986a. "If Fish Could Fly: Timucuan Population and Native American Historical Demography." *Journal of Interdisciplinary History* 4 (Spring 1986): 701–20.

———. 1986b. "Primary Source by Primary Source? On the Role of Epidemics in New World Depopulation." *Ethnohistory* 33 (Summer 1986): 293–312.

Henry, James A., Kenneth M. Portier, and Jan M. Coyne. 1994. *The Climate and Weather of Florida.* Sarasota: Pineapple Press.

Higgs, Charles D. 1951. "The Derrotero of Alvaro Mexia, 1605." Appendix A in Irving Rouse, "A Survey of Indian River Archeology." *Yale University Publications in Anthropology* 44: 265–74.

Hoffman, Charles. 1983. "A Mammoth Kill Site in the Silver Springs Run." *Florida Anthropologist* 36, nos. 1–2: 83–87.

Hoffman, Paul E. 1993. "Hernando De Soto: A Brief Biography." Pp. 421–59. In Clayton, Knight and Moore, eds., 1993, q.v., 421–59.

Howard, E. B. 1940. "Studies Bearing upon the Problem of Early Man in Florida." *Carnegie Institute of Washington Yearbook* 39: 309–12.

Hoyt, J. H. 1967. "Barrier Island Formation." *Bulletin of the Geological Society of America* 78, no. 9: 1125–36.

Hoyt, J. H., and J. R. Hails. 1974. "Pleistocene Stratigraphy of Southeastern Georgia." Pp. 191–205 in *Post-Miocene Stratigraphy: Central and Southern Atlantic Coastal Plain,* edited by R. Q. Oaks and J. R. Dunbar. Logan: Utah State University Press.

Hoyt, J. H., V. J. Henry, Jr., and J. D. Howard, eds. 1966. *Pleistocene and Holocene Sediments, Sapelo Island, Georgia and Vicinity.* Guidebook for field trip no. 1, Geological Society of America, Southeastern Section.

Hudson, Charles. 1997. *Knights of Spain, Warriors of the Sun: Hernando de Soto and the South's Ancient Chiefdoms.* Athens: University of Georgia Press.

Hulton, Paul, ed. 1977. *The Work of Jacques Le Moyne de Morgues, A Huguenot Artist in France, Florida and England.* London: British Museum Publications.

Jacksonville, Tampa, and Key West System and East Coast Line. 1891. "Standard Guide" map of the state of Florida. Buffalo, N.Y.: Matthews, Northrup & Co., Art Printing Works.

Jahn, Otto L., and Ripley P. Bullen. 1978. *The Tick Island Site, St. Johns River, Florida.* Florida Anthropological Society Publications 10.

Jeffreys, Thomas. 1762. *A Description of the Spanish Islands and Settlements on the Coast of the West Indies.* London: Printed for T. Jeffreys.

Jennings, Francis. 1975. *The Invasion of America: Indians, Colonialism, and the Cant of Conquest.* Chapel Hill: University of North Carolina Press.

Johnson, A. Sydney, H. O. Hillestad, S. F. Shanholtzer, and G. F. Shanholtzer. 1974. *An Ecological Survey of the Coastal Region of Georgia.* National Park Service Scientific Monograph Series 3. Washington, D.C.

Kimber, Edward. 1744. *A Relation or Journal of a Late Expedition to the Gates of St. Augustine, on Florida.* Facsimile reproduction of the 1744 edition, with an introduction and index by John Jay TePaske. Gainesville: University of Florida Press, 1976.

Klos, George. 1995. "Blacks and the Seminole Removal Debate, 1821–1835." Pp. 128–56 in *The African American Heritage of Florida,* edited by D. R. Colburn and J. L. Landers. Gainesville: University Press of Florida.

Lanier, Sidney. 1875. *Florida: Its Scenery, Climate, and History.* A facsimile reproduction of the 1875 edition, with introduction and index by Jerrell H. Shofner. Gainesville: University of Florida Press, 1973.

Larson, Lewis H. 1980. *Aboriginal Subsistence Technology on the Southeastern Coastal Plain during the Late Prehistoric Period.* Gainesville: University Press of Florida.

Laudonnière, René. 1586. *Three Voyages.* Translated and with an introduction and notes by Charles E. Bennett. Gainesville: University of Florida Press, 1975.

Le Conte, John. 1822. "Observations on the Soil and Climate of East Florida, John Le Conte, Captain, U.S. Army, February and March 1822." Pp. 17–36 in *Le Conte's Report on East Florida,* edited by Richard Adicks. Orlando: University of Central Florida Press.

Le Moyne de Morgues, Jacques. 1965. "The Narrative of Jacques le Moyne de Morgues." In Lorant, ed., 1965, q.v., 33–86.

Leontyev, O. K., and L. G. Nikiforov. 1965. "Reasons for the World-wide Occurrence of Barrier Beaches." *Oceanology* 5, no. 4: 61–67.

Liebhardt, Barbara. 1988. "Interpretation and Causal Analysis: Theories in Environmental History." *Environmental Review* 12 (1): 23–36.

Lockey, Joseph B. 1949. *East Florida, 1783–1785.* Berkeley: University of California Press.

Lorant, Stefan. 1965. *The New World: The First Pictures of America.* 2d edition. Edited and annotated by Stefan Lorant. New York: Duell, Sloan, and Pearce.

Ludlum, David M. 1963. *Early American Hurricanes, 1492–1870.* Boston: American Meteorological Society.

Lundelius, Ernest L., Jr., Russel W. Graham, Elaine Anderson, John Guilday, J. Alan Holman, David W. Steadman, and S. David Webb. 1983. "Terrestrial Vertebrate Faunas." In Wright, ed., 1983, q.v., vol. 1, pp. 311–53.

McAlister, Lyle N. 1984. *Spain and Portugal in the New World, 1492–1700.* Minneapolis: University of Minnesota Press.

McHarg, Ian L. 1969. *Design with Nature.* New York: Natural History Press.

MacKay, John, and J. E. Blake. 1839. "Map of the Seat of War in Florida compiled by order of Bvt. Brigr. Genl. Z. Taylor, principally from the surveys and reconnaissances of the Officers of the U.S. Army, by Capt. John MacKay and Lieut. J. E. Blake, U.S. Topographical Engineers."

MacNeil, F. S. 1950. "Pleistocene Shorelines in Florida and Georgia." U.S. Geological Survey professional paper 221-F. Washington, D.C.

Martin, Paul S. 1967. "Prehistoric Overkill." Pp. 75–120 in *Pleistocene Extinctions: The Search for a Cause,* edited by P. S. Martin and H. E. Wright, Jr. New Haven: Yale University Press.

Martin, Richard A. 1972. *The City Makers.* Jacksonville: Convention Press.

Martin, Robert A., and S. David Webb. 1974. "Late Pleistocene Mammals from the Devil's Den Fauna, Levy County." Pp. 114–45 in *Pleistocene Mammals of Florida,* edited by S. David Webb. Gainesville: University of Florida Press.

Martin, Sidney Walter. 1944. *Florida during the Territorial Days.* Athens: University of Georgia Press.

Mexia, Alvaro. 1605. "Derrotero of Alvaro Mexia, 1605." Translated and with an introduction by Charles D. Higgs. Appendix A in Irving Rouse, *A Survey of Indian River Archeology,* Yale University Publications in Anthropology 44.

Milanich, Jerald T. 1994. *Archaeology of Precolumbian Florida.* Gainesville: University Press of Florida.

Milanich, Jerald T., and Charles H. Fairbanks. 1980. *Florida Archaeology.* New York: Academic Press.

Milanich, Jerald T., and Charles Hudson. 1993. *Hernando de Soto and the Indians of Florida.* Gainesville: University Press of Florida.

Milanich, Jerald T., and Susan Milbrath. 1989. *First Encounters: Spanish Explorations in the Caribbean and the United States, 1492–1570.* Gainesville: University of Florida Press.

Miller, James J. 1980. "Coquina Middens on the Florida East Coast." *Florida Anthropologist* 33, no. 1: 2–16.

Mitchem, Jeffrey M. In press. "Expeditions to East Florida by Clarence Bloomfield Moore." Introduction in C. B. Moore, *Excavations in East Florida*. Tuscaloosa: University of Alabama Press.

Mooney, James M. 1928. *The Aboriginal Population of America North of Mexico*, edited by John R. Swanton. Smithsonian Miscellaneous Collections 80, no. 7. Washington, D.C.

Morison, Samuel Eliot. 1974. *The European Discovery of America: The Southern Voyages, A.D. 1492–1616*. New York: Oxford University Press.

Mowat, Charles L. 1943. *East Florida as a British Province, 1763–1784*. Berkeley: University of California Press. Facsimile reproduction, with an editorial preface by Rembert W. Patrick. Gainesville: University of Florida Press, 1964.

Mueller, Edward A. 1962. "East Coast Florida Steamboating, 1831–1861." *Florida Historical Quarterly* 40: 241–60.

National Oceanic and Atmospheric Administration. 1976. Bathymetric map, Jacksonville, Florida. Jacksonville NH 17–5 (OCS), Washington, D.C.: National Ocean Survey.

———. 1978. Jacksonville, Florida. Local climatological data, annual summary with comparative data. Environmental Data and Information Service. Asheville, N.C.: National Climatic Center.

Neill, Wilfred T. 1953. "Notes on the Supposed Association of Artifacts and Extinct Vertebrates in Flagler County, Florida." *American Antiquity* 19, no. 2: 170–71.

Newsome, Lee. 1987. "Analysis of Botanical Remains from Hontoon Island (8VO202), Florida: 1980–85 Excavations." *Florida Anthropologist* 40, no. 1: 47–84.

Northeast Florida Regional Planning Council. 1987. Northeast Florida Comprehensive Regional Policy Plan, July 1, 1987. Jacksonville: Northeast Florida Regional Planning Council.

———. 1990. Northeast Florida Comprehensive Regional Policy Plan, 1990 evaluation. Jacksonville: Northeast Florida Regional Planning Council.

———. 1991. Adopted amendments to the Northeast Florida Comprehensive Regional Policy Plan. Jacksonville: Northeast Florida Regional Planning Council.

Parry, J. H. 1966. *The Establishment of European Hegemony: 1415–1715*. New York: Harper & Row.

———. 1974. *The Discovery of the Sea*. New York: Dial Press.

Patrick, Rembert W. 1954. *Florida Fiasco*. Athens: University of Georgia Press.

Petulla, Joseph M. 1977. *American Environmental History: The Exploitation and Conservation of Natural Resources*. San Francisco: Boyd & Fraser Publishing Company.

Proby, Kathryn Hall. 1974. *Audubon in Florida*. Miami: University of Miami Press.

Proctor, Samuel. 1963. "Jacksonville During the Civil War." *Florida Historical Quarterly* 41, no. 4: 343–55.

Purdum, Elizabeth D., James R. Anderson, Jr., and Peter A. Krafft. 1988. *Florida County Atlas and Municipal Fact Book*. Institute of Science and Public Affairs. Tallahassee: Florida State University.

Puri, H. S., and Robert O. Vernon. 1964. *Summary of the Geology of Florida and a Guidebook to the Classic Exposures*. Special Publication 5. Tallahassee: Florida Geological Survey.

Pyne, S. J. 1982. *Fire in America*. Princeton: Princeton University Press.

Quinn, David B. 1977. *North America from the Earliest Discovery to the First Settlements: The Norse Voyages to 1612*. New York: Harper & Row.

Ribaut, Jean. 1927. *The Whole and True Discouerye of Terra Florida*. A facsimile reprint of the 1563 London edition, with a preface by Jeanette Thurber Connor. DeLand: Florida State Historical Society.

Roberts, William. 1763. *An Account of the First Discovery, and Natural History of Florida*. A facsimile reproduction of the 1763 London edition, with an introduction and index by Robert Gold. Gainesville: University of Florida Press, 1976.

Romans, Bernard. 1775. *A Concise Natural History of East and West Florida*. Reprint of the 1775 New York edition, with modernized typography and corrected errata. New Orleans: Pelican Publishing, 1961.

Rosenau, Jack C., Glen L. Faulkner, Charles W. Hendry, Jr., and Robert W. Hull. 1977. *Springs of Florida*. Florida Bureau of Geology Bulletin 31. Tallahassee: Florida Department of Natural Resources.

Rouse, Irving. 1951. *A Survey of Indian River Archeology, Florida*. Yale University Publications in Anthropology 44.

Russo, Michael. 1992. "Chronologies and Cultures of the St. Marys Region of Northeast Florida and Southeast Georgia." *Florida Anthropologist* 45, no. 2: 107–26.

———. 1993. *The Timucuan Ecological and Historic Preserve Phase III Final Report*. Southeast Archeological Center Accession 899, Department of Anthropology. Gainesville: Florida Museum of Natural History.

St. Johns River Water Management District. 1998. *Land Acquisition and Management Five-Year Plan, 1998*. Palatka. Florida.

Sauer, Carl Ortwin. 1966. *The Early Spanish Main*. Berkeley: University of California Press.

———. 1971. *Sixteenth Century North America, The Land and the People as Seen by the Europeans*. Berkeley: University of California Press.

Saunders, Rebecca. 1993. "Architecture of the Missions Santa Maria and Santa Catalina de Amelia." Pp. 35–61 in *The Spanish Missions of La Florida*, edited by B. G. McEwan. Gainesville: University Press of Florida.

Semken, Holmes A., Jr. 1983. "Holocene Mammalian Biogeography and Climatic Change in the Eastern and Central United States." In Wright, ed., 1983, q.v., vol. 2, pp. 182–207.

Shafer, Daniel L. 1995. "Freedom Was as Close as the River." Pp. 157–84 in *The African American Heritage of Florida*, edited by David R. Colburn and Jane L. Landers. Gainesville: University Press of Florida.

Siebert, Wilbur Henry. 1929. *Loyalists in East Florida 1774 to 1785*. Vol. 2,

Records of Their Claims for Losses of Property in the Province. DeLand: Florida State Historical Society.

Simmons, William Hayne. 1822. *Notices of East Florida.* A facsimile reproduction of the 1822 Charleston edition, with an introduction and index by George E. Buker. Gainesville: University of Florida Press, 1973.

Smith, Bruce D., ed. 1990. *The Mississippian Emergence.* Washington, D.C.: Smithsonian Institution Press.

Smith, James M., and Stanley C. Bond, Jr. 1984. "Stomping the Flatwoods." MS. St. Augustine: Historic St. Augustine Preservation Board.

Smith, Marvin T. 1987. *Archaeology of Aboriginal Culture Change in the Interior Southeast: Depopulation during the Early Historic Period.* Gainesville: University Press of Florida.

Snell, L. J., and Warren Anderson. 1970. *Water Resources of Northeast Florida (St. Johns River Basin and Adjacent Coastal Areas).* Report of Investigations 54. Tallahassee: Florida Bureau of Geology.

Solís de Merás, Gonzalo. 1567. *Pedro Menéndez de Avilés, Memorial by Gonzalo Solís de Merás.* A facsimile reproduction of the 1923 edition, translated from the Spanish with notes by Jeanette Thurber Connor, with a new introduction by Lyle N. McAlister. Gainesville: University of Florida Press, 1964.

Sparke, John. 1565. "The Voyage made by Master John Hawkins . . . to the Indies of Nova Hispania, Begun in A.D. 1564." Pp. 360–96 in *Hakluyt's Voyages,* edited by Richard David. Boston: Houghton Mifflin, 1981.

Stapor, Frank W., and William F. Tanner. 1977. "Late Holocene Mean Sea Level Data from St. Vincent Island and the Shape of the Late Holocene Mean Sea Level Curve." Pp. 35–68 in William F. Tanner, ed., *Coastal Sedimentology.* Tallahassee: Geology Department, Florida State University.

Steward, Julian H. 1958. *Theory of Culture Change: The Methodology of Multilinear Evolution.* Urbana: University of Illinois Press.

Stilgoe, John R. 1982. *Common Landscape of America, 1580 to 1845.* New Haven: Yale University Press.

Stoltman, James B., and David A. Baerreis. 1983. "The Evolution of Human Ecosystems in the United States." In Wright, ed., 1983, q.v., vol. 2, pp. 252–68.

Stork, William. 1769. *An account of East-Florida, with a Journal, kept by John Bartram of Philadelphia, Botanist to His Majesty for the Floridas; Upon a journey from St. Augustine up the River St. John's as Far as the Lakes.* 3d ed. London: W. Nicoll.

Stringfield, V. T., and H. H. Cooper, Jr. 1951. *Geologic and Hydrologic Features of an Artesian Spring East of Florida.* Report of Investigations 7. Tallahassee: Florida Geological Survey.

Sturtevant, William C. 1977. "The Ethnological Evaluation of the Le Moyne–De Bry Illustrations." In Hulton, ed., 1977, q.v., 69–74.

Swanton, John R. 1946. *The Indians of the Southeastern United States.* Bureau of American Ethnology Bulletin 137. Reprint, 1979. Washington, D.C.

Swift, W. H. 1829. "Map of the Territory of Florida from Its Northern Boundary to

Lat: 27 °, 50'." Annexed to the report of the Board of Internal Improvement dated February 19, 1829.

Tebeau, Charlton. 1971. *A History of Florida*. Coral Gables: University of Miami Press. 2d ed., 1980.

TePaske, John Jay. 1964. *The Governorship of Spanish Florida, 1700–1763*. Durham, N.C.: Duke University Press.

Thunen, Robert L., and Keith H. Ashley. 1995. "Mortuary Behavior along the Lower St. Johns: An Overview." *Florida Anthropologist* 48, no. 1: 3–12.

U.S. Coast Survey Office. 1864. Northern part of Florida. Compiled by A. D. Bache, superintendent. U.S. Coast Survey Office.

U.S. Geological Survey. 1966. Jacksonville Sheet, 1:250,000. Reston, Va.: U.S. Geological Survey.

————. 1972. Daytona Beach Sheet, 1:250,000. Reston, Va.: U.S. Geological Survey.

————. 1975. Hydrologic Unit Map-1974, State of Florida. Reston, Va.: U.S. Geological Survey.

————. 1976. State of Florida, 1:500,000. Reston, Va.: U.S. Geological Survey.

————. 1984. "Water Resources Data, Florida, Water Year 1983." *U.S. Geological Survey Water-Data Report* FL–83–1A, vol. 1A: *Northeast Florida Surface Water*. Orlando: U.S. Geological Survey Water Resources Division.

U.S. House. 1843. *Report of the Committee of Claims*. Report no. 104, 27th Cong., 3d sess.

————. 1844a. *Actual Settlements in Florida under the Armed Occupation Law*. Document 70, 28th Cong., 1st sess.

————. 1844b. *Report of the Committee of Claims, Joseph M. Hernandez*. Report no. 58, 28th Cong., 1st sess.

U.S. Water Resources Council. 1970. *Water Resources Regions and Subregions for the National Assessment of Water and Related Land Resources*. Washington, D.C.: U.S. Water Resources Council.

Vignoles, Charles. 1823. *Observations upon The Floridas*. A facsimile reproduction of the 1823 New York edition, edited and with an introduction and index by John Hebron Moore. Gainesville: University of Florida Press, 1977.

Waller, Ben I. 1983. "Florida Anthropologist Interview with Ben I. Waller." *Florida Anthropologist* 38, nos. 1–2: 31–39.

Waterbury, Jean. 1983. "The Castillo Years." Pp. 57–90 in *The Oldest City*, edited by Jean Waterbury. St. Augustine: St. Augustine Historical Society.

Watts, William A. 1969. "A Pollen Diagram from Mud Lake, Marion County, North-Central Florida." *Geological Society of America Bulletin* 80: 631–42.

————. 1971. "Postglacial and Interglacial Vegetation History of Southern Georgia and Central Florida." *Ecology* 52: 676–90.

————. 1983. "Vegetational History of the Eastern United States 25,000 to 10,000 Years Ago." Pp. 294–310 in Wright, ed., 1983, q.v., vol. 1, pp. 294–310.

Watts, William A., and M. Stuiver. 1980. "Late Wisconsin Climate of Northern Florida and the Origin of Species-Rich Deciduous Forest." *Science* 210: 325–27.

Webb, S. David. 1974. "Chronology of Florida Pleistocene Mammals." Pp. 5–31 in

Pleistocene Mammals of Florida, edited by S. David Webb. Gainesville: University Press of Florida.

Weber, David J. 1992. *The Spanish Frontier in North America*. New Haven: Yale University Press.

West, Frederick Handleigh. 1983. "The Antiquity of Man in America." In Wright, ed., 1983, q.v., vol. 1, pp. 364–82.

Whitaker, Arthur Preston, trans. and ed. 1931. *Documents Relating to the Commercial Policy of Spain in the Floridas*. Publications of the Florida State Historical Society 10. DeLand.

White, Leslie A. 1959. *The Evolution of Culture*. New York: McGraw-Hill.

White, William A. 1970. *The Geomorphology of the Florida Peninsula*. Florida Bureau of Geology. Geological Bulletin 51.

Whitmore, F. C., Jr., K. O. Emery, H. B. S. Cooke and D. J. P. Swift. 1967. "Elephant Teeth from the Atlantic Continental Shelf." *Science* 156: 1477–81.

Williams, John Lee. 1837a. Map of Florida by J. Lee Williams. New York: Greene & McGowran.

————. 1837b. *The Territory of Florida: or Sketches of the Topography, Civil and Natural History, of the Country, the Climate, and the Indian Tribes*. A facsimile reproduction of the 1837 New York edition, with an introduction and index by Herbert J. Doherty, Jr. Gainesville: University of Florida Press, 1962.

Wright, H. E., Jr., ed. 1983. *Late-Quaternary Environments of the United States*. Vol. 1, *The Late Pleistocene*, edited by Stephen C. Porter. Vol. 2, *The Pleistocene*, edited by H. E. Wright, Jr. Minneapolis: University of Minnesota Press.

Index

Florida Museum of Natural History
The Ripley P. Bullen Series
Jerald T. Milanich, General Editor